HARRY LEE POE & JIMMY H. DAVIS

GOD AND THE COSMOS

DIVINE ACTIVITY IN SPACE, TIME AND HISTORY

IVP Academic

An imprint of InterVarsity Press
Downers Grove, Illinois

InterVarsity Press
P.O. Box 1400, Downers Grove, IL 60515-1426
World Wide Web: www.ivpress.com
E-mail: email@ivpress.com

InterVarsity Press® is the book-publishing division of InterVarsity Christian Fellowship/USA®, a movement of
students and faculty active on campus at hundreds of universities, colleges and schools of nursing in the United States
of America, and a member movement of the International Fellowship of Evangelical Students. For information
about local and regional activities, write Public Relations Dept., InterVarsity Christian Fellowship/USA, 6400
Schroeder Rd., P.O. Box 7895, Madison, WI 53707-7895, or visit the IVCF website at <www.intervarsity.org>.

All Scripture quotations, unless otherwise indicated, are taken from the Holy Bible, New International Version®.
NIV®. Copyright ©1973, 1978, 1984 by International Bible Society. Used by permission of Zondervan Publishing
House. All rights reserved.

Design: Cindy Kiple
Images: paper background: © Sasa Milosevic/iStockphoto
        solar system: © Baris Simsek/iStockphoto
        portrait of architect Bramante: School of Athens—detail of right grouping including Euclid (portrait of
        architect Bramante) explaining a problem of geometry by (Raffaello Sanzio) Raphael at Stanza
        della Segnatura. Erich Lessing/ Art Resource, NY
        Illustrations by Benjamin Watson

ISBN 978-0-8308-3954-4

Printed in the United States of America ∞

Library of Congress Cataloging-in-Publication Data

Poe, Harry Lee, 1950-
 God and the cosmos: divine activity in space, time, and history /
Harry Lee Poe and Jimmy H. Davis.
     p. cm.
 Includes bibliographical references (p.   ) and index.
 ISBN 978-0-8308-3954-4 (pbk.: alk. paper)
 1. Providence and government of God—Christianity. I. Davis, Jimmy
H., 1948- II. Title.
 BT135.P57 2012
 231.7—dc23

                                                                     2011051588

P   24   23   22   21   20   19   18   17   16   15   14   13   12   11   10   9   8   7   6   5   4   3   2   1

Y   32   31   30   29   28   27   26   25   24   23   22   21   20   19   18   17   16   15   14   13   12

CONTENTS

Illustrations 7

Acknowledgments. 9

Introduction: *Where Is God?* 13

PART ONE: *What Kind of God Interacts with the World?* . . 31

   1. Religious Views of God and Nature 33

   2. Traditional Christianity 69

   3. The Process Theology Option 101

   4. Beyond the God of the Gaps 122

PART TWO: *What Kind of World Allows God to Interact?* . . 146

   5. Cosmology and the Emergence of Everything 148

   6. God, Uncertainty and Openness 179

   7. God and Life 208

   8. God and History 249

   9. Conclusion 284

Name and Subject Index 293

Scripture Index 304

ILLUSTRATIONS

0.1 Peacocke's Levels or Hierarchies of Complexity 27

1.1 The Paths Within Hinduism 37

1.2 The Major Branches of Buddhism 43

1.3 The Major Groups Within Islam. 53

2.1 Perkins's Golden Chain. 80

5.1 Aristotle's Earth-Centered Universe 151

5.2 Ptolemy's Cosmology 153

5.3 Copernican Heliocentric Universe 154

5.4 The Complexity of the Copernican Model. 155

5.5 Tychonic System 156

5.6 Stellar Parallax 158

5.7 Big Bang Model 162

5.8 Level 1: Physical World of Peacocke's Levels of Complexity. 168

5.9 Shell Structure of the Earth and Location of the Lithosphere 171

6.1 De Broglie Matter-Wave 184

6.2 Probability Density for Electron Position 185

6.3 Lorenz Data Plot 192

6.4 Population Changes 193

6.5 Bifurcations to Chaos. 194

6.6 Example of a Fractal, the Koch Snowflake. 195

7.1 The History of Life Reflected in the Geological Column
and Timeline 212

7.2 Homologous Structures Mentioned by Darwin 216

7.3 Range of the Tibetan Greenish Warbler 219

8.1 Aristotle's Influence 282

9.1 Rate of Expansion of Space 286

9.2 Increase in Diversity of Elements 287

9.3 Increase in Diversity of Body Forms 287

9.4 Diversity of Cultural Artifacts 288

ACKNOWLEDGMENTS

✦✧✦

M ANY BOOKS REPRESENT an effort to prove a thesis. Such books take a position on an issue and present material that will support their views and undermine contrary views. These books play an important part in the examination of an issue by putting forward in as strong a way as possible one of the sides in a debate. This book does not represent an effort to prove a thesis.

Another kind of book explores a question. This book began with a question that formed in the mind of a chemistry professor. The resulting book represents a fifteen-year conversation between that chemistry professor and a theologian. Over the course of fifteen years we have eaten many meals and written several books, each preparation for the next. We have taught a course together on the relationship between science and faith. All along the way we have sought to understand our faith and our understanding of the physical world in light of each other. This book is not a Christian apologetic in the sense that we have tried to argue for the existence of God. The book begins with our assumption of faith. Given our common faith in the God of the Bible, we have sought to understand how God acts in a world in which laws of nature operate consistently.

We have had the pleasure of many conversations with colleagues at Union University through the years, especially with Randall Bush, Ben Mitchell, Kelvin Moore, Geoffrey Poore, Greg Thornbury, Bill Nettles, Michael McMahon, Wayne Wofford, Jennifer Gruenke and Fonsie Guilaran. Two conferences provided the occasion for us to engage in prolonged discussion of an unsystematic nature that formed the germ of the idea for this book, and we wish to thank the organizers and plenary speakers of these conferences: "Christianity and the Soul of the

University: Faith as a Foundation for Intellectual Community" at Baylor University in 2004, and "Austin Farrer Centenary Conference" at Oxford University in 2004. Many of the ideas in this book began to crystallize for us in 2007 at the STARS Conference in Cancún, Mexico, sponsored by the Center for Theology and the Natural Sciences. We had profitable discussion at the conference with Marco Bersanelli, Trinh Xuan Thuan, John Barrow, Don Howard, Susan D'Amato, Ted Davis, Donald Petcher, Peter Colyer and Bob Russell. We are also most grateful for dialogue partners in the American Scientific Affiliation, especially Ted Davis, Terry Morrison, Bob Fay, Randy Isaacs and Jennifer Wiseman.

The introductory chapter began its life as a paper presented by Jimmy Davis to the Chemistry Colloquium at Union University in 2005 and in an expanded form as "Where Is God?" a paper presented at the 2006 Christianity in the Academy Conference at the Germantown Campus of Union University.

Several sections of the book were originally given as papers at various conferences by Hal Poe: "Constructing an Evangelical Alternative to Process Theology" at the annual meeting of the Evangelical Theological Society in 2003; "Beyond the God of the Gaps" at the 2003 annual Christianity in the Academy Conference; "Religious Pluralism and the Science and Religion Dialogue" at the annual meeting of the American Academy of Religion; "The Reformation and the Rise of Modern Science" at the annual meeting of the American Scientific Affiliation in Edinburgh, Scotland. The discussion of the Trinity includes a section from Hal Poe's conclusion to *What God Knows*, ed. Harry Lee Poe and J. Stanley Mattson (Waco, Tex.: Baylor University Press, 2005), and his paper "Trinitarian Implications of Einstein's Universe" presented at the Einstein, God, and Time conference of the Ian Ramsey Center at Oxford University in 2005.

Hal Poe's work on imagination comes from a series of lectures he presented in 2009 in commemoration of the bicentennial of the birth of Edgar Allan Poe. These lectures were given in connection with the annual meeting of the American Scientific Affiliation at Baylor University; a special lecture for Metanexus Institute in Philadelphia; and a series of lectures at Russian universities sponsored by the U.S. Department of State, the U.S. Consulate in St. Petersburg, the U.S. Embassy in Moscow and the U.S. Consulate in Yekaterinburg. The Russian lectures were delivered at Herzen Pedagogical University and St. Petersburg State University, in St. Petersburg; Moscow State University, Russian University for the Humanities, and Gorky Institute for Literature, in Moscow; Ural State University, in Yekaterinburg; and Perm State Pedagogical University, in Perm.

The staff of the Emma Sumer Watters Library at Union University has been most helpful in securing resources through interlibrary loan without which assistance this book could not have been written. We are most grateful to Mykle Johnson for reading the manuscript. We have the privilege of teaching at a university that has encouraged our work through the years, and we wish to acknowledge our appreciation to the trustees of Union University and to David S. Dockery, our president, Carla Sanderson, provost, Gene Fant, vice president for academic affairs and Greg Thornbury, dean of the school of theology and missions. Gary Deddo, our editor at InterVarsity Press, believed in this project and guided it through the approval process. We thank the staff of InterVarsity Press for their work in turning a manuscript into a book, and we are grateful that they allowed us the time to nurture our ideas. Finally, we congratulate Benjamin Watson on the fine illustrations he has provided for his first book project. We are grateful to him for taking on this task in his senior year at Union University and we look forward to his many successes in the future.

Our wives must deal with us when the lights go out at school. Christine Menzel and Mary Anne Poe have been our constant companions and supporters through the process of writing a book that took many years longer than we had anticipated. We thank them for their never-failing encouragement.

Harry Lee Poe
Jimmy H. Davis

INTRODUCTION

WHERE IS GOD?

✦✧✦

IN THE MOVIE *Galileo: The Challenge of Reason*, Galileo's assistant asks, "Where is God?" in the new sun-centered model of the universe. The screenwriter's Galileo replies, "He is not up there, not up there spinning the universe like some great child's toy. Not up there. How should I know? I am a mathematician not a theologian."[1]

POSING THE QUESTION: A SCIENTIFIC QUERY
—BY JIMMY H. DAVIS

When I first saw the movie *Galileo* I thought Galileo's answer was lame. I still do, but now I have more sympathy for Galileo's struggle in answering. Lately, I have been asking myself the same question in regard to how I understand and practice chemistry. As a Christian, how will my practice of chemistry differ with that of a non-Christian theist, a deist or an atheist? How will my chemistry differ from that of a practitioner of one of the world's other religions? Should my chemistry be different? Before you assign me to the lowest circle of Dante's *Inferno*, let's consider a chemical reaction that I have enjoyed doing for as long as I can remember.

Take a bowl, cover the bottom of the bowl with baking soda and cover the baking soda with vinegar. Voilá, a most amazing thing happens. The

[1]*Galileo: The Challenge of Reason* (Northbrook, Ill.: Learning Corporation of America, 1978), DVD.

white powder and clear liquid are transformed into thousands of effer-
vescing bubbles that rapidly foam toward the top of the bowl. The foam
dissipates quickly and we are left with a white solid, a clear liquid and a
dying effervescence. (If we add a lot of vinegar, we produce so much foam
that it overflows the bowl, as my wonderful mother knows.)

When we add more vinegar, the process repeats itself another glo-
rious time. Vinegar can be repeatedly added with effervescence each
time. Finally, all the white powder will be used up and adding more
vinegar has no effect. What is going on here?

How would a chemist describe this reaction? The common term
baking soda would be replaced with the term *sodium hydrogen carbonate*
and *vinegar* would be replaced with *acetic acid*. Rather than saying
baking soda and vinegar produced a foam, the chemist would say
sodium hydrogen carbonate reacts with acetic acid to produce sodium
acetate, water and carbon dioxide. Furthermore, these names would be
symbolically represented by formula: sodium hydrogen carbonate
($NaHCO_3$), acetic acid (CH_3COOH), water (H_2O) and carbon dioxide
(CO_2). The chemists would go further and translate the sentence
[sodium hydrogen carbonate reacts with acetic acid to produce sodium
acetate, water, and carbon dioxide] into a chemical equation:

$$NaHCO_3 + CH_3COOH \rightarrow NaCH_3COO + H_2O + CO_2$$

Now the chemist is ready to explain the observations. When the
aqueous solution of acetic acid touches the solid sodium hydrogen
carbonate, the solid dissolves in the water. In the process of dissolving,
the sodium hydrogen carbonate dissociates into sodium ions (Na^+)
and hydrogen carbonate ions (HCO_3^-). The HCO_3^- is classified as a
base; it immediately reacts with the acid, acetic acid, forming carbonic acid (H_2CO_3). Carbonic acid is unstable and immediately de-
composes into water (H_2O) and carbon dioxide (CO_2). The time it
takes to form the bubbles of carbon dioxide is much shorter than the
time it takes to describe what is happening at the molecular level. The
effervescence results from the formation of carbon dioxide gas. (The
reaction of carbonates with an acid producing carbon dioxide gas is
the basis of using baking soda as a rising agent in baking and using

carbonates as antacids.) Vinegar is not a pure substance but is a 5 percent solution of acetic acid dissolved in water. In contrast, the baking soda is a pure substance; it is 100 percent sodium hydrogen carbonate. The extent of the reaction is limited by the reactant which has the lowest concentration; thus, chemists would say that acetic acid is the limiting reagent. Although it looks like you are adding equal amounts of solid and liquid, you are not adding as much acetic acid as sodium hydrogen carbonate. The acetic acid is quickly consumed, leaving the leftover sodium hydrogen carbonate (white solid) and a water solution of sodium acetate (clear liquid). Adding more vinegar brings more acetic acid in contact with sodium hydrogen carbonate which produces more carbon dioxide gas. Once the entire white solid disappears, there is no longer any carbonate present and adding more vinegar does not cause any reaction (effervescence). This fun reaction exposes us to a lot of chemistry—atoms and molecules, states of matter (solid, liquid and gas), acids and bases, stability of compounds, limiting reagents, and kinetics.

By now you may be asking what this discussion has to do with the question Where is God? To me it has everything to do with the question. Consider: the reaction behaves the same no matter whether one is in North America, Europe, Africa or Asia. Also, a chemist in all these locations would give the same chemical explanation for the reaction. Further, the reaction proceeds the same way whether a man, a woman, a child or an adult is doing the mixing. Furthermore, the same is true whether the mixer is a Christian, deist, Hindu, Buddhist, Muslim, agnostic or atheist. No special prayers or incantations are needed for the reaction to proceed. The description of the experiment (the chemical explanation) is 100 percent natural. So, where is God in this process?

The previous two paragraphs reflect how modern science functions. *Modern science assumes that all physical events have physical causes. In order to find these causes, modern science breaks the event down into parts and looks for some mechanism (pattern of connections) that give rise to the event being studied.* Modern science explains natural phenomena in terms of natural events and does not invoke supernatural intervention. Paul de Vries, a philosopher at Wheaton College, coined the term *methodological naturalism* to describe how science functions in the modern world.[2] Our example of the reaction of baking soda and vinegar was explained in terms of the interaction of molecules with no mention of the supernatural. Naturalists who are also Christian have a long tradition of seeking natural explanations for events.[3] Some examples are Galileo Galilei (1564-1642), Francis Bacon (1561-1626), Johannes Kepler (1571-1630), Robert Boyle (1627-1691), Isaac Newton (1642-1727), John Herschel (1792-1871), Charles Lyell (1797-1875) and Asa Gray (1810-1888). Each sought to discover the laws of nature, which to them testified to God's existence. The discovery of these laws was a religious act.

The previous explanation for the reaction of baking soda and vinegar was religiously neutral; it could be used whether the scientist is Christian or atheist. Historically, however, many Christians have feared that the exclusive explanation of natural phenomena by natural causes might undermine the belief in God. This fear is a response to the philosophy of scientific naturalism.[4] Scientific naturalism states that empirical science is the only valid source of knowledge and that there is no place for the supernatural. Naturalists who could be classified this way include Georges-Louis Leclerc, Comte de Buffon (1707-1788); Pierre-Simon de Laplace (1749-1827); Thomas H. Huxley (1825-1895); and John Tyndall (1820-1893).

Christians thank God for food; a scientific naturalist replies that food is "nothing but" an agriculture cycle which is "nothing but" a water cycle and nutrition cycle. Christians thank God for comfort in times of trial; a scientific naturalist replies that these thoughts are "nothing but" our psychology which is "nothing but" our physiology. The British neuroscientist Donald M. MacKay (1922-1987) categorized this type of thinking as "nothing-buttery." As he said, "Nothing-

---

[2]Paul de Vries, "Naturalism in the Natural Sciences," *Christian Science Review* 15 (1986): 388-96. He seemed to have coined the phrase *methodological naturalism* at a 1983 conference at Wheaton College.

[3]Those who study nature have been called natural philosophers, naturalists and scientists. The term *scientist* was coined by the Englishmen William Whewell (1794-1866) in the 1830s.

[4]The term *scientific naturalism* was coined by Thomas H. Huxley (1825-1895) in 1892. De Vries used the term *metaphysical naturalism* to contrast with *methodological naturalism*.

buttery is characterized by the notion that by reducing any phenomenon to its components you not only explain it, but *explain it away.*"[5]

To those who hold the view of scientific naturalism, our explanations of natural events are a zero-sum game. To them a 100 percent natural explanation means a 0 percent divine involvement. Do the following relationships hold? If there is a process for which we do not have a physical explanation, can we say that this process involves 100 percent divine involvement? As we gain physical understanding, does the divine involvement now become less than 100 percent? And finally, does a full physical understanding equal 0 percent divine involvement? During the celebrations of the fiftieth anniversary of the discovery of the structure of DNA, James Watson (b. 1928) remarked, "Every time you understand something, religion becomes less likely."[6] In this statement Watson assumes that 100 percent natural means 0 percent divine. Watson's statement expresses scientific naturalism. He is saying that nature is nothing more than the natural process; there is no involvement of the supernatural. He is saying that everything can be explained by using natural phenomena such as mass, forces, energy and so forth.

So what is a Christian who is a scientist to do? What vocabulary is available to describe what they do and how God relates to the physical world? When we try to include God in the naturalistic explanation of science, we hear something like the following: God exists. God created the universe. God established the laws of the universe. When one mixes baking soda and vinegar, one observes the action of these laws. God seems to be stuck back at the beginning. I am beginning to think that scientists who are Christian function as methodological deists.

Are we stuck functioning as methodological naturalists and thinking like methodological deists? The question Where is God? addresses the fundamental question of causation and our ability to identify it accurately. Further, this question is one that Christian theologians and natural philosophers have dealt with since the beginning of Christi-

---

[5]Donald M. MacKay, *The Clockwork Image* (Downers Grove, Ill.: InterVarsity Press, 1974), p. 43.

[6]James Watson, quoted in Roger Highfield, "DNA Pioneers Lash Out at Religion," *London Daily Telegraph*, March 24, 2003.

anity. Several key incidents over the last two thousand years illustrate the problem.

In the patristic period, Augustine of Hippo (354-430) expressed the view that all truth is God's truth when he stated, "Let every good and true Christian understand that wherever truth may be found, it belongs to his Master."[7] Although he believed that the ultimate reality is spiritual, he used natural knowledge to interpret Scripture. Further, the regularity of the natural order causes some to cease to wonder and miss that God is the primary cause, Augustine said,

> But there is one kind of natural order in the conversion and changeableness of bodies, which, although itself also serves the bidding of God, yet by reason of its unbroken continuity has ceased to cause wonder. . . . And so the vanity of philosophers has found license to assign these things also to other causes, true causes perhaps, but proximate ones, while they are not able to see at all the cause that is higher than all others, that is, the will of God."[8]

During the Middle Ages, Christian theologians and philosophers, in considering how to determine the extent of God's activity in nature, provided the following contributions to the development of modern thought. On the one hand, they saw God almost always acting in nature through secondary causes. Why? Although they believed that God could do anything that he wished, they believed that God almost always restricts himself with the *cursus communis naturae* (the common course of nature). This restriction assures the validity of investigations into an almost constant world. Because of this belief that God acts through secondary causes, natural philosophers promoted the use of observation and experiment in addition to reason when studying the *cursus communis naturae:*

- English theologian Robert Grosseteste (c. 1175-1253), bishop of Lincoln, affirmed that experiments should be used in order to verify a theory, testing its consequences.

---

[7]Augustine, *On Christian Doctrine* 2.18 (28), J. F. Shaw translation, www9.georgetown.edu/faculty/jod/augustine/ddc.html.
[8]Augustine, *On the Trinity* 3.2 (7), www.newadvent.org/fathers/130103.htm.

- Dominican friar and theologian Albert the Great (c. 1200-1280) promoted searching for the underlying causes of events in nature.

- English Franciscan friar and theologian Roger Bacon (c. 1214-1294) implemented the observation of nature and experimentation as the foundation of natural knowledge; he was responsible for making the concept of laws of nature widespread.

- English Franciscan friar and philosopher William of Occam (c. 1285-c. 1350) developed the concept known as Occam's Razor: when comparing equally possible explanations for an event, the simplest one should be chosen. This became a foundation of the scientific method and reductionism in science.

A second effect of this emphasis on the *cursus communis naturae* was that it put the visible activity of God outside the common course of nature. Of course to the medieval philosophers God was the primary cause behind the secondary causes and thus involved in everything. The Dominican priest and theologian Thomas Aquinas (1225-1274), in his great work *Summa Theologica*, reaffirmed that secondary causes can be used to study nature but that all events are directed by God:

> Since God wills effects to proceed from definite causes, for the preservation of order in the universe, it is not unreasonable to seek for causes secondary to the divine will. It would, however, be unreasonable to do so, if such were considered as primary, and not as dependent on the will of God.
>
> But the causality of God, Who is the first agent, extends to all being, not only as to constituent principles of species, but also as to the individualizing principles; not only of things incorruptible, but also of things corruptible. Hence all things that exist in whatsoever manner are necessarily directed by God towards some end. . . . Since, therefore, as the providence of God is nothing less than the type of order of things toward an end, . . . it necessarily follows that all things, inasmuch as they participate in existence, must likewise be subject to divine providence.[9]

---

[9]Thomas Aquinas, *The Summa Theologica* 1.19.8; 1.22.2 (Benziger ed., 1947), trans. Fathers of the English Dominican Province, www.ccel.org/a/aquinas/summa/FP.html.

At the Protestant Reformation, John Calvin (1509-1564) reaffirmed Augustine's idea that all truth is God's truth by stating, "If we reflect that the Spirit of God is the only fountain of truth, we will be careful, as we would avoid offering insult to him, not to reject or condemn truth wherever it appears. In despising the gifts, we insult the Giver."[10] The English philosopher and pioneer in the scientific revolution Francis Bacon (1561-1626) urged study and proficiency in "the two books of God":

> Let no man upon a weak conceit of sobriety or an ill-applied moderation think or maintain, that a man can search too far, or be too well studied in the book of God's word, or in the book of God's works; divinity or philosophy: but rather let men endeavour an endless progress or profi-cience in both; only let men beware that they apply both to charity, and not to swelling; to use, and not to ostentation; and again, that they do not unwisely mingle or confound these learnings together.[11]

The American Presbyterian theologian B. B. Warfield (1851-1921), who served as professor of didactic and polemic theology at Princeton Seminary for thirty-four years, reaffirmed the thoughts of Aquinas when he stated:

> All the modifications of the world-stuff have taken place under the di-rectly upholding and governing hand of God, and find their account ultimately in his will. But they find their account proximately in second causes. . . . What account we give of these second causes is a matter of ontology—how we account for their existence, their persistence, their action. And the relation we conceive them to stand in to God, the up-holder and director as well as the creator of them. . . . [Calvin] ascribed to second causes as their proximate account the entire series of modifi-cations by which the primal indigested mass called heaven and earth has passed into the form of the ordered world which we see.[12]

---

[10]John Calvin, *Institutes of The Christian Religion* 2.2.236, trans. Henry Beveridge, www.ccel .org/ccel/calvin/institutes.i.html.

[11]Francis Bacon, *Advancement of Learning*, chap. 1, www.gutenberg.org/dirs/etext04/adlr10 .txt.

[12]B. B. Warfield, *Evolution, Science, and Scripture: Selected Writings*, ed. Mark A. Noll and David N. Livingstone (Grand Rapids: Baker, 2000), pp. 308-9. This was first published as "Calvin's Doctrine of Creation," *Princeton Theological Review* 13 (April 1915): 190-255.

Another way of stating this is to say that processes of the physical universe are 100 percent divine and 100 percent natural. Warfield is saying that it is not a zero-sum game. God is the ultimate governor of his creation. Yet God chooses to govern the cosmos by regular cause-and-effect relations that can be understood as we observe the world. To paraphrase Warfield, every chemical reaction is the action of God in the world.

But the emphasis on the *cursus communis naturae* and on the regularity of the laws of nature put Western scientific thought on a path that led some thinkers to position God as an absentee first cause (deism), to have no need for God in the explanation (methodological naturalism), and to conclude that there is no God (ontological naturalism). Why? The problem that Galileo's assistant and our chemist narrator have is letting a model of some aspect of the universe substitute for the actual universe. In science, models are mental pictures to represent things that are difficult to observe, such as objects or processes that are too small to be seen (atoms), too slow to be observed (coal formation), or too vast and far away to be observed at once (universe). The model of a phenomenon never contains all the information within that phenomenon.

Since the ancient Greeks, naturalists have tried to confine the universe to the model of a machine. In astronomy, the model of the universe was a machine of earth-centered nested spheres (Eudoxus of Cnidus, 408-355 B.C., and Aristotle, 384-322 B.C.) to the addition of deferents, epicycles and equants to the spheres (Ptolemy, A.D. 83-161), to sun-centered nested spheres (Copernicus, 1473-1543), to the clockwork machine (Robert Boyle),[13] to a mathematical model (Newton). Each step in the process resulted in a more self-contained machine. Aristotle had a Prime Mover on his outermost sphere, which caused

---

[13]Robert Boyle, *A Free Enquiry into the Vulgarly Received Notion of Nature*, eds. Edward Bradford and Michael Cyril William Hunter (1686; reprint, Cambridge: Cambridge University Press, 1996), p. 13. Boyle was influenced by the astronomical clock located in the Cathedrale Notre-Dame of Strasbourg, France. This clock has a perpetual calendar and a planetary dial displaying the positions of the sun, moon, and lunar and solar eclipses. In addition, at half-past midday, a procession of figures representing Christ and the apostles occurs, while a rooster crows three times.

the other spheres to move; Thomas Aquinas was able to give God a place in the universe by making him the Prime Mover. After Newton, the notion of a self-contained clock-work universe developed that had no need for God to explain the motions of the heavenly bodies. Although Newton believed God was needed to keep the solar system stable, Pierre-Simon Laplace presented a model of the solar system that explained it fully from its origin as a nebula to its orbits today. When Napoleon asked where was God in his model, Laplace replied that he did not need that hypothesis.[14]

Although the Newtonian model seems complete when it describes the orbit of one planet, the flight of a cannon ball or the need for car safety belts, much of nature is chaotic where the determinism of Newtonian mechanics breaks down. As will be discussed in chapter six, chaotic systems, such as turbulent flow, three-body planetary motions and weather, make up a great deal of our universe, yet Newtonian mechanics does not give a good description of their behavior. Likewise the atomic model of the atom, which can be traced back to Democritus (c. 460–c. 370 B.C.), presents a nice closed system where all the behavior of matter is explained by the interactions of atoms. Yet the well-behaved billiard ball model of the atom, at its very subatomic heart, is a system of probabilities. Quantum mechanics will also be discussed in chapter six. In biology the closed model is natural selection and genetics with the iron rule of genetics determining the survivability of the organism. Yet even here openness is present in the form of epigenetics. As discussed in chapter seven, the environment can regulate how the genes are expressed with two organisms with the same genetic code having vastly different health histories.

Although scientists continually, consciously or unconsciously, construct models that are closed machines, nature has a lot of openness that is ignored by these machine models. As MacKay stated, "There is all the difference in the world between describing and analyzing a particular system as a mechanism, and claiming that the 'real' explanation, the only worthwhile or objective explanation to be had of the situation,

---

[14]W. W. Rouse Bell, *A Short Account of the History of Mathematics*, 4th ed. (New York: Dover, 1908), p. 363.

is the explanation you get in terms of machine analogies."[15] Chaos, quantum phenomena and epigenetics are three examples of the openness found throughout nature. This openness is an internal part of nature, not a God-of-the-Gaps ignorance that will one day be removed. We suggest in this monograph that God is there not only in the working of the "machine" but in the underlying software that tells the "machine" how to behave in a particular situation. It is an open universe providing an open vista on which the master Artist can craft what he wills.

Recognizing the Issues: A Theological Response —by Harry Lee Poe

Still, the old question persists. How does God relate to the physical world? Some would argue that the idea of God is a matter of mass psychosis, a mental disorder of the mass human collective. Others call the God idea a "theotoxin"—a poisonous notion at work in some corner of the brain. Whether or not God exists is a different question than the one before us, but it is not completely unrelated. If God exists, then how does God relate to the physical world? If God does not relate to the physical world, then why do we even have an idea of God? The problem of the idea of God lies behind Anselm's ontological argument for the existence of God. Freud suggested that the idea is a projection on the universe of both our longing and our guilt. This hypothesis suffers from enormous anthropological and cultural problems. Because so many of Freud's theories have been discredited by modern psychology, psychiatry and neuroscience, his religious theories tend to linger as a harmless bit of his legacy as the founder of a great discipline. Whereas his other theories have suffered rigorous clinical examination, his religious ideas do not lend themselves to rigorous experimental scrutiny anymore than the God idea does. This inaccessibility of God for experimental research in a scientific age only exacerbates the question of how a nonphysical being might act on matter and energy in a physical universe.

For most people the real problem with God goes back to the problem

---

[15]MacKay, *Clockwork Image*, p. 12.

of pain and suffering in the world. How could a good, all-powerful God allow such things to happen? C. S. Lewis pointed out the real problem with this question when he asked where we ever got the idea of a good God in the face of a world of sickness, pain and death. Projecting a monster or monsters, as most primitive cultures seem to have done, makes sense, but how did people get the idea that a benevolent God lies behind all the suffering and death? The ability to ask about suffering, a question laden with moral assumptions of goodness, justice, beauty and love, suggests the presence of something breaking in from the outside to lift the human race above the givenness of existence. Beauty, justice, goodness and love simply are not natural.

Any exploration of how God relates to the physical world, then, must deal with how God relates to people who have such lofty, unnatural ideas. People share physical existence along with the rest of nature. We must not only ponder what God has to do with a chemical reaction, but also what God has to do with people in the course of their lives. How do people know about God if God really exists? And what does God have to do with the course of human history? The physical world is big and involves both space and time. The universe has a complex organization of matter and energy relationships that seem to involve only four fundamental forces on which all the other laws of nature depend. One of the greatest frustrations for physics for the last hundred years has been the effort to reduce these four forces (gravity, electromagnetism, strong nuclear force and weak nuclear force) down to just one great primordial unified field.

To a certain extent we live in a time of paradigm shift away from the science of the last five hundred years, which focused on experimentation, and back to the earlier Greek model of Plato and Aristotle, who developed theories of how the universe works which provided the basis for scientific thought for the next two thousand years. String theory and M theory provide mathematical models for the universe, but without a current proposal for how to test the models experimentally. The new theories work mathematically, as Ptolemy's earth-centered universe did, and younger postmodern theorists do not have the same attachment to empiricism as the scientists of the Enlightenment tradition. While the absence of an experimental base causes concern among traditionalists in physics, the new theories have a compelling charm for those who seek a final reductionist explanation for the universe. It would be the new grand metanarrative.

Answers to the question of how God acts on the universe have tended to be reductionist. As such, they have tended to be unhelpful. More complicated answers seldom gain a hearing because people prefer simple, black-and-white, either-or explanations. Politicians learned this trait of human nature long ago; thus, the trait has charm both for fundamentalism and for unbelief.

When we consider how God relates to the physical world, we do well to remember how many disciplines have come into being over the last five hundred years whose task it is to study different levels of organization of the physical world. Each discipline has its own method and vocabulary for describing and explaining what it observes at different levels of complexity. Arthur Peacocke has drawn attention to the significance of this growing complexity and its accessibility (fig. 0.1).[16] At the simplest level of organization, physics explores elementary particles and atoms. At a more complex level of organization, chemistry explores atoms, molecules and compounds. Geology explores minerals and rocks, while cosmology, astronomy and astrophysics explore different aspects of planets, stars, galaxies and other parts of the heavens. Along the way of organizational complexity the physical world does something in these later days that it has never done before. It comes alive! The biological sciences and neurosciences explore the different levels of organization of living things as cytology, cell biology, physiology, anatomy, botany and zoology, and their many subspecializations describe and explain what they observe. The next level of organizational complexity involves the social sciences as they study animal and human behavior, such as anthropology, archaeology, history, psychology, sociology, economics, political science and philosophy. No single methodology allows all of these sciences to do their work, because each level of organization is a different world. Something dramatic happens when

---

[16]Arthur Peacocke, *Theology for a Scientific Age*, 2nd ed. (London: SCM Press, 1996), pp. 214-18.

matter and energy move from simplicity to complexity. The old aphorism that the whole is greater than the sum of its parts describes the phenomenon of the universe. It can be described in terms of its parts, but its individual parts do not explain the whole. Just as scientists relate to different levels of the universe in different ways, a nonreductionist view of the activity of God would suggest that God relates to different levels of organization of the universe in different ways (if God relates to them at all). Neither reductionist science nor reductionist theology help us understand this universe where one kind of rule applies at the level of human experience and another kind of rule applies at the quantum level of subatomic particles.

We also do well to recall that in our universe all of the levels of organization may exist concurrently now but have not always done so. The universe began some fourteen billion years ago as a rather simple expression of energy that took on characteristics of mass. Since then the universe has grown progressively more complex. The four forces appeared over time—a rather short period of time from our perspective looking back, but as it was occurring from the perspective of the singularity and the beginning of time and space, their appearance would have involved eons since it involved all the time that had ever happened until the moment the four forces began to appear and do something.

Freedom of the triune God. Most attempts to deal with the question of how God relates to or acts on the universe limit God in some way. Some limit God to acting in only one level of organization, such as the quantum level or the human level. Some limit God to only acting in one way, such as beginning creation but standing aloof from it or by determining every event at all levels. In most cases these reductionist approaches intend to preserve some important value to the culture these explanations emerged from. To a certain extent the theological limitations of God in the West, with its historical association with Christianity, represent a rejection of the orthodox trinitarian view of God. The different models tend to choose one person of the Trinity for their God while leaving little, if any, place for the other members of the Trinity. This entails the problem of viewing the Trinity as three gods rather than as one God in three persons. Those

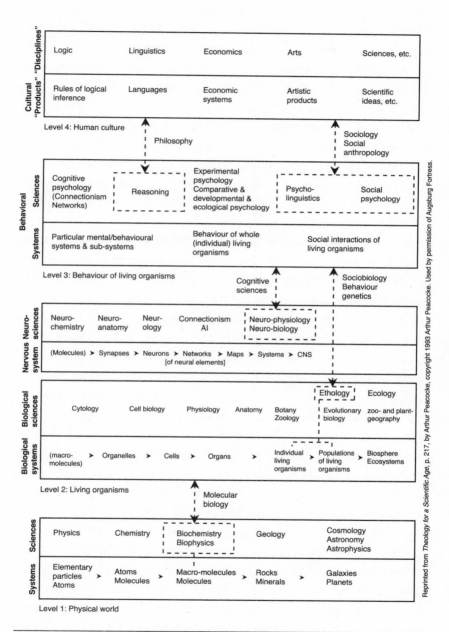

Figure 0.1. Peacocke's levels or hierarchies of complexity

who restrict God's relationship to the universe as a self-emptying, self-limiting model, have adopted the incarnational model of the Son, who gave up aspects of his majesty when he took on flesh. Those who restrict God's relationship to the universe as the ordination of all things by fiat have adopted a monarchical model of the Father while leaving the Son and the Spirit to carry out the orders. Those who restrict God's involvement to a nondirective presence in the process have adopted a model of the Holy Spirit who animates the universe but has no plans of his own. Only a truly trinitarian model of one God can help us move to a clearer understanding of how God might relate to such a complex structure as the universe in appropriate ways for different levels of physical complexity.

Directional universe: Simplicity to complexity. If the universe is not created by God, and if God is not involved in the universe, then the universe tells us nothing about God. If, on the other hand, God did create the universe and continues to be involved with it, then it may be a source of information about God. At every level of the universe the physical world moves from simplicity to complexity. The complexity of the universe occurs over time, which gives time and space a direction. Every branch of science has a direction that moves from simplicity to complexity. From energy to matter to elements, the universe continues to move until elements compose living organisms that grow in complexity from one-cell creatures to self-conscious, sexual beings that live in community and alter the universe to suit them. The universe is not static. It has a direction. It is organized in such a way that humans can interfere with it and manipulate its laws to suit our imaginations. We can split atoms and alter genes. We can violate gravity because we have learned that the interrelatedness of the universe allows one law to trump another law, like the children's game of rock-paper-scissors.

The cosmos moves forward and leaves behind. This linear direction of all the sciences suggests more than a mere static universe would suggest. During the Enlightenment of the eighteenth and nineteenth centuries, when the pioneers of modern science still believed in the static, eternal universe of Aristotle, it made sense to believe that the universe has no meaning or purpose. A static universe just *is*. A dynamic universe, on the other hand, does things. It appears to make things out of itself.

Progress: A value-based goal. This directional, dynamic universe also appears to have a deeply embedded value that we might call "progress." The universe works in such a way that it favors the movement from simplicity to complexity, long before we see this distinction in life forms. Darwin believed that he recognized a process of selection of organisms in nature similar to the process at work in the breeding of dogs, cows and horses. He attributed this process to nature rather than to God, because his reductionist theology viewed God as autocrat who acted by fiat. If animals changed over time, then he concluded God could not have been involved since this view violated his theological assumptions. Apparently, it never occurred to Darwin that his theological system was wrong and that God could be involved in the selection. In *Eureka* (1848), Edgar Allan Poe's original proposal of a big bang theory and the origin of life, Poe described the interaction of elements and life forms in adaptation in terms of a grand narrative. He said, "The plots of God are perfect. The Universe is a plot of God."

Open universe. Modern science has also discovered a remarkable aspect of our universe that previous generations never imagined. At every level of organization, in spite of increasing complexity, the universe possesses "openness." Though the forces of nature operate according to patterns that we call the laws of nature, they do not operate in the deterministic way we once thought. Odd, strange and unexpected things happen along the path of growing complexity. The universe has an open door at every level of complexity for the personal (whether human or divine) to interact, intervene, interrupt and alter the course of nature while never violating the laws of nature. Science and the ability for personal minds to develop science provides us with the empirical evidence that a personal mind may interfere with the laws of nature without altering them. Rather than hiding in the gaps, God is involved in the big observables that science describes.

Instead of proposing the single way God acts on the universe, or the one level of physical organization at which God operates, this study proposes that God is present and active at all organizational levels of the universe in a way appropriate to each level; otherwise God is not involved at all. We have divided the discussion into two questions that will help sort out the issues: (1) What kind of God interacts with the world, and (2) What kind of world allows God to interact?

PART ONE

What Kind of God Interacts with the World?

Most people on our planet believe in the divine. We have differing conceptions of the divine, but almost everyone believes that something is out there besides us. While books that attack the existence of God in the context of a discussion of science may have sensational value, they are mere diversions from serious inquiry into how the divine relates to the world. In the West the generic term *God* has referred to the God of the Bible, but that traditional terminology has changed gradually over the last fifty years.

While people in the United States, Canada, Europe, Australia and New Zealand tend to have a tolerant view of religion and accept the validity of many religious beliefs and practices, they also tend to think of other religions in terms of their own cultural beliefs and values. Most people in these countries are not practicing Christians, but their beliefs and assumptions about religion take their cue from the Christian faith. Thus, it is not unusual to hear Westerners talking about all people going to heaven when they die, even though Hinduism and Buddhism do not share this understanding of what happens after death. Likewise, Westerners may be heard speaking of all people worshiping the same God, when in reality the religions of the world have vastly different conceptions of God. While some religions value a God who loves us, other religions do not conceive of the higher power as a self-conscious personal mind who is aware of us, much less capable of loving us.

These various conceptions of God frame the background for a Western consideration of what kind of God would or could interact with the physical world. The question only arises because of the development in the West of modern science with its laws of how the physical world operates. The conception of laws of nature that arose in the West has its intellectual and conceptual basis in the Western view of a God who created the universe and established the laws of its operation, just as he established moral laws for the conduct of people. This line of thought in the late Middle Ages gave rise to the scientific revolution. It is not necessary to believe in the God of the Bible in order to accept the model of the universe that this theological and philosophical revolution produced. If one accepts the scientific model of a concrete, knowable universe, however, the options for the kind of God that can and does interact with that universe begin to narrow.

In pursuing the question of what kind of God interacts with our world, we will first explore the religious outlook of non-Western cultures that produced other approaches to science over centuries in highly developed civilizations that flowered long before the appearance of the modern scientific revolution in the West. Then we will explore in broad strokes the leading options for how Christians, and to a certain extent Jews, have dealt with the question.

1

RELIGIOUS VIEWS OF
GOD AND NATURE

✦✧✦

Before exploring the question of God's involvement in the world, it may be helpful to put the question in global context alongside religions other than Christianity. Different cultures and their religions have different concepts of what kind of God and what kind of universe exist. This question does not mean the same thing in cultures with different religious understandings, and it might even be regarded as naive or absurd not only because of their different views of God but also because of different views of the nature of reality. Modern science, with its view of a physical world that operates according to observable patterns that can be understood, is a product of Christianity and the Western culture it produced. When the question of how God relates to the physical world arises in the West, it assumes a common understanding of what is meant by *God* for the last fifteen hundred years. In Western culture the God of religion is the God of the Bible, whom Jews, Christians and Muslims all acknowledge is the all-powerful Creator of all things. A self-conscious being capable of communication, God is concerned for people in all aspects of their lives, from their moral to their physical well-being.

Historically, when people in the West have pondered how God relates to the physical world in light of what we know about science, they think in terms of the personal God of the Bible. Before dealing with this issue, however, it may be helpful to compare the God of the

Bible with other conceptions of deity among the major world religions. The thinking that gave birth to modern science arose within
the Christian educational institutions that served the late medieval
church. The assumptions about physical reality that made science
possible are rooted in the biblical view of a real physical world separate from God combined with Aristotle's understanding of
knowledge and how it is acquired. The Western question of how
God relates to the physical world assumes an enormous intellectual
and faith tradition that most people who ponder the question are
ignorant of. Realizing how other cultures think about the divine and
nature, however, may help to clarify the question and suggest some
aspects of a solution.

For many years the science-and-religion dialogue in the West assumed that *religion* meant Christianity. The rare scholar made reference to Judaism, with passing reference to Maimonides, though
rarely did the mainstream of the science-and-religion dialogue explore the uniquely Jewish perspective on the question. At one level
this marginalization of non-Christian perspectives represents what
might be expected from any entrenched establishment. At another
level, however, the science-and-religion dialogue emerged in the
West as an issue for Christianity and to a certain degree for Judaism.[1]
The discussion in the West began as an internal conversation within
Christianity.

Every culture has some form of science. Even the most primitive
societies have discovered something about nature that they consistently rely on. Such discoveries may include the medicinal value of
plants or the movement of the heavenly bodies. Each culture also has
its dominant religious understanding of reality. When Francis Bacon
proposed what came to be known as the scientific method in the early
seventeenth century, he began a conversation within Christianity that

---

[1]The Jewish community provided major contributions to science and to the science-and-religion
dialogue in the West during the medieval period and in the late modern period. But from the
late medieval period until the nineteenth century Jews were not allowed access to the new
learning of the universities in many countries in the West. Jews and Baptists could not attend
Oxford and Cambridge; thus, they were not in a position to be engaged at the same level as
those Christians who had access to the academy.

had implications for how Christians related their faith to the world around them.[2]

Within the broad umbrella of Christianity, however, major groups have understood the questions posed by modern science differently, as they have also arrived at different ways of relating science and religion. Catholic, Protestant and Orthodox Christians have had different attitudes toward the project over time. Thus, we cannot speak with any consensus about *the* Christian view of science. We must speak of different approaches by Christians to the issues related to science and religion.

The issues of science and religion normally occur as internal conversations within a religious community—until major intercultural change takes place. Colonialism breeds such change as products of one culture cross-fertilize with products of another. The scientific method is one such product that cultures around the world have adopted. This adoption has changed the practice of science around the world, achieving a rare standard of behavior. The common agreement of methodology has created a global scientific culture that cuts across the more traditional understandings of geographically or racially identifiable cultures. The common scientific culture, however, creates the need to be aware of the plurality of religious perspectives that exist within the scientific community.

Each religion has its own internal issues that arise as a result of the rise of modern science. As the science-and-religion dialogue takes on a global dimension that involves participants from many religious perspectives, the importance of understanding the issues of each particular religion has grown in importance. Just as it is inappropriate to speak of *the* Christian perspective on a particular issue raised by a scientific breakthrough, it is inappropriate to speak of *the* Buddhist, Islamic, Hindu or Jewish perspective. Each of these religions contains major subgroups that differ on important teachings or conceptions of their common religion.

---

[2]The period following Bacon also coincides with the imperial expansion of European kingdoms through the conquest and colonization of many traditional Islamic, Buddhist and Hindu empires. Muzaffar Iqbal explores the effects of European colonial expansion on the scientific tradition of Islam in *Islam and Science* (Aldershot, U.K.: Ashgate, 2002).

Just as a fundamentalist Protestant may have a different view than a Thomist Catholic of many questions related to science, so too will variety be found among the other religions of the world. The issues, however, will tend to be different from the issues dealt with by Christians.

HINDUISM

S. A. Nigosian refers to the caste system of India as based on "accidents of birth."[3] Within Hinduism, however, there are no "accidents of birth." Instead, *samara* (rebirth) and *karma* (action) determine the caste into which a person is born.[4] The process of rebirth or reincarnation has no beginning and no ending because it is the expression of the One, Brahman, Absolute Being. The world of experience is not created by the One. Rather, the world of experience is the expression of the One.

An individual self may attain identification with the universal self (Brahman) and thus find release from the cycle of rebirths. The Upanishads (800-500 B.C.), a large collection of sacred texts by many authors, which contain the philosophical foundation for Hinduism, refer to this liberation as *moksha*. Within the broad umbrella of Hinduism, however, various interpretations of the ultimate state of the individual knowing self in relation to Brahman have arisen, each with its own method for the self to escape the cycle of rebirth (fig. 1.1). Hindus recognize three major approaches to the problem of escaping the endless cycle of death and rebirth: *karma marga, jnana marga* and *bhakti marga*.[5]

Karma marga: Path of duties. The *karma marga* or "path of duties" involves the observance of the rituals, ceremonies, customs, social obligations and dietary laws of one's caste. These various duties for each caste are enumerated in the *Code of Manu*, compiled in the second century.[6] Manu is believed to be the father of the human race and the one who established the duties and order of society. Mohandas "Mahatma" Gandhi followed the "path of duties," which involved him in issues of justice and freedom as he involved himself in the issues facing his so-

---

[3]S. A. Nigosian, *World Religions: A Historical Approach*, 3rd ed. (New York: Bedford/St. Martin's, 2000), p. 23.
[4]Ibid., pp. 34-35.
[5]Ibid., p. 37.
[6]Ibid., p. 28.

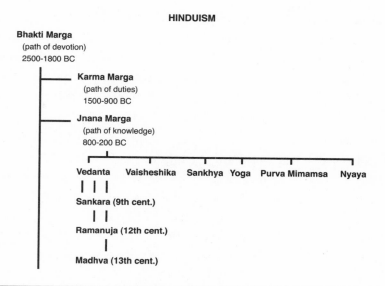

Figure 1.1. The paths within Hinduism

ciety.[7] This approach is rooted in early expressions of Hindu religion, with a tradition dating back to the period of the Vedas (1500-900 B.C.), the earliest Hindu texts comprising primarily hymns, chants and directions on ritual, spells, chants and incantations.[8]

Jnana marga: Path of knowledge. The *jnana marga* or "path of knowledge" involves the intellectual or philosophical approach to ultimate bliss. This approach is rooted in later developments of Hinduism and dates from the period of the Upanishads (800-200 B.C.). Mystic figures like Sri Ramana Bhagavan "Maharishi" have followed the "path of knowledge."[9] The path of knowledge has six major alternative systems in practice: Vedanta, Vaisheshika, Sankhya, Yoga, Purva Mimamsa, and Nyaya.

Vedanta system. The Vedanta system takes a philosophical approach to release based on the Upanishads, also known as Vedanta. Three distinct approaches to the Vedanta system have emerged.

---

[7]A. L. Herman, *A Brief Introduction to Hinduism: Religion, Philosophy, and Ways of Liberation* (Boulder, Colo.: Westview Press, 1991), pp. 1-8.
[8]Ibid., pp. 50-63.
[9]Ibid., pp. 63-87, 8-15.

- Sankara (ninth century A.D.) taught that the individual self and the physical world are illusions. The only true reality is Brahman, the only existent, who is not a "who," because Brahman is impersonal. Brahman's existence involves neither space nor time. In the Sankara tradition, liberation from the cycle of rebirths involves complete identification with Brahman.[10]

- Ramanuja (twelfth century A.D.) taught that the individual self and the physical world are not illusions at all. Rather, they form the "body" of Ultimate Reality or the manifestation of Brahman. The Ramanuja interpretation of the Upanishads regards Brahman as a personal being known as Vishnu, who is described as having every perfection, in contrast to the Sankara view of Brahman as impersonal and indescribable. Instead of complete identification with or absorption into Brahman, the ultimate state for the knowing self is an eternal state of conscious bliss in the presence of Brahman.[11]

- Madhva (thirteenth century A.D.) provided a third interpretation of the monism of the Upanishads which does not regard an individual knowing self as either one with Ultimate Reality or as the physical manifestation of the Ultimate Reality. Individual selves are freed from the cycle of rebirths by Vayu, the son of Vishnu, who breathes power into those he sets free. Those who are not set free by Vayu experience an eternity of rebirths.[12]

Besides the Vedanta system, other philosophical approaches to Hinduism explore how the self might escape the cycle of rebirths. These systems illustrate the variety of ways that various branches of Hinduism conceive of the Ultimate Reality and its relation to the world of experience. Let us briefly explore these various approaches.

Vaisheshika. The Vaisheshika system uses logic to explore the external world of experience, which is regarded as a self-existent combination of eternal and indivisible "atoms." The process of combination

---

[10]Nigosian, *World Religions*, p. 41.
[11]Ibid.
[12]Ibid., p. 42.

and recombination of atoms occurs through the power of Advishta, "the divine 'unseen force.'"[13] The eternal Self is the source of all individual selves. The eternal Self, individual selves and individual atoms all exist alongside each other eternally.

Sankhya. The Sankhya system recognizes two eternal categories of being: matter and self. Individual selves do not come from a higher eternal Self but are eternal in themselves. The self that is associated in one body after another through the cycle of rebirth may escape the cycle by the experience of "higher intelligence" *(budhi).* Through this experience of insight, ignorance and matter are both destroyed and the self is free to experience eternal existence without the physical constraints of endless rebirth.[14]

Yoga. The Yoga system has several expressions, but they have in common the disciplines of controlling the body and mind in order to free the individual self from the physical and mental distractions that prevent it from realizing unity with the Ultimate Reality. This discipline allows the attainment of pure consciousness in which the self, "emptied of all content and no longer aware of either object or subject, is absorbed into the Ultimate and is one with the One."[15]

Purva Mimamsa. The Purva Mimamsa system is the least philosophical of the philosophical approaches because it regards the Vedas as inspired in a way not normally found in Hinduism. The Vedas are regarded as eternal without human authorship. They have Ultimate Reality as their author, without mixture of error. By keeping the literal meaning of the Vedas and observing their rites and ceremonies, individual selves escape the cycle of rebirth. Obedient observance of the Vedas is rewarded by the "Supreme God." The philosophical or intellectual dimension of Purva Mimamsa involves the study and proper interpretation of the Vedas.[16]

Nyaya. The Nyaya system focuses on correct reasoning. The evil actions that result in individual selves experiencing evil consequences in

---

[13]Ibid., p. 38.
[14]Ibid.
[15]Ibid., p. 39.
[16]Ibid., p. 40.

rebirth come from faulty reasoning. Freedom from the cycle of rebirth, therefore, comes from correct reasoning.

The first path—the path of duties—is the path best known to the realm of activism and social involvement in the West. The second path—the path of knowledge—is the path best known to the philosophical and scientific communities of the West. Discussions of science and religion from a Hindu perspective tend to come from this area of Hinduism. Exports to the West include the Theosophical Society, Transcendental Meditation and the Divine Light Mission.[17] While these paths tend to receive the most attention in the West, they would be the less attractive forms of Hinduism in India today. The third path is by far the most popular expression of Hinduism in India.

Bhakti marga: Path of devotion. The third path, *bhakti marga* or the "path of devotion," allows adherents to attain freedom from the cycle of rebirth through devotion to a particular deity. This path has its origins in the ancient Harappan civilization that preceded the Aryan invasion of the Indus Valley (2500-1800 B.C.).[18] The *bhakti marga* may appear to be monotheistic or polytheistic because a god like Vishnu may assume a variety of forms and corporeal manifestations or *avatars*. In the twentieth century A. C. Bhaktivedanta Swami Prabhupada, founder of the International Society for Krishna Consciousness, is known to the West as someone who followed the "path of devotion."[19] The path of devotion involves an understanding of deities who affect disease, drought, wealth, luck, fertility, political power, love and every other aspect of the world of experience. Besides the three principle deities and their consorts, Hindu tradition acknowledges some 300 million other deities

---

[17]David M. Knipe, *Hinduism* (New York: HarperSanFrancisco, 1991), p. 150.

[18]Herman, *Brief Introduction to Hinduism*, pp. 38-49.

[19]Ibid., pp. 17-28. In 1972 a Hindu mystic named Swami Chinmayananda lectured at the University of South Carolina, where I served as chair of the lectures committee of the university during my undergraduate days. I helped to arrange the visit in cooperation with a group of students at the university who came from India. The swami represented the path of knowledge. He gave a highly engaging lecture that involved a reasoned argument for the existence of God. He was genial and generous of spirit to his audience, who knew little about India or Hinduism. He dealt with ignorance in a kind and comforting way. After the meeting, however, as we were leaving, a devotee of Krishna and follower of Swami Prabhupada approached him in the parking lot. He flew into a rage as the woman began to ask questions, and he ordered her to go away, cursing her as a heretic.

who may serve as village or household gods or goddesses.[20]

Against this simple sketch of the much more complex reality of the variety of religious and philosophical understandings within Hinduism, the science-and-religion dialogue takes place. We cannot simply speak of a Hindu view of science. Different branches of Hinduism regard the phenomenal world in different ways.

Observations. The common feature of Hinduism does not rest in a common understanding of Ultimate Reality or Brahman, nor in a common understanding of the nature of the world of experience. Hindus may manifest expressions of monism, pantheism, monotheism or polytheism. Nonetheless they share a common view that the human problem involves bondage to an endless cycle of death and rebirth. Religion is the means of liberation.

BUDDHISM

Buddhism does not quite fit the Western notion of religion, yet it does not quite qualify as a philosophy either. Nonetheless, it combines both philosophy and religion, for Buddhism is a way of life.[21] Buddhism emerged as a separate system from the path of knowledge of Hinduism at the end of the Upanishad period (c. 500 B.C.), but it continues to assume the Hindu problem of the unending cycle of rebirth and death. Buddhism begins with the present condition of existence, with the goal of attaining enlightenment, or a state of perfect freedom in existence.[22]

The founder of Buddhism was Siddhartha Gautama, a prince who struggled to understand why there was suffering and pain in the world. In his quest for enlightenment, Gautama identified the Four Noble Truths that Buddhists hold:

1. Human existence is characterized by suffering that involves (1) physical pain and mental anguish, (2) change, and (3) not being free. This form of human existence is impermanent, imperfect and dependent.[23]

2. Suffering is caused by dependent existence (conceived of by Ther-

---

[20]Nigosian, *World Religions*, pp. 44, 49.
[21]Richard A. Gard, *Buddhism* (New York: George Braziller, 1961), p. 14.
[22]Ibid., pp. 15-16.
[23]Ibid., pp. 109-10.

avada Buddhists as plurality of elements *(dharmas)* and by Mahayana
Buddhists as a relativity *(sunyata)* of elements.[24]

3. Freedom from suffering comes through the elimination or cessation
of causation.

4. The elimination of causation and attainment of *nirvana* comes
through the interdependent practice of right thought and right
conduct, which results in right being.[25]

The Four Noble Truths of Buddhism, by which Siddhartha Gautama
attained enlightenment and became the Buddha, should be understood
in the West as involving more than the cognitive/epistemological dimension of truth. They should also be understood as the metaphysical
experience of truth when taken together as a whole.[26] Buddhism involves
two major streams with particular variations in different countries that
interpret the Four Noble Truths in different ways (see fig. 1.2).

Theravada. Theravada Buddhism regards the self as the coordinated
combination of its component elements but having no true reality as a
thing in itself.[27] Causality involves the relationship of eternal unchanging elements. The eternal elements combine and then recombine
to represent the world of perceived reality, but it is not the world of ultimate reality.[28] The oldest group of Buddhism, Theravada, gives
central place to the Buddha as the great Master who embodies the life
of discipline that renounces the world. The Buddha is only a man, but

---

[24]Ibid., pp. 118-19. *Sunyata* is often interpreted as "void" or "nonexistence," Gard insists that the
concept has more the idea of "devoid of independence" or "relative." Nigosian, however, prefers
"void" or "emptiness" (see Nigosian, *World Religions,* p. 92).

[25]Ibid., p. 124. See also Dalai Lama, "Understanding and Transforming the Mind," in *Buddhism
& Science: Breaking New Ground*, ed. B. Alan Wallace (New York: Columbia University Press,
2003), pp. 91-92. The present Dalai Lama stresses that the experience of suffering involves
feeling as it relates to consciousness. The origin of suffering comes in *karma* or actions that
proceed from volitional consciousness. *Nirvana* comes through subduing of consciousness. If
consciousness is not subdued, *samsara* continues.

[26]Gard, *Buddhism,* p. 107.

[27]Theravada Buddhism is the older form of Buddhism found primarily in India and Southeast
Asia. It derives its name from the *theras* or "elders" and considers itself the champion of the
early orthodox understanding of Buddhism. *Mahayana* is a term variously translated as "Expansive Way" and "Great Vehicle." In contrast to itself, Mahayana has spoken of Theravada as
Hinayana or "Small Vehicle." While Theravada rejects the Hinayana terminology, Mahayana
insists that it has incorporated the Small Vehicle into the Great Vehicle.

[28]Gard, *Buddhism,* pp. 116-17.

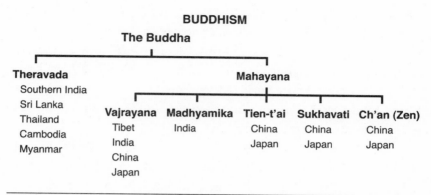

Figure 1.2. The major branches of Buddhism

he exemplifies the way to *nirvana*. A person may not follow the way of the Buddha in the present life, but eventually in a future life he or she must renounce the world in order to escape the cycle of death and rebirth. Theravada Buddhism is found primarily in India, Sri Lanka, Thailand, Cambodia and Myanmar.

Mahayana. Mahayana Buddhism does not regard anything as real that depends on something else. Thus, it does not regard the combination of eternal elements as real in any sense, not even in the nominal or momentary sense of Theravada Buddhism. Because of the interdependent nature of the eternal elements of Theravada Buddhism, not even the individual elements are regarded as real by Mahayana Buddhism because they depend on each other.[29] Mahayana Buddhism has many sects found in Tibet, Mongolia, China, Korea and Japan, the largest of which require some discussion. This study will examine five of the major sects.

Madhyamika. Madhyamika Buddhism arose in India and represents a philosophical approach to enlightenment that rejects the validity of extreme positions. The truth will be found somewhere between opposite positions. Never a large group, Madhyamika Buddhism has nevertheless had an influence on the major groups of Buddhism.

---

[29]Ibid., pp. 117-18. According to Gard, Theravada represents a form of radical pluralism while Mahayana represents a form of radical monism.

Tien-t'ai or Tendai. Tien-t'ai Buddhism arose in China and spread to Japan as Tendai. This approach has never been widely accepted. It affirms several approaches to Buddhism that in the West would be seen as mutually exclusive, but Tien-t'ai holds them as mutually inclusive: (1) all things are empty and void, without substantial reality, (2) all things have a temporary, passing existence, and (3) all things are both void and temporary at the same time.

Sukhavati. Amitabha, the Buddha of infinite light, called Sukhavati, the Western Paradise, into being by the power of his infinite merit. The Western Paradise is an intermediate state, also known as the Pure Land, where devotees of Amitabha have an easier way of escaping the endless cycle of death and rebirth. This popular approach to Buddhism in China and Japan includes the worship of Amitabha through prayers, songs of praise, chanting sacred texts and a variety of other acts of devotion that would correspond to (but by no means be equivalent to) aspects of popular Hinduism that venerate individual deities.

Vajrayana. Vajrayana Buddhism under the influence of Hindu tantricism follows Mahayana Buddhism in its philosophical understanding. This tantric form of Mahayana practiced in Tibet adds a nonspeculative dimension that includes esoteric beliefs and practices that involve physical exercises, gestures, sounds, rituals and visual aids. Because all things are one in the Mahayana system, this way views physical processes of equal value with mental processes as a way to Enlightenment.[30] The Tibetan Buddhist cosmology consists of millions of worlds, heavens and hells. Gods, goddesses and lesser spirits inhabit the heavens, the local places of earth and the nether world of hell. The gods of the earth and the nether world continually interact with people and require tribute (sacrifice) and worship.[31] Unique among Tibetan Buddhists is the recurring manifestation of Buddha in the *bodhisattvas*, those who have attained Enlightenment but defer *nirvana* for a time in order to help others in their journey. Tibetan Buddhism involves many

---

[30]Heinrich Dumoulin, *The Cultural, Political, and Religious Significance of Buddhism in the Modern World* (New York: Macmillan, 1976), pp. 161-62. Gard, *Buddhism* , p. 28. Nigosian, *World Religions*, pp. 91-92.

[31]Robert B. Ekvall, *Religious Observations in Tibet: Patterns and Function* (Chicago: University of Chicago Press, 1964), pp. 77-79.

lamas who are the living manifestation of *bodhisattvas*, "saviors," the most important of which are the Dalai Lama and the Panchen Lama.[32] These two, however, are not the only recurring *lamas*. There are many, and they reflect the spiritual levels or hierarchies connected with Tibetan Buddhism.

Ch'an or Zen. Ch'an Buddhism grew up in China and spread to Japan, where it is known as Zen. Whereas Western Paradise Buddhists believe that the Buddha has immeasurable merit that he bestows on his followers, Ch'an or Zen Buddhists do not believe that the Buddha has any merit at all to bestow. This school of Buddhism does not allow for understanding the Buddha as deity. One escapes the bondage of death and rebirth by meditation that leads to emptiness. The Zen meditation exercises focus on escaping rationality and the illusion of physical reality and individual existence.

Observations. Buddhism retained the Hindu problem of the cycle of death and rebirth, but the meaning of the individual knowing self has had an ambiguous career. The branches of Buddhism disagree over the nature of the phenomenal world as having either temporary reality or no reality at all.

Observations on the religions of reincarnation. The varieties of Hinduism and Buddhism share a common belief in the continuing cycle of death and rebirth rather than a common view of the divine. The various traditions within these two broad umbrellas of faith have a wide variety of views of God. The question of how God relates to the physical world does not have the same significance within these traditions. First, these religions do not have a tradition of divine revelation from a self-conscious being as the monotheistic religions do. Thus, they do not have a tradition of claims by a God who describes his activity in creation and history. Second, these religions and the cultures they produced do not have a dynamic view of the universe that led to the development of experimental science like that spawned by Christianity.

The understanding of reincarnation precedes written history. Its antiquity points to an agricultural community that lived by the cycles

---

[32]Ibid., p. 47.

of the seasons. The death and burial of the seed that grows to new life only to die again formed the central story for many ancient cultures from Egypt and Canaan to China. This prehistoric view of the world did not have the benefit of the rise of consecutive civilizations with their technological advances or the rise of modern science with its dynamic understanding of the universe, and picture of the development of the universe and its structures over fourteen billion years, to guide its thinking. Viewed locally in time and space, the universe appears like a static, cyclical place, but when we stand back seven thousand years in the history of human civilization and fourteen billion years in the history of the universe, the cycle of death and re-birth seems less compelling.

Whereas modern science challenges some traditional Christian theologies of how God relates to the physical world, modern science challenges the traditional Hindu and Buddhist views of nature.

JUDAISM

The Western world has been most familiar with Judaism of all non-Christian religions. Judaism had spread throughout the Roman Empire before the birth of Jesus Christ. Jesus Christ was Jewish, and the sacred books of ancient Israel became the foundational documents of the early Christians before the apostles of Jesus wrote the Christian Scriptures. Perhaps because of this familiarity with an aspect of ancient Judaism, the Christian West has assumed it understood Judaism more than it has.

Judaism comes from the faith of the people of the ancient kingdom of Judah, which became the Roman province of Judea. From this territory the Jews derive their name. Judaism and the Jews descend from the faith of the patriarch Abraham, who lived in the Fertile Crescent some four thousand years ago. Unlike the other ancient religions of the world, which deified the forces and cycles of nature, the descendants of Abraham worshiped a single God whom they believed had created the heavens and the earth. Not only had this God created all things, but he exercises power over all things as King and Ruler. This view of God and the created order would prove critical for the development of experimental science in the modern era. Instead of capricious spirits and deities governing the forces of earth and weather, a wise and righteous Creator held sovereignty over all forces. Instead of the heavenly bodies determining the fate and destiny of people and nations, a single, holy God brought about his purposes.

According to the ancient national story of Abraham's descendants, the God of Abraham made himself known to Moses by the name of Yahweh and commissioned Moses to be his representative to appear before the pharaoh of Egypt, the mightiest ruler on earth, and to demand that pharaoh free the enslaved descendants of Abraham. In the story of the exodus of the slaves from Egypt, Yahweh demonstrates his authority over all the forces of nature and establishes his faithfulness in keeping a promise to Abraham.

When Yahweh first speaks to Abraham, he appears to be little more than a household god, common among the cultures that stretched from Egypt to China. Yahweh makes small promises involving protection, prosperity, the gift of an heir to aged parents, and the promise that all the nations would be blessed through him. Over several generations Yahweh renews his promises to Isaac, Abraham's son, and then Jacob, Abraham's grandson. Yahweh gives Jacob the new name Israel and promises to extend his blessings to the children of Israel. As they grew in number, migrated to Egypt and eventually became a slave caste, the descendants of Abraham through Jacob come to be known as Israel.

When Yahweh freed Israel from Egyptian slavery, he established a covenant with the entire nation that involved promises on both sides.[33] Yahweh would be the God of Israel and Israel would keep the covenant commandments of Yahweh. This covenant established the religion of Yahweh worship that involved a hereditary priesthood, an elaborate sacrificial system and a highly restricted locus of worship that could only be practiced at one location. In addition to the cultic ritual, the covenant included expansive instructions on how people were to treat each other and how people were to practice their piety throughout the

---

[33]The dual nature of the Mosaic covenant appears most clearly in Deuteronomy with its lengthy statement of blessings if Israel kept the covenant and curses if Israel did not. Paul drew a strong contrast between the nature of the covenant of the Mosaic law and the covenant of grace mediated by Jesus Christ (Gal 3:1–5:1).

course of their lives, including the practice to cease all labor on the last day of their seven-day week.

For purposes of this discussion, one of the most important aspects of the religion of Israel was the understanding that God not only has absolute rule over all nature but also over the progress of history. The Jews came to have a linear view of reality as opposed to the cyclical view that predominates within nature religion. A linear view of time, space and the universe is critical for the development of a program of scientific discovery. The nation of Israel split in two following a civil war several centuries after the exodus. The northern kingdom of Israel was conquered by Assyria in 722 B.C. and the southern kingdom of Judah was conquered by Babylon in 586 B.C. The people of the northern kingdom disappeared, but the people of Judah persisted in their identity as followers of Yahweh until Persia conquered Babylon and allowed the people of Judah to rebuild their temple and resume their sacrificial system some seventy years after the fall of Jerusalem. Persia was conquered by Alexander the Great, and the territory of Judah passed from empire to empire until absorbed by the Romans in 63 B.C., when Pompey successfully laid siege to Jerusalem.

Following the fall of Jerusalem in 586, when the people of Judah could no longer fulfill the sacrificial system because the temple had been destroyed, a Jewish group arose that placed emphasis on studying the Scriptures and practicing the piety that each individual could follow with emphasis on keeping the day of rest. This movement grew and flourished among the Jews dispersed throughout the ancient world from India to Spain. Known as Pharisees, their weekly gatherings came to be known by their Greek term *synagogue*. With the restoration of temple worship, however, another group arose that placed emphasis on the temple cult. They were the Sadducees. Whereas the Pharisees accepted the prophecies and the wisdom literature of ancient Israel as revelation from Yahweh, the Sadducees only accepted the books of the law that focused on temple worship.

Under Roman rule, through a local Idumean collaborator, the temple worship was defiled when Herod politicized the office of high priest. Breaking with the tradition of the ceremonial law governing the priesthood, Herod made it an appointive office. Local hostility grew against Rome and the Herod family until the Jewish Revolt of A.D. 66 brought full-scale war. As a result of the war, Jerusalem was captured and the temple razed to the ground in A.D. 70, at which time the sacrificial system of the law of Moses came to an end. Without temple, priesthood and sacrifice, the religion of ancient Israel ended, but the faith of Abraham continued. The Sadducee party faded away, but the Pharisees, who had established synagogues in every major city in the Roman and Persian Empires, continued to observe the traditions. The city of Jamnia on the Palestinian coast south of Joppa became a center of Pharisaical Judaism under the leadership of Johann ben Zakkai, a student of Hillel, most prominent of ancient rabbis. Through this center the Pharisees' determination of the Hebrew Scriptures was defined.

The rabbis or teachers of the law relied on the continuity of the oral tradition of scriptural interpretation, which formed the Mishnah. Over the centuries following Jamnia, the commentary on the Mishnah grew into the Talmud. The Jews kept their identity and their faith within pagan Rome, Persia and India through attention to the teachings of the law and the observation of the traditions handed down from generation to generation. By this means they flourished in a broad array of cultures, yet without cultural assimilation.

After the rise of Christendom, several distinct ethnic groups of Jews developed in different regions. Ashkenazi Jews were identified with central and eastern Europe. This group makes up some 80 percent of the worldwide Jewish population and is the group of Jews most familiar to the American experience. Sephardi Jews were located on the Iberian Peninsula. Mizrahi Jews can be found across North Africa and the Middle East. The Mizrahi community would have been the most prominent during the first thousand years of modern Judaism, flourishing in the intellectual and commercial centers of the Islamic world. Maimonides, the great Jewish philosopher, theologian and physician of the twelfth century, fled Spain for the more open climate of Egypt. Smaller groups include the Yemenite Jews found in the Southern Arabian Peninsula and the Beta Israel Jews of Ethiopia.

For the most part, Jews were excluded from university study in

Europe until the modern period. Until the modern period, university study meant religious study because the universities were collections of monastic orders. Jews had their own schools for preserving the traditions and studying the Torah and Talmud. The result of this difference in religious education meant that Jews were not involved in the changing nature of education and learning in the European universities. Within the Islamic world, however, different conditions existed from time to time. During the time of Maimonides, for instance, a Jewish philosopher living in Egypt had intellectual opportunities that neither Jews nor Christians had in twelfth century Germany. Living as a distinct people within the medieval feudal society of Christendom, the Jews of Europe had a different task from that of Christians: the primary task of survival.

Following the upheaval of the Reformation and the initial blast of the scientific revolution in the late eighteenth century, the relationship of Jews to the broader society of Europe began to change. In England, Jews and even Baptists were allowed to enter the universities. In a short time Jews would make monumental contributions to the study of the natural sciences. In this climate, however, Judaism would suffer from the challenge to tradition. The same fractions to religious tradition that occurred in all the other world religions would come to Judaism in the modern period with several alternative forms of practice.

Orthodox Judaism. Orthodox Judaism continues the traditional practice of Judaism from ancient times, with gradual accommodation to local culture and practice in matters not touched on by tradition. The Orthodox Jews hold to the teachings of Maimonides on the thirteen principles that constitute Jewish faith.

Conservative Judaism. Conservative Judaism upholds the inspiration of the Torah by God but does not agree with Orthodox Judaism that it was dictated by God to Moses. Conservative Jews acknowledge the tradition of interpretation but allow for a continuing interpretation of the law in light of modern realities.

Reform Judaism. Reform Judaism moves in a more liberal direction in its departure from holding to tradition. Reform Judaism places its emphasis more on moral and ethical behavior than on the rituals and ceremonies of the past. Corporate worship involves an egalitarian atmosphere of participation not found in the older male-dominated forms of Judaism.

Besides these groups, several new and smaller groups began in the twentieth century that deemphasize the place of tradition and the classic Jewish understanding of God as the center of Jewish identity. Among these are Reconstructionist Judaism, which began in the 1920s and views God as the sum of all natural processes rather than as a personal being. Under Reconstructionist thought, Judaism has more to do with cultural ethnicity than with religion.

Judaism continues to work out the relationship between tradition and innovation in the context of the modern world. As a tiny minority on earth, the Jews continue to deal with issues of survival as a people. They continue to be a great historical problem in explaining how a group scattered across the globe can retain their identity for 2,500 years. In the context of survival, the question of God's protection and even God's existence has haunted the Jewish community since the horrors of the Nazi genocide. The problem of suffering poses a major issue in Jewish thought when considering how God relates to the physical world.

ISLAM

Islam emerged on the Arabian Peninsula in the seventh century under the leadership of the prophet Muhammad (571-632), who called the tribal people of the region to faith in the God of Abraham, the only God, who created the world. According to tradition, the Arabs descend from Abraham's eldest son, Ishmael. The God of Abraham is a personal being, perfect in all attributes, who exercises sovereign power over all creation. He created with purpose and intention and will one day judge all people with justice and mercy as he rewards the faithful with eternal bliss in paradise or punishes the wicked with eternal torment in hell. God cannot be known in any way except as he reveals himself through his prophets, the last and greatest of whom was Muhammad. God revealed to Muhammad his definitive revelation, the Qur'an, which means "recitation." This revelation came by means of the angel Gabriel, who recited it to Muhammad, who in turn recited it to his followers who wrote it down. The collection of many recitations was edited during the time of Caliph Uthman (644-656).[34] Muslims believe that the 114 chapters of the Qur'an are the perfect expression of the will of God and are copies of the original texts in heaven.

Islam includes two main groups, each with a variety of subgroups that differ over matters of succession from the Prophet and approaches to interpretation of the Qur'an (see fig. 1.3). When the Prophet died, the elders elected Abu Bakr, Muhammad's first adult male convert and his father-in-law, to serve as caliph (successor). The Sunni Muslims accept the legitimacy of this succession and constitute the majority group of Muslims. Many Muslims believed, however, that Muhammad had intended for Ali, his cousin and son-in-law, to succeed him. Abu Bakr appointed Omar as his successor, but Omar was assassinated. Six electors appointed by Omar chose Uthman to succeed him, but he was also assassinated. In 656, Ali finally became caliph through the support of the Hasimite tribe. War broke out when Muawiya, governor of Syria, refused to support Ali. A third group, the Khariji (seceeders), emerged in the midst of the strife and rejected both Ali and Muawiya. One of these Khariji assassinated Ali, whereupon Muawiya succeeded to the caliphate and founded the Umayyad Dynasty. The eldest son of Ali accepted a pension instead of pressing his claims. The younger son, Hussain, agreed not to press his claim during Muawiya's life. When Muawiya died and named his own son Yezid to succeed him, Hussain raised a following known as the Shi'ah (partisans) of Ali. The Battle of Karbala (680) ensued in which Hussain and all of his followers were killed by a much larger army.[35]

Shiites. Since the Battle of Karbala, the Shiite Muslims have insisted that only the descendents of Muhammad could be legitimate successors or caliphs to the Prophet. They believe that the line of descent flows through Ali. The descendants of Muhammad who succeeded him took the title of imam or spiritual head, instead of caliph. The Shiite group

---

[34]N. J. Dawood, "Introduction," *The Koran*, trans. N. J. Dawood (London: Penguin Classics, 1999), pp. 1-4.
[35]Ruqaiyyah Waris Maqsood, *Islam* (Chicago: Contemporary Books, 2003), pp. 24-27.

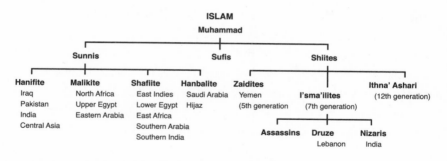

Figure 1.3. The major groups within Islam

had to modify its understanding of the succession as the different lines of the Prophet's descendants came to an end. The Shiites divided over which line of descent they considered the true line. The Zaidites of Yemen believe that the line continued to the fifth generation. The Ithna' Ashari (Twelvers) of Iran believe that the line continued for twelve generations. The I'sma'ilites (Seveners) believe that the line continued for seven generations.[36] This group includes the Assassins of legendary fame, the Druze of Lebanon and the Nizaris of India under the leadership of the Aga Khan.[37] All of the groups of Shiites have in common the belief that the last legitimate, lineal successor to the Prophet did not die. The last imam mysteriously disappeared but continues to maintain a mystical presence with the world and the course of history as the Hidden Imam. The Hidden Imam will someday return as the Mahdi, who will usher in the end of the world.[38]

The concern for the legitimate successor to the Prophet has deep theological roots. By believing in a successor determined by blood descent, the Shiites affirmed that the successor would be determined by Allah and not left to human error. This view reflects the Shiite understanding that God determines all natural processes but does not determine human action. As the successor to the Prophet designated by God, the imam has sole authority in the interpretation of the Qur'an.

---

[36]Will Durant, *The Age of Faith*, The Story of Civilization 4 (New York: Simon & Schuster, 1950), pp. 261-62.
[37]Ibid., pp. 309-10.
[38]Maqsood, *Islam*, p. 29. See also Durant, *Age of Faith*, p. 217.

Sunnis. The Sunnis constitute the vast majority of Muslims. The term comes from the word *sunna*, which conveys the idea of the consensus of the community, or the tradition.[39] While the Shiites regard the majority Sunnis as a corruption of true Islam, Sunnis believe that they carry on the true tradition of Islam that is "practical, tolerant, and compassionate."[40] Instead of vesting interpretive authority in the imam, the Sunnis rely on tradition (*sunna*) and the consensus of scholars (*ijma*) for the interpretation of the Qur'an. The tradition has grown through the centuries, but four major approaches to interpretation have developed: Hanifite, Malikite, Shafiite and Hanbalite.[41]

Hanifite. The Hanifite constitute a more liberal approach to interpretation as regards practice. It has major support in Iraq, Pakistan, India and Central Asia.

Malikite. The Malikite interpret practice according to the Qur'an and the Hadith, the traditional sayings ascribed to the Prophet that were collected in various versions by his followers. The Malikite rely on the consensus opinion of the Medina community in their teaching of the Qur'an and Hadith. The Malikite approach has strong following in North Africa, upper Egypt and eastern Arabia.

Shafiite. The Shafiite approach developed a "science" of interpreting the law that combined elements of the other approaches for application in an expanding Islam. This approach has adherents in the East Indies, lower Egypt, east Africa, southern Arabia and southern India.

Hanbalite. The Hanbalite approach has stressed the letter of the law. It emerged in response to the decadence of the court in Baghdad. Its strongest following is in Saudi Arabia and Hijaz.

Sufis. Alongside the Shiites and Sunnis, the Sufis represent the mystical element of Islam. Sufism developed largely in reaction to the

---

[39]Nagosian, *World Religions*, p. 326. Maqsood, *Islam*, p. 29.

[40]Maqsood, *Islam*, p. 28.

[41]Muzaffar Iqbal insists that the various approaches to the interpretation of the Qur'an should not be referred to as "schools," which suggests a division of Islamic law. Islamic law should not be seen as divided since the collective literature of these four "traces its origins to the universally applied twin sources of Islamic law—the Qur'an and the Sunna of the Prophet of Islam" (*Islam and Science* [Aldershot, U.K.: Ashgate, 2002], pp. 147-48). The ones for whom these approaches are named are Abu Hanifa (d. 767), Malik b. Anas (d. 795), al-Shafi'i (d. 820) and Ahmad b. Hanbal (d. 855).

perceived legalism and ritual of the dominant expression of Islam at the time. The Sufis have held that leadership should go to the one who most emulates the lifestyle of the Prophet in humility, piety and simplicity. Sufis have been criticized and at times persecuted by orthodox Muslims for some of their heterodox beliefs and practices. The emphasis on personal union with God, the use of music and other means to induce transcendental experience (as with the dervishes), veneration of teachers and saints, and the formation of separate groups, has set the Sufis apart as a noticeable group within Islam.[42]

Observations on Islam and nature. All branches of Islam share the fundamental belief that Allah, the only God, is one and has created all the physical and nonphysical worlds. Muzaffar Iqbal explains, "The Physical cosmos observes a Divine Law just as humans are supposed to."[43] All Muslims also believe that Muhammad is the prophet of Allah. The Qur'an is the revelation of Allah and is perfect in its teaching. The science-and-religion dialogue in the West has historically involved a dialogue between science and Christian theology rather than a dialogue between science and the Bible. Within the Islamic world, however, the dialogue must deal with nature as described in the revealed text of the Qur'an.[44] Though Muslims agree that everything that happens within the universe is ordained by God without randomness or chance, they disagree over the extent of human free will.

REFLECTIONS ON SCIENCE AND RELIGION

Nature religions typically promote a cyclical view of reality as expressed in the concept of reincarnation. The seasons that agriculture depends on constantly reinforced this cyclical view. People who live in a preliterate, prehistoric agrarian society would notice the cycle of the seasons and the rhythm of the tides. Prescientific peoples live in a small world with a narrow view of the way the universe works. The sun sets, the sun also rises. The moon waxes and wanes. The stars move in their courses

---

[42]Maqsood, *Islam*, pp. 132-39; Nagosian, *World Religions*, pp. 326-27.

[43]Iqbal, *Islam and Science*, p. 33.

[44]Muzaffar Iqbal, "Islam and Modern Science: Questions at the Interface," *God, Life, and the Cosmos: Christian and Islamic Perspectives*, ed. Ted Peters, Muzaffar Iqbal and Syed Nomanul Haq (Aldershot, U.K.: Ashgate, 2002), p. 16.

and come 'round again. Close up, the world is an endless cycle of repetition. Given a perspective of fourteen billion years and a good radio telescope, however, the motion of nature looks different. From the vantage point of twenty-first-century biology, chemistry, physics and astronomy, we have a perspective to recognize the progressive, linear or evolutionary character of nature.[45] Likewise, we have a historical perspective that the preliterate world lacked. We can reflect on the past since the invention of writing, which tells us that human culture has a direction that contrasts with a cyclical view. As religion in India has developed from a polytheistic nature religion to a philosophical monism, it has retained a commitment to a cyclical understanding of reality while shedding both the theological and prescientific bases for that view. For the various expressions of Hinduism and Buddhism, the question of how the divine relates to the physical world is framed by an entirely different mindset than people in the West take for granted.

In contrast with the nature religions of antiquity, the ancient Hebrews had a different notion of reality. The children of Israel did not have a broad enough historical or scientific perspective to develop a linear view of nature or history. Culture had not changed in a significant way. Technology had not advanced sufficiently to notice the development of civilization. The experience of the community had not persisted long enough to see beyond the appearance of the cycles, yet Israel abandoned a cyclical view of reality in favor of a linear view that would not become apparent until modern times. One of the great anthropological problems concerns how the Hebrews could adopt a faith in a God of purpose, hope and progress so at odds with human experience of seasons and the cultural understanding that prevailed at that time. Though scientific investigation depends on a linear nature to time, scientific understanding of a linear development of the universe and its components did not become available until the modern era.

Islam follows Judaism and Christianity in affirming the Creator

---

[45]The idea of a cyclical expansion and contraction of the universe continued to have appeal until the most recent observations revealed that the expansion rate of the universe has accelerated, making a contraction most unlikely. This aspect of cosmology will be explored more fully in chap. 5.

God of nature and history. As we have seen, however, Islam has a focus on the will of God that goes beyond affirmations of most Jewish and Christian groups. Islamic groups have disagreed over how they interpret the Qur'an's teaching about God's will, but the challenge for Muslims involved in the sciences concerns how to allow for contingency, variation, flux, randomness and chance in a world dictated by the will of God. Unlike the Bible, which contains a variety of models for how God relates to the physical world, the Qur'an focuses on the submission of all things to the will of God. Whatever transpires is the will of God.

To a certain extent, the religions of India and Islam represent the extreme alternatives for how the divine relates to the physical world. The Qur'an speaks of God as totally other from the world which is under his absolute control. The philosophical branches of Hinduism or Zen Buddhism, on the other hand, conceive of the divine as inseparable from the world, yet uninvolved in its direction.

This brief survey of the complexity of diversity within the major non-Western religious traditions suggests the need for discretion in representations of what the various traditions believe about the nature of physical reality, the nature of transcendent reality and the relationship between the two. Each of the religious traditions surveyed has some diversity of understanding about the physical and the transcendent. Members of a strand of a tradition may tend to think of their strand's understanding as representative of the thinking of their entire tradition. Likewise, those from other traditions or no religious tradition may tend to generalize and categorize all the strands of a tradition in terms of a single strand with which they have some familiarity.

Against the backdrop of this complex variety of religious perspectives on physical reality lies another feature of the science-and-religion dialogue that may arise as a result of the global culture of science. A scientist's religious views may not necessarily represent the perspective of his or her own religious tradition.

Compartmentalization has been a feature of the Western intellectual tradition that allows a scientist (or anyone else) to hold contradictory ideas by relegating them to different areas of life. This dynamic may come as an aspect of the complexity of knowledge and could be expected to occur in non-Western traditions as well. On the other hand, some scientists alter their theological understanding as a result of their scientific work. Within the West this dynamic has resulted in the dramatic transformation of approaches to Christian theology in the modern era. We could expect that the same dynamic occurs in non-Christian settings as well. In these situations the perspective of a scientist, or a theologian influenced by modern science, may no longer represent the traditional understanding of the religious tradition he or she comes from. This distinction becomes important in a pluralistic discussion when someone represents new insights as the view of his or her religious community. When we add racial, ethnic and gender diversity within subgroups, the need for discretion in our assertions becomes even more compelling.

Modern science in faith perspective. We have briefly explored the variety of conceptions of the universe and of how deity might relate to it from a world religions perspective. Each culture has developed some form of science or knowledge of the physical world. Astronomy is one of the most ancient sciences, largely because of how the heavens related to the concept of deity among the ancient nature religions. Modern science, however, arose in a culture that had a late start. Western culture lagged far behind the great cultures of the East. The emergence of modern experimental and theoretical science took place as an expression of the core beliefs and values of the culture in which it appeared. Beliefs have consequences. Often it is the unintended consequences of belief that have some of the most profound and far-reaching impact.

A matter of continuing curiosity concerns why modern science emerged in northern Europe instead of in a region that had a longer and more developed intellectual tradition such as the Indus River valley, the Yellow River valley, the Nile River valley or the Tigris and Euphrates basin. China, India and the Islamic world made remarkable discoveries about the physical world and the world of mathematics when northern Europe was still semibarbaric, yet northern Europe made sudden and dramatic gains in scientific knowledge beginning in the sixteenth century.

This discussion of the basic beliefs of the major world religions suggests one aspect of an answer to why the method of modern science did not arise in other cultures. Ancient nature religions were not inclined to develop a system of studying natural phenomena when all phenomena were seen as the activity of nature gods, spirits or demons. In the same way, when the world is seen as an illusion, the intellect turns in another direction. When the world is seen as a single expression of deity, then the idea of the kind of differentiation necessary for scientific study does not happen. When all phenomena in an objective, physical world are seen as the will of God rather than as events that follow an established law, then one is not inclined to seek to discover natural laws. Basic beliefs about God and nature set the context in which modern science developed as an expression of those beliefs in the West such that we can describe the course of science as "methodological theism."

The nature of deity among Christians differs from the understanding of deity by the two other great monotheistic religions that believe in a Creator. The God of Christian faith exists in three divine persons: Father, Son and Spirit. While the Father exhibits the authority and intent of the God of Judaism and Islam, the Son expresses the identification of God with the physical world associated with Hinduism, and the Spirit manifests the force that holds all reality together that we find in Buddhism. The basic gospel faith of Christians allowed them to think of the world in a different way.

While the other cultures had the intellect for science, they lacked one ingredient that came from an unlikely source as the modern world would count likely sources for scientific discovery. They never experienced anything comparable to the Protestant Reformation, which rejected tradition as the final authority in matters of religion. While Christians of the medieval period had the same faith as Christians of the early modern period, they were bound by another aspect of their worldview that had nothing to do with the Bible and their faith. Medieval Western Europeans believed in the philosophy of Plato as firmly as they believed the gospel because Augustine had utilized Plato in the development of his theological system in the fifth century. In fact, they read their Bible through the grid of a Platonic understanding of reality.

This Platonic reading of the Bible cast their intellects to the contemplation of the "other world," the world beyond the physical. In the thirteenth century, Thomas Aquinas broke with Augustine and based his theological system on the philosophy of Aristotle. Not until Western Europeans grew warm to the philosophy of Aristotle, with its focus on knowledge of the physical world, did they have the tools in place for the scientific revolution. With the spirit of reformation, however, they obtained the method they needed for scientific research and the intentional pursuit of knowledge.

In his discussion of the rise of modern science, Alfred North Whitehead dismissed the Protestant Reformation as a "domestic affair" and a "popular uprising" that "drenched Europe in blood."[46] He manages to think of modern science as somehow unrelated to religion, when modern science is the product of religion, and more specifically, it is the product of a heated debate within the Christian communities of learning in the West. In the Reformation the principle issue at stake was one of authority. In the sixteenth century the science faculty did not observe with detached bemusement the discussions of the theology faculty. The science faculty *was* the theology faculty. The university was a monastic community. All disciplines were subdisciplines of theology. Theology was the "queen of the sciences" and philosophy was her handmaiden. The Protestant Reformation was not only a debate about authority in matters of religion but also authority in politics and all areas of scholarship, including what we now call science.

Scripture and tradition. The change of mind that we call the Reformation began to take place at least 150 years before Luther's posting of his ninety-five theses, and it would continue to unfold 150 years afterward. Rather than the product of the later Renaissance as Whitehead suggests,[47] this way of conceiving authority had begun at least by the time of John Wycliffe (d. 1384), long before the observations of Copernicus (d. 1543). We might even argue that it played a large part in the thought of William of Occam (d. c. 1350).

---

[46]Alfred North Whitehead, *Science and the Modern World* (New York: Free Press, 1967), pp. 1-2.

[47]Ibid., p. 8.

Occam repudiated the philosophical theology of the Scholastic tradition, the speculative approach to theology of the late medieval period. He regarded natural theology as an impossible project and insisted on Scripture as the ultimate authority in religion. He ascribed to it an authority above pope or ecclesiastical hierarchy. The interpretation of Scripture belonged not to clergy only but also to "the discretion and counsel of the wisest men sincerely zealous for justice without respect to persons, if such can be found—whether they be poor or rich, subjects or rulers."[48] Williston Walker observed that "in his contest with what he deemed a derelict papacy he taught that Scripture, and not the decisions of councils and Popes, is alone binding on the Christian. No wonder that Luther, in this respect, could call him 'dear master.'"[49]

Occam did not create a new way of thinking. He merely modified a growing intellectual stream of thought that reached back earlier in the medieval period. The medieval world built upon the Augustinian tradition that looked to Plato and the Thomist tradition that looked to Aristotle. Though Plato and Aristotle differed greatly over the reliability of sensory observation of the world of experience, they both appealed in some way to the universal forms and how the physical world relates to them. The great revolution in thought came with the nominalists, who argued that universal forms had no existence other than as names for things in the world of experience. In contrast to the nominalists, the realists affirmed that the universals exist. In the twelfth-century debate over transubstantiation, the nominalists lost and transubstantiation was declared dogma by the Fourth Lateran Council in 1215. William of Occam appropriated nominalism, but tried to make it fit within the limits of church dogma.

By the time of Wycliffe a great schism divided the Church of Rome, with multiple popes and intricate political machinations between popes, kings and emperors. It was a time during which religious orders grew

---

[48]William of Occam, *De Imperatorum et Pontificum Potestate*, p. 27, 11. 17-20, as cited in Ernest A. Moody, "William of Ockham," *The Encyclopedia of Philosophy*, ed. Paul Edwards (New York: Macmillan, 1972), 8:317.

[49]Williston Walker, *A History of the Christian Church*, 3rd ed. (New York: Charles Scribner's, 1970), p. 252.

wealthy in the accumulation of lands that had formerly been attached to parish churches to support the local priest through the income from the farm. This problem led to the practice of "multiple livings," whereby a priest might have two or three parishes widely separated and which he might visit just a few times a year, if at all.[50] In the face of these and other issues, Wycliffe turned to the Bible as his authority. He rejected transubstantiation, which had been the official teaching of the Roman Church for over 150 years. With a multiple papacy, Wycliffe rejected the authority of the pope as head of the church. Instead, he regarded Christ as the head of the church.[51] In these and other matters he reached his conclusions through a study of Scripture freed from the accumulated traditions of the church since the first century.

The translation of the Bible into the vernacular, which Wycliffe promoted, came about because of the place that Scripture held in Wycliffe's theology. While Wycliffe's controversial teachings addressed the abuses and corruption of the Roman Church and its place in society, the basis for his teachings all went back to the Bible as his authority. Wycliffe insisted that "faith depends on the Scriptures," and that "to ignore the Scriptures is to ignore Christ."[52] Wycliffe respected the doctors of the church and utilized their arguments for support, particularly the arguments of Augustine. Nevertheless, he never placed the tradition of the church on the same level of authority as Scripture.[53] It is particularly important to note that Wycliffe used the category of "law" when speaking of the Bible rather than one of the philosophical terms associated with the philosophical tradition of medieval theology. Herbert Winn, editor of Wycliffe's works, argued that Wycliffe's understanding of Scripture "formulated the great Protestant ideal of

---

[50]George Macauley Trevelyan, *England in the Age of Wycliffe* (New York: Longmans, Green, 1935), pp. 121-26.

[51]John Wycliffe, *Select Writings, by John Wycliffe*, ed. Herbert E. Winn (Oxford: Oxford University Press, 1929), p. 132. Wycliffe declared that Christ "is the heed of the Chirche; and He ordeynede a lawe to men, and confermede it with his lyf, for to reule holi Chirche, and teche how that men shulde lyve."

[52]John Wycliffe, quoted in John Stacy, *John Wyclif and Reform* (Philadelphia: Westminster Press, 1964), p. 80.

[53]Ibid., pp. 81, 94.

freedom from authority and validity of the private judgment."[54]

Wycliffe belonged to a stream of thought within the Church of Rome prior to the Reformation. John Hus (d. 1415), a disciple of Wycliffe from Bohemia, brought Wycliffe's understanding of Scripture and tradition back with him from England to the University of Prague, where he expounded on these ideas. Hus argued,

> For this truth, because of certitude, a man ought to expose his life to the danger of death. And, in this way, every Christian is expected to believe explicitly and implicitly all the truth which the Holy Spirit has put in Scripture, and in this way a man is not bound to believe the sayings of the saints which are apart from Scripture, nor should he believe papal bulls, except in so far as they speak out of Scripture, or in so far as what they say is founded in Scripture simply.[55]

For his opinion Hus was condemned by the Council of Constance and burned at the stake. For good measure, the council ordered that Wycliffe's bones be exhumed from his grave and burned as well. As for the Bible, the council decided that it was too dangerous for the common folk and it was restricted to use by the clergy. Once out in the open, however, the idea that tradition might somehow inhibit one's grasp of the truth had become firmly planted in the consciousness of the church, even if only as an idea to condemn. Wycliffe and Hus did not merely reject tradition. They also insisted on going to a reliable source for truth. They insisted on going to the primary source rather than to tradition about that source.

According to Dorothy L. Sayers, "It was the rise of the New Learning, which led eventually to the Reformation, to the Renaissance and to the invention of Scientific Method."[56] Sayers argued that the old world fell apart because the professionals who ran the old world grew lazy in their habits and old-fashioned in their ideas. In other words, they were bound by the traditions they were inextricably a part of. Rather than the professional leadership of the church, "It was certain amateur thinkers who

---

[54]Winn, ed., *Select Writings by John Wycliffe*, p. xviii.

[55]John Hus, *The Church*, trans. David S. Schaff (Westport, Conn.: Greenwood Press, 1976), p. 71.

[56]Dorothy L. Sayers, *Begin Here* (New York: Harcourt, Brace, 1941), p. 36.

hit upon that new method of thought which we now call 'scientific'; by
which we mean the method that collects facts by observation, uses them
to form a theory, and then tests the theory by fresh experiments with
facts."[57]

Sayers viewed the explosion of knowledge in astronomy and physics
as a piece with the new notions of art and literature that accompanied
the new way of thinking about religion. The renaissance in art merely
swept aside the accumulated medieval tradition as the new thinking in
theology had swept aside the accumulated tradition of the church in
favor of an older, more authentic and reliable source. The arts found
their older source in the ancient world into which Christ was born.

When Martin Luther raised the issue of authority in 1517, he operated out of the conviction that tradition could not lead to ultimate
truth and salvation. He believed in the priority of Scripture as his ultimate authority. As a professor of Old Testament, Luther developed
his theology from an examination of the Bible rather than through the
scholastic method of philosophical categories that had dominated in
the church for centuries. In particular, Luther rejected the authority of
Aristotelian philosophy in the interpretation of the Bible.

The scientific method of Francis Bacon. The work of Francis Bacon
(d. 1626) in developing what we now call the "scientific method"
emerged in the context of the working out of the English Reformation.
The Puritans hoped to carry the English Reformation further than
Henry VIII had been willing to go. The concerns of the Puritans coincided with the method of Bacon. First, like the earlier Reformers,
they proposed to eliminate the traditions of the English Church,
whether in theology or ceremony. Second, they proposed to introduce
a preaching ministry to England that spoke plainly, rather than in the
allegorical literary style that had prevailed for centuries. Third, they
intended to discover God's laws for the governance of his church as
laid down in Scripture.

The proposal Bacon made for scientific research involved nothing
less than a rejection of the received philosophical tradition as the deter-

[57]Ibid., pp. 37-38.

minative starting point for understanding the physical world. His initial thoughts on what has come to be known as the scientific method were published as *Novum Organum* in 1620. The *Novum Organum* or *New Organon* was a takeoff on Aristotle's treatise on rational thinking titled *Organon*.[58] Though Aristotle's philosophy had been the catalyst for engaging the physical world during the high Middle Ages, by the time of Bacon it had become a straight jacket. Just as the Reformers had insisted on going to the Bible as God's revealed Word for its authority, Bacon insisted on going to creation as God's handiwork to understand the physical order. The Puritans and their theological forebears had rejected the authority of tradition and insisted on immediate examination of the written text. Bacon rejected the authority of philosophical tradition and insisted on the immediate examination of the observable data. The purpose of the scientific method was not to protect scientific inquiry from the assumption that God had made everything. Rather, the purpose of the scientific method was to protect science from the speculative philosophical systems that explained the world rationalistically by theory without recourse to experimentation. The philosophical explanations, instead of the "God hypothesis," hampered science in understanding how the world works.[59]

The most famous case of this sort occurred with Galileo, who was attacked and prosecuted by the academy for holding ideas that conflicted with Aristotle's explanations of the world. Though Aristotle focused attention on the physical world, which created a climate for scientific observation, he also offered deductive explanations for much of scientific phenomena. Galileo's great case was not a conflict of science and religion, but of science and Aristotelian philosophy. The

---

[58]Aristotle had included his categories and his ideas about interpretation in his collection on analytics that was named *Organon* (instrument). The significance of Bacon naming his work the *New Organon* was not lost on anyone. In his preface Bacon began, "Those who have taken upon them to lay down the law of Nature as a thing already searched out and understood, whether they have spoken in simple assurance or professional affectation, have therein done philosophy and the sciences great injury. For as they have been successful in inducing belief so they have been effective in quenching and stopping inquiry; and have done more harm by spoiling and putting an end to other men's efforts than good by their own."

[59]I first developed the preceding ideas in Harry Lee Poe, "Christianity and the Future of Higher Education," *Findings*, Winter 2004, www.breakpoint.org/features-columns/articles/entry/12/9192.

arrest of Galileo (d. 1642) illustrates Bacon's concern. The academic community could not tolerate his rejection of Aristotle's cosmology. The fact that his telescope demonstrated that the moon is not the perfect sphere Aristotle's philosophy had demanded held little weight against the ingrained philosophical view of the academy.[60] The questioning of tradition had not only been a problem in far-off Prague and Oxford with Hus and Wycliffe, but the local situation in Florence where Galileo lived had erupted in revolution just a few years earlier with Savonarola. Galileo stood in the tradition of rejecting tradition.

The great advance in scientific knowledge began with Francis Bacon's argument that the acquisition of knowledge cannot blossom through reliance on ancient philosophy or tradition.[61] Instead, his scientific method involved experimentation through trial and error. Bacon proposed replacing Aristotle's method of *deductive* reasoning from unquestionably true premises with a new method of *inductive* reasoning based on the raw evidence found in nature. Bacon's method proceeds through a process of elimination rather than from an axiom of affirmation. He explained that

> If the mind attempts to do this affirmatively from the beginning (as it always does if left to itself), fancies will arise and conjectures and poorly defined notions and axioms needing daily correction, unless one chooses (in the manner of the Schoolmen) to defend the indefensible.[62]

Just as the Reformers had rejected the heavily philosophically grounded deductive method of medieval scholasticism in favor of exposition of the Bible, Bacon rejected the philosophically based science of the medieval period inherited from the Greeks in favor of the exposition of nature.

In his discussion Bacon distinguished between the *metaphysics* of the philosopher and the *physics* of the scientist. Metaphysics deals with the eternal world of forms and final causes, while physics deals with effi-

---

[60]I first expressed these ideas in Harry Lee Poe, *What God Knows: The Question of Time and Divine Knowledge* (Waco, Tex.: Baylor University Press, 2006), p. 6.

[61]For a concise discussion of the development of the scientific method, see the narrative by Jimmy H. Davis in Harry L. Poe and Jimmy H. Davis, *Science and Faith* (Nashville: Broadman & Holman, 2000), pp. 3-15.

[62]Francis Bacon, *The New Organon*, ed. Lisa Jardine and Michael Silverthorne (Cambridge: Cambridge University Press, 2000), pp. 126-27.

cient and material causes.[63] Bacon regarded final cause as unhelpful in understanding the actual operation of the physical world, and it tends to distort science. Bacon believed that "the task and purpose of human Science is to find for a given nature its Form."[64] By "form," Bacon did not mean the old Greek philosophical conception of forms found in Aristotle, which had preoccupied the Schoolmen. Instead he meant "those laws and limitations of pure act which organize and constitute a simple nature, like heat, light or weight, in every kind of susceptible material and subject. The form of heat, therefore, or the form of light is the same thing as the law of heat or the law of light."[65] In rejecting the old philosophical notion of science as related to the eternal forms, Bacon chose the language of the Reformers of the church from the time of Wycliffe. He proposed to discover the *laws* of nature. These were not the laws that an allegorized Natura laid down. Rather, they were the laws that God laid down for the governance of the physical world.

Bacon lived in the world of the Puritans, who had prevailed upon James I, whom Bacon served as Chancellor, to authorize a new translation of the Bible. The Puritans had acquired their pejorative nickname because of their efforts to purify the Church of England through the discovery of God's law for the church found in Scripture. Bacon appropriated not only their methodology but also their terminology of laws in the tradition of Wycliffe.

Bacon also lived in a world that was fast losing its poetic imagination. He was born into a world in which allegory had reigned supreme in literature, song and preaching for one thousand years. In 1596, shortly before his death, Edmund Spenser published the last expanded version of *The Fairie Queen*, the last great allegorical poem in English. William Shakespeare retired from play writing and returned to Stratford in 1613 when the popular tastes changed and the public no longer enjoyed listening to people speak in verse. They had been persuaded by the most popular show in town, the Puritan preachers, that language should be plain spoken and clearly understood. Language

---

[63]Ibid., p. 109.
[64]Ibid., p. 102.
[65]Ibid., p. 128.

itself was shifting from the poetic to the mere transmission of facts and information. That Bacon succeeded can be seen in those who followed his lead, such as Robert Boyle (1627-1691), who further refined the scientific method in his experiments on gases.[66]

CONCLUSION

For all the many scientific discoveries that occurred within China, India and the Islamic world, these rich cultures lacked one element present within the Western church at the beginning of the second millennium. They lacked a mass intellectual movement that rejected tradition in the same way that the Protestant Reformation rejected religious tradition in the West. With faith in objective revelation from God (the Bible) and an objective world created by God (nature), the West had a basis for knowledge that did not depend on cultural tradition for its authority. People could go directly to the sources of knowledge. The intellectual movement that gave birth to the Reformation and the scientific revolution did not stand outside or alongside the Western church. Instead, it grew up within the Western church over a period of five hundred years, with slight modifications in outlook over time until it came to full bloom.

One other feature of the human phenomenon of religion bears noting. The major families of the world's religions have three primary ways of conceiving of deity's relationship to the physical world. Some conceive of deity as relating to the world essentially as its detached and transcendent ruler. Some conceive of the physical world as somehow the manifestation of an immanent but impersonal deity. Some conceive of deity as a spirit that permeates everything and is nonpersonal. Christianity affirms aspects of all three of these conceptions of deity as God the Father, Son and Holy Spirit, but also a God who is personal and interested in people and the world.

---

[66]Harry Lee Poe, *Christianity in the Academy* (Grand Rapids: Baker, 2004), pp. 140-41. This paragraph comes with minor alteration from my earlier book.

2

TRADITIONAL CHRISTIANITY

❖❖❖

IN THE WESTERN WORLD, little children learn who God is when they ask big questions about the world.

"Momma, where did the trees come from?"
"God made the trees."
"Momma, where did the clouds come from?"
"God made the clouds."
"Momma, where did the mountains come from?"
"God made the mountains."

Biblical faith begins with an understanding of God as the Creator of all things. The activity of God in relation to the physical world is the beginning of the biblical understanding of who God is. Apart from God's identity as Creator, the rest of the biblical story makes no sense. The exclusive claims to deity by the God of Israel are the foundation statement for all of Jewish law. The Bible begins by explaining who God is, and whenever the people who have faith in the Creator meet people of other religious experiences, they explain what they mean when they speak of God. Jonah explained who the God was that he worshiped in this way: "I am a Hebrew and I worship the Lord, the God of heaven, who made the sea and the land" (Jon 1:9).

BIBLICAL FAITH

In a surprisingly transparent way, the Bible tells the story of God's dealings over centuries with Abraham and his descendants. From the time of Israel's four-hundred-year sojourn in Egypt until the destruction of Jerusalem (586 B.C.) by the armies of Babylon a thousand years later, the Hebrew people had an ambiguous relationship with the God of Abraham, Isaac and Jacob. They regularly flirted with the nature deities from the cultures around them. After the Babylonian captivity, however, we never again find the children of Israel doubting that the Creator God is the only God.

The Christian faith arose within the Jewish community and shares a common faith in the God who made all things. With the Christian faith, however, we find the most dramatic instance of God interacting with the physical world. Christians believe that God entered into the time-space continuum by taking on flesh and entering into humanity. Two important events mark human experience: birth and death. Without God's involvement in the course of nature, faith in Jesus as God has no foundation. The birth, death and resurrection of Jesus all represent extreme, unavoidable examples of divine involvement in the normal course of nature.

John's Gospel begins by explaining that when he speaks of God, he means the one who created the world and then entered into it (Jn 1:1-3, 14). Paul's sermons in Lystra (Acts 14:11-18) and in Athens (Acts 17:16-34) begin this way. The apostles consistently described God as the Creator and explained the rest of their faith in light of this belief (Heb 1:1-4; Col 1:15-20; Rom 1:20-23; 1 Pet 4:19).

In the days of the early church during persecution by the Roman Empire, the Christians explained their faith to the authorities and to others within the empire by explaining what they believed, beginning with there is only one God, who had created all things. The vast collection of documents written from the period of the apostles until the legalization of the Christian faith under Constantine (A.D. 313) consistently emphasizes that the Christian faith begins with the assumption that God created the world. Irenaeus (c. 185) clarified the Christian faith in *Against Heresies* when he said that Christians believe "in one God, the Father Almighty, Maker of heaven and earth, and the sea, and all things that are in them; and in one Christ Jesus, the Son of God, who became incarnate for our salvation."[1] In the next

---

[1]Irenaeus, *Against Heresies*, 1.10.1.

generation Tertullian (d. c. 225) affirmed this first article of faith when he wrote in *On Prescription Against Heretics* that Christians believe "that there is one only God, and that He is none other than the Creator of the world, who produced all things out of nothing through his own Word, first of all sent forth."[2] Though Origen (d. c. 254) had some rather esoteric teachings that he derived from his attempts to integrate Greek philosophy with the Bible, he stood solidly with the other great teachers of the church in declaring that Christians believe "That there is one God, who created and arranged all things, and who, when nothing existed, called all things into being."[3] These representative theologians speak for the faith of Christians in the centuries following the resurrection of Christ.

With the end of persecution and the legalization of Christianity under Constantine, the Christians met in universal council several times over the next few centuries to deal with major theological questions that arose in the context of a pluralistic culture. Beginning with the Council of Nicaea in 325 and continuing with the Council of Constantinople (381), the Council of Ephesus (431) and the Council of Chalcedon (451), the leaders of the Christian faith issued theological statements designed to address the new questions. Because these statements address what Christians believe, they are known by the Latin word that begins each proposition (*credo*—"I believe") and are called the creeds. The most popular of these early creeds became elements of regular worship among the Christians and continue to be repeated by the congregations in churches to this day. The Apostles' Creed begins "I believe in God the Father Almighty, Maker of heaven and earth." The Nicene Creed begins "We believe in one God the Father Almighty, Maker of heaven and earth, and of all things visible and invisible."

For the first three hundred years of the Christian faith, theology tended to involve a commentary on the implications of the gospel message about Jesus. Living in Alexandria, where the Jewish community had embraced Greek philosophy in its interpretation of Scripture, Origen delved into a project to blend Greek philosophy with

---

[2]Tertullian, *On Prescription Against Heretics*, 13.
[3]Origen, *De Principiis*, pref.

the Bible and Christian faith. The use of philosophy as a framework for understanding and interpreting Christianity, however, did not come to full flower until Augustine.

THE RISE OF PHILOSOPHICAL THEOLOGY

Augustine (354-430) was born in present-day Algeria to a heathen father and Christian mother. As a young man Augustine loved the good life and kept a concubine by whom he fathered a son. Intellectually gifted, Augustine pursued a career as a rhetorician and in 384 obtained a post as teacher of rhetoric in Milan, the new capital of the Western Roman Empire. During his young adult years Augustine became of follower of the Manichaean religion. Manichaeism was a syncretistic religion founded by Mani and based on a dualism of good and evil. Mingling elements of Buddhism, Zoroastrianism and Christianity, the Manichaean religion regarded the physical world as the result of a primordial victory of evil over good, which resulted in a mixture of the two. The religion aimed at freeing souls from the captivity of the material world. The Manichaeans abstained from sexual intercourse because procreation extended the domination of darkness over light. Within the hierarchy of Manichaeism, the elect were those who had surrendered to the strict ascetic rules of Mani. Augustine could not bring himself to give up sex, so he remained a "hearer" who awaited further illumination.

Within the belief system of Manichaeism, the Christian faith made little sense to Augustine. First of all, he did not conceive of the world as good and the result of the creative activity of a good God. If the God of the Bible created the world and made humans in his image, then the God of the Bible must be fleshly and darkness. Second, he could not conceive of a good God entering into the physical world to "be defiled by the flesh." Third, he had learned from the Manichaeans to regard the crucifixion as a symbol of human suffering that had no objective meaning.

Augustine finally abandoned the Manichaean view of the relation between the physical and spiritual world when the Manichaean view came into conflict with the best science of his day. As an educated man

Augustine had studied the mathematical calculations by which the Greeks had plotted the motions of the heavenly bodies. The Manichaeans had an elaborate cosmology that placed Christ in the sun, which the Manichaeans represented as a triangular window through which the eye of Christ beheld the world, and his wisdom in the moon. The Holy Spirit dwelt in the air; God the Father dwelt in a secret light. Through the normal bodily functions of the elect, a portion of the divine light is released from its physical captivity and rises through the air (the Holy Spirit) to the moon (wisdom of Christ) which grows larger as it fills with light. Once full, the moon transports the light to the sun (Christ) and is empty again. The sun then transports the light to the secret light (God the Father). Augustine concluded that Ptolemy had the better explanation for the cycles of the heavenly bodies and turned his back on his religion.

The next critical step in Augustine's intellectual journey to faith came in his rejection of a dualism of good and evil. Through Neo-Platonic thought, Augustine came to regard evil as a corruption of the good rather than as an independently existing substance. He could then understand how the physical world could be created by a good God as good, and yet it could suffer from corruption.

The final barrier to Augustine's acceptance of the gospel of Jesus Christ involved his attitude toward the Bible. Augustine, like many modern people, suffered from a severe case of "literalism." He was a skilled rhetorician rather than a poet. He was versed in the manipulation of language for pragmatic purposes. As he read the Bible, he found that people are made in God's image. People are physical, therefore God must be physical. He also found that God had a long arm, a face and all manner of physical characteristics. Not until he heard the preaching of Ambrose, the bishop of Milan, did Augustine understand that the Bible uses metaphorical or poetic language to speak of God by analogy.

Augustine became the new model for theology in the West during a cataclysmic period in world history. He died in 430 as the Vandal hordes laid siege to his city of Hippo, near present-day Bona, Algeria. The West ceased to be part of the Roman Empire, whose capital had moved to Constantinople, far to the east. Augustine's approach to theology dominated Western thought in all spheres of life for the next thousand years. Science and philosophy had been the dominant elements in Augustine's conversion, with the Bible playing only a small part until the final moments of his conversion. His primary questions had been scientific and philosophical rather than theological. When he became a Christian, his understanding of science and philosophy provided the structure through which he would read the Bible and develop his theological system.

The system that Augustine developed relied heavily on the Neo-Platonic school of thought, which contained aspects of the ascetic demands of Manichaeism while allowing for the God of the Bible.[4] While Augustine maintained a healthy balance between Scripture and his philosophical influencers, medieval Christianity, the further removed in time from Augustine, grew into an ascetic, otherworldly religion with little interest in the present world, which was seen more as a means to an end.[5] We might say that Augustine valued Platonic thought more for its apologetic value in his *Confessions* and *The City of God* than for its theological value, but by the tenth century Plato held an intellectual ascendency over Western theological thought. The West was the shadow lands of Platonic thought, not the real place. The married priesthood of old Christianity was replaced by a celibate priesthood in the new Christianity of the West. Within this world the Platonic hierarchy prevailed with the king on the top of the social order, followed by nobles, knights, yeomen and serfs. With the Western church the same Platonic hierarchy provided an organizational structure with the bishop of Rome and his archbishops, bishops, clergy and laity. Augustine provided the intellectual and conceptual basis for the feudal system that held society together for a thousand years after the social fabric of the Roman Empire had been torn to bits by a suc-

---

[4]Augustine discusses his dependence on "the Platonic books" in his *Confessions*, 7.8 (12)-21 (27). Augustine also discusses his affinity with the Platonists in *The City of God*, 1.36, 8.5-14. Augustine critiques the failures of Platonic philosophy, particularly as it allows for polytheism, but found it helpful in his own conversion and theological development.

[5]C. S. Lewis traces this development in the theologians' views of sex in *The Allegory of Love* (New York: Oxford University Press, 1958), pp. 14-17.

cession of invasions. In the arts, the realistic painting of the classical world was replaced by painting that sought to present the spiritual world. Icons abandoned the earlier three-dimensional representational art as symbolism replaced realism. Allegory became the normal form for literature as diverse as poetry and sermons.[6]

Within this cultural milieu which prevailed until the Renaissance, people assumed that God created the world and ruled it. This cultural milieu, however, placed its emphasis on the other world. People were asking basic survival questions in the chaos that accompanied the collapse of society. It was an age of strong and fierce leaders who slew their enemies. People did not question the motives or means of the tribal chieftains who came to be called kings. Little more did they question how God went about ruling his world.

Augustine's world and the understanding of God's place in it began to change forever with the birth of Thomas Aquinas in 1225. Alexander of Hales and Albertus Magnus had reintroduced the study of Aristotle to the West, but it was Thomas Aquinas who engaged Aristotle creatively to make him the foundation for the Roman Church's new theology. While the theology of Augustine, with its dependence on Neo-Platonism, ultimately relied on Plato for its emphasis on the world of ideas rather than the world of physical experience, the theology of Thomas would rely on Aristotle for its emphasis on the world of experience. While Plato's system argued that all knowledge comes to the soul prior to birth and is gradually recalled, Aristotle taught that the mind is a blank slate at birth and all knowledge comes after birth. Thus Thomas placed great emphasis on what reason can learn through experience. The truths that come by revelation from God in the Bible cannot come through reason, but the truths of revelation are never contrary to reason.

Thomas gave the medieval church a new project with his approach to theology. Theology remained the queen of the sciences, with phi-

---

[6]For a fascinating discussion of the change from classical to medieval culture and how Augustine and the medieval theologians appropriated aspects of Platonic thought, see C. S. Lewis, *The Allegory of Love* (New York: Oxford University Press, 1958), pp. 44-111. Lewis provides a helpful discussion of the key influencers of the development of the medieval mind in *The Discarded Image* (Cambridge: Cambridge University Press, 2000), pp. 45-91.

losophy as her handmaiden, but all the fun was to be had with the handmaiden. Augustine had fully explained God. The only thing left to do was to learn everything else that could be known. No contradiction existed between theology and philosophy because all knowledge comes from God, so theologians were free to learn what they could about the physical world.

As far as how God relates to the world that can be known, Thomas was a good Augustinian. God determines all things. As to what this determination looks like, Thomas was a good Aristotelian. Philosophically and scientifically, for the two were the same discipline at the time, God is the First Cause, the Designer, the reason there is something rather than nothing. Like Plato, Augustine placed his emphasis on "universals," or the eternal ideas of which physical matter is merely the expression. By following Aristotle, Thomas Aquinas opened the door to another way of thinking. Aristotle placed his emphasis on the particular or individual things encountered in the world. Thomas followed Augustine in placing primary emphasis on universals, but his critic John Duns Scotus (c. 1265-1308), who was also an Aristotelian, placed his emphasis on the individual or the particular. This shift has enormous implications for scientific inquiry. Reference to universals made scientific inquiry irrelevant because the universals explained everything to the medieval mind. The study of individual or particular cases, however, resulted in a new way of thinking about universals. William of Occam (d. c. 1350), a follower of Duns Scotus, carried the line of thought on individuals one step further. He argued that only individual objects exist. Universals are only mental concepts created to speak of the collective experience of individual objects.

The ideas that theology and philosophy cannot contradict each other and that all truth is God's truth are both happy thoughts, but they became impossible to sustain following Occam. Multiple philosophical outlooks had appeared during the high Middle Ages that created intellectual battlegrounds. Aristotle knew he had created a philosophical system that contradicted Plato's. The theological debates raged because so many theological and philosophical ideas were at loggerheads, and no one was in a position to declare the truth except the pope or a church council. Given the scandalous situation in the medieval papacy, however, Occam said that Scripture alone had reliable authority as a source of truth.

THE SPIRIT OF REFORM

It is a mistake to identify the Reformation too closely with Martin Luther and John Calvin. They stood at the end of a long line of people who represented a way of thinking about reliable authority that included people like William of Occam. The roster also included people like John Wycliffe (c. 1328-1384) and John Hus (c. 1372-1415). These theologians held that only revelation from God had reliable authority because of the tendency for people to develop traditions over time that distort the Bible. These early Reformers regarded transubstantiation, claims of papal infallibility, indulgences, penitential practices and a variety of other Catholic Church traditions that had arisen over the previous millennium to be without validity.[7] They argued that tradition had distorted the truth of the Christian faith and made it unrecognizable when compared to the biblical model.

This same spirit of reform was at work among scholars concerned with examining particular phenomena in the world. As scholars like Copernicus (1473-1543) discovered, they could make observations of particulars, but the explanations of how those particulars ultimately worked was laid down by the Greek philosophical tradition. Copernicus described his sun-centered heaven with planets in circular orbits, not because he observed circular orbits, but because the Greek scientific-philosophical tradition established by Aristotle said that the heavenly bodies move in circles. Kepler remarked of Copernicus that he was "interpreting Ptolemy rather than nature."[8] The philosophical framework determined how scientists thought about their observations,

---

[7]Transubstantiation is a Western Christian concept that arose in the Celtic territories of northern Europe and was debated during the reign of Charlemagne but not adopted as dogma until 1215. Papal infallibility had been a growing teaching through the Middle Ages but was not defined as dogma until the First Vatican Council of 1870. The immaculate conception of the Virgin Mary would not be declared a teaching of the Church until 1854, contrary to the teaching of Thomas Aquinas.

[8]A. Koestler, "Johanes Kepler," *The Encyclopedia of Philosophy* (New York: Macmillan, 1972), 4:329.

just as the philosophical framework determined how theologians thought about God.

The breakthrough in science and theology came when theologians following William of Occam determined to scrape away the mountain of accumulated tradition and go back to the Bible as the authoritative source for beginning theology. The Reformation spirit of going back to the original source was adopted by Kepler and Galileo, who determined to ignore the accumulated philosophical tradition that explained nature. They would go back to the original source: creation. Theologians like Johannes Kepler (1571-1630) regarded the Bible and nature as the direct handiwork of God. For Kepler, the stationary sun, the fixed stars and the planets provided an analogy of the creative activity of God the Father (represented by the stationary sun), God the Son (represented by the stationary stars) and God the Holy Spirit (represented by the moving planets). Though he was never able to describe it adequately, Kepler believed that multiple forces operated within the world to cause elliptical orbits beyond Aristotle's Prime Mover. He never doubted, however, that God was responsible for the forces.

Two of Kepler's contemporaries contributed substantially to the emancipation of scientific discovery from the Greek philosophical tradition: Galileo Galilei (1564-1642) and Francis Bacon (1561-1626). Galileo did not run afoul of the academic authorities for challenging the Bible. His trouble arose when he challenged Aristotle's teaching that the heavenly bodies must be perfectly smooth spheres—a principle which did not allow for craters on the moon. Francis Bacon, who operated in Protestant England as minister to the Calvinist King James I, had the advantage of an intellectual climate that had already recognized the problems of the medieval philosophical tradition as applied to theology. Bacon argued that natural philosophy, as science was then called, had not produced any significant discoveries since ancient times because it was chained to unwarranted philosophical metaphysics that explained natural phenomena. Bacon proposed a method for the increase of knowledge that relied upon the accumulation of data, experimentation and scrupulous interpretation. The spirit of the Renaissance with its love of classical learning and dependency on all things ancient could never lead to new discovery. The Reformation spirit of returning to the primary source would fuel the scientific revolution.

Just as nature abhors a vacuum, the reforming spirit of theologians and scientists quickly sought a new philosophical master. The followers of Calvin found their new philosophy in the thought of Peter Ramus (1515-1572), a French logician and rhetorician who attacked Aristotle and embraced French Protestantism. He was killed on the third day of the St. Bartholomew massacre. The method of Ramus involved dividing every subject into two parts and dichotomizing each subdivision. Ramist logic simplified or reduced every question into a choice between two options. When William Perkins (1558-1602) popularized the theology of John Calvin in his theological text *A Golden Chain* (1590), he relied on the philosophical system of Ramus.[9] To make the method more vivid, however, Perkins included an elaborate diagram that divided all of theology from before creation until after the last judgment into a dichotomy of the two eternal decrees of God: election and reprobation (see fig. 2.1). The idea of conceiving theology as a massive dichotomy represents a major innovation by Perkins to the earlier theology of Calvin.

Like Plato's hierarchy or Aristotle's chain of being, Perkins's *Golden Chain* provides his audience with a way to conceive of God's causal involvement in the world. God is the King who issues decrees, and from these decrees there issues forth an unbroken chain of cause and effect. The caption for the Golden Chain diagram stresses the idea of causality: "A survey, or Table declaring the order of the causes of Salvation and Damnation, according to God's word." Significantly, Perkins created a system of philosophical theology, but he believed he had provided the secret key to biblical theology.[10] Calvinist theologians who

---

[9]For a brief introduction to the method of Ramus and how Perkins adapted it to his service, see Donald K. McKim, "William Perkins' Use of Ramism as an Exegetical Tool," in William Perkins, *A Commentary on Hebrews 11 (1609 Edition)*, ed. John H. Augustine (New York: Pilgrim Press, 1991), pp. 32-45.

[10]Timothy George has noted Calvin's caution about saying too much about predestination owing to the limits of God's revelation on the subject, and adds, "Perkins belonged to those who were not afraid to rush where Calvin had feared to tread" (Timothy George, *John Robinson and the English Separatist Tradition*, NABPR Dissertation Series 1 [Macon, Ga.: Mercer University Press, 1982], p. 63). For a fascinating discussion of the revisionism of Calvin's theology by Perkins and other English Puritans, see R. T. Kendall, *Calvin and English Calvinism to 1649* (Oxford: Oxford University Press, 1981).

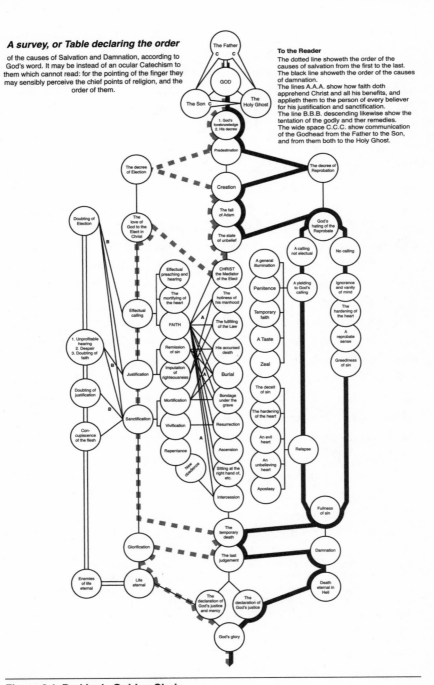

A survey, or Table declaring the order

of the causes of Salvation and Damnation, according to God's word. It may be instead of an ocular Catechism to them which cannot read: for the pointing of the finger they may sensibly perceive the chief points of religion, and the order of them.

To the Reader

The dotted line showeth the order of the causes of salvation from the first to the last. The black line showeth the order of the causes of damnation.
The lines A.A.A. show how faith doth apprehend Christ and all his benefits, and applieth them to the person of every believer for his justification and sanctification.
The line B.B.B. descending likewise show the tentation of the godly and ther remedies.
The wide space C.C.C. show communication of the Godhead from the Father to the Son, and from them both to the Holy Ghost.

Figure 2.1. Perkins's Golden Chain

stand in the Perkins tradition rather than the Calvin tradition continue to be consumed with establishing the correct sequence of cause and effect in the "order of salvation," but no commonly agreed sequence has yet been established.

Perkins's theology, with its helpful diagram, took the English-speaking world by storm. Perkins eclipsed Calvin in book sales and *A Golden Chain* became the dominant theological text in England, Scotland, Massachusetts and Holland. Perkins not only shifted the major teachings of Calvin to create a new form of Calvinism that would be institutionalized by Perkins's followers at the Synod of Dort and the Westminster Assembly, but he created an intellectual climate that would affect political and scientific thought as well. When Bacon described the goal of scientific inquiry, he spoke of discovering the "laws" of nature. The conceptual framework for exploring the world of physical phenomena was based on the model that Perkins popularized. It was not necessary to be a Calvinist along the lines of Perkins in order to use the conceptual framework of Puritanism. It had been the language of the court of King James I for over twenty years when Bacon wrote his *New Organum* in which he proposed the scientific method of inquiry.

In the medieval world influenced by Augustine and his Neo-Platonic framework, God exercised his dominion over the world through his angelic servants, who populated the heavens and had oversight of all regions of the earth and the individuals who dwelt upon it. The medieval world took the biblical understanding of spiritual beings in the service of God and blended it with Plato's notion of a hierarchy of spiritual beings that extended from the lowest form of life upward through the levels of the celestial realms to the great unconscious God. Of course, the Prime Mover of Aristotle does not exercise care or concern for the physical world. The God of the philosophers is not concerned with people and has no purpose for the physical order. Nonetheless, the Greek philosophers have an unbroken chain of cause and effect from the first cause, even if the first cause was unintentional or nonconscious. The Christian adaptation of the Greek systems of Plato and Aristotle replaces the unconscious God of Plato and the self-absorbed God of Aristotle with a loving God who cares about the physical world. Michelangelo's *Last Judgment* in the Sistine Chapel illustrates the medieval conception of the divine hierarchy in God's governance of the world. In Perkins's *Golden Chain*, the angels of the medieval world no longer have any place. God exercises his dominion through his royal decrees, which he enforces by the sheer exercise of his will. The laws of nature are inviolate because they are the decrees of God. Calvin had made clear at the outset of his *Institutes of the Christian Religion* that God not only created the world but also governs it, and this government does not involve merely the establishment of general principles but of specific incidents. God does not sit "idly in heaven" and look "on at what is taking place in the world"; God "holds the helm, and overrules all events."[11]

Robert Boyle (1627-1691) was an early disciple of Bacon's inductive method of gathering data and developing general principles from the observation of many particular situations. The general principle that Boyle concluded from his study of the relationship of pressure and volume of gas is known as "Boyle's law." When Isaac Newton (1642-1727) studied the movements of bodies on earth and in the heavens, his conclusions became known as the "law of universal gravitation" and the three "laws of motion." It was not necessary for Boyle and Newton to be Calvinists for them to imbibe the intellectual frame of reference that saw all of nature determined by God's laws of nature.

The intellectual mode of thought that dominated the English-speaking world also had its influence on the continent through the religious ferment that animated Europe during the Thirty Years' War, which coincided with the Catholic Counter-Reformation. We have seen that Kepler and Galileo had developed ideas about method similar to those of Bacon, who sought to free science from the domination of philosophy. We have also seen that the spirit of reformation had run through Catholic thought for centuries before Luther and did not cease with Luther's break with Rome. René Descartes (1596-1650), a French physicist and mathematician, regarded mathematics to be the key to scientific method because it provided the means of attaining absolute

---

[11]John Calvin, *The Institutes of the Christian Religion*, trans. Henry Beveridge (Grand Rapids: Eerdmans, 1957), 1:175.

certainty. To this approach Descartes added a dynamic skepticism that doubted all things as the starting point of finding what was undoubtable and true. Descartes argued that belief depends on an exercise of the will. This view of belief stood at the heart of Perkins's system in contrast to Calvin who had regarded belief as a form of knowledge. Thus, we see Descartes participating in the intellectual climate of the age. Perkins's system had gone to Holland with William Ames, in the early days of the reign of James I, when he could not accept the terms of conformity laid down by the Church of England. In Holland Perkins's teachings found an eager audience. Descartes went to Holland in 1618 with the army of Maurice of Nassau on the eve of the Synod of Dort, which depended on Perkins's interpretation of Calvin.

The method of Descartes in pursuing what can be known resonated with Perkins's method. Within Perkins's system the important question was how a person might know he or she is among the elect. Perkins developed a system of questioning that would help a person arrive at the answer to this question. This method is known as "casuistry." Medieval Catholicism had an earlier version of casuistry, but Perkins's version stands on the shoulders of Ramus philosophy and aims at reducing a question to a dichotomy that leaves only two options. Perkins's approach had such a far-reaching impact on the English-speaking world because he applied his system to all issues in decision making. Through Perkins's casuistry, educated people learned how to explore every kind of decision they faced, from moral questions to business questions, by reducing the issue into the two opposing options. Whether Descartes self-consciously followed the Perkins model or merely represented the way people had begun to think as a result of the pervasive intellectual rigor of the Puritan movement, he arrived at a dichotomy between mind and body that leads to a dichotomy between the physical world and the spiritual world. Because of the Puritan revolution of the seventeenth century, this way of thinking fit well with the English Enlightenment of the eighteenth century.

Descartes conceived of the world as a great mechanical continuum in which all matter existed as a whole. Unable to accept a vacuum on the grounds laid down by Aristotle, he conceived of all space between discernible objects as filled with moving matter. A material aether filled all of space so that no vacuum was left. Thus the entire material universe was in motion. God set it all in motion and established the laws by which it operated, but it operated like a machine. Even living things were mechanical in nature. Thus the human mind is not "natural" to its body but was joined to a body by an act of God. The material/physical world has a mechanical structure characterized by space and duration, but the mental/spiritual has neither. Descartes' physics gained little support and proved unsustainable, but his concept of a rigid dichotomy between the physical/material on the one hand and the spiritual/metaphysical/mental on the other hand gained wide support, probably because the intellectual climate of his day had grown accustomed to looking for dichotomies wherever they could find them.

Descartes had a love for Augustine, which is apparent in his discussion of time and space, for Augustine had argued that time came into being when God created matter. Descartes' approach, with its skepticism of what can be known through the senses, also reflects an influence from Plato. Descartes' God is still the ruler of the universe, but by laying down the decrees at the beginning, as Perkins described in *The Golden Chain*, God need not be continually involved in creation. While a sophisticated theologian may have assumed the activity of the Holy Spirit throughout the world, Perkins's diagram kept the Holy Spirit in eternity. A mechanical world can run on its own once it is set in motion. Though Galileo and Bacon repudiated the philosophical explanations of the universe laid down by Aristotle, they reflect Aristotle's confidence in empirical observation. Descartes' love of mathematics as the key to scientific understanding blended with his Platonic biases turned his method toward rationalism.

The Puritan hegemony collapsed in England following Oliver Cromwell's military dictatorship and the restoration of King Charles II with his Arminian church. In contrast to the Perkins version of Calvinism, which believed that God predestined the individuals who would be saved, the Arminian branch of the Reformed tradition believed that God predestined all those who would have faith in Christ to be saved. This difference resulted in a variety of other differences related to the working of election, atonement and perseverance. The generation after Descartes inherited the preference for dichotomies that Perkins had introduced to the European consciousness, but without the same theological commitments. Mathematics and physics made huge strides through the work of Isaac Newton. Newton accepted fully the mechanical model of the universe and set about describing it. When he was criticized for not explaining the cause of gravity, Newton replied that it was enough to show that gravity exists and behaves according to certain laws. Newton attempted to keep science a descriptive discipline without reference to philosophical explanations of why things happen the way they do. Not all scientists are as scrupulous. People continue to associate science with philosophical explanations, and they find it hard to separate their method from their philosophical convictions.

The scientific world had long accepted the idea of the aether that filled all of space. This aether provided the medium by which objects at distance could have a mechanical relationship to each other. Newton's early work on motion and gravity, accomplished during the eighteen-month period following his graduation from Cambridge in 1665, was carried out with the assumption of the presence of the aether. In later years, however, Newton adopted an atomic theory of the composition of the universe and conceived of gravity as a force that might act at a distance without the aid of aether. Descartes' universe was filled with a continuous medium, but Newton conceived of atoms that need not touch one another in order to exert force on one another. Furthermore, the movement of all matter, from atoms to planets, began to be seen as the cause for every effect.

Within this climate, questions about how God ruled the universe arose. Perkins's scheme still worked perfectly well in the context of the new scientific thinking. To a great extent, implications of Perkins's view of soteriology were applied to cosmology. God ruled the world by his decrees before the foundation of the world. The chain of cause and effect is the result of all things having been set in motion, just as the salvation of the elect and the damnation of the reprobate resulted from the chain of causation issuing from the decrees of God. God need not have any involvement in the administration of the world once he set it in motion and established the basic laws it would run by.

A sovereign God who creates perfectly has no need to interfere with the world after creation, and the movement known as deism adapted this position to theology. When Calvin had spoken of those who conceived of an idle God who looked on as the world went about its business, he was addressing the kind of mindset that years later manifest itself in deism. Not until the scientific community had fully developed a mechanical model of the world that fit with the respectable Puritan notion of the decrees of God did deism become a respectable intellectual alternative. John Toland (1670-1722) initiated deism as a significant movement in 1696 with the publication of *Christianity Not Mysterious*. The deists rejected miracles and revelation from God. They advocated a view of God based on reason and the natural moral law, which everyone possessed. While deism allowed for a moral, Creator God, it left no place for God taking on flesh, dying for the sins of the world and rising from the dead. Constitutional monarchy had come to heaven. God was still King, but the people had charge of their own affairs.

The responses to deism carried theology further into speculative philosophy as the foundation for religion. George Berkeley (1685-1753) built on Descartes' skepticism to say that only mind and ideas truly exist because what we call nature is merely the result of impressions within the mind. By attacking nature Berkeley attacked the mechanical model and proposed in its place the mind of God. This highly speculative approach proved less than compelling. Joseph Butler (1692-1752) answered the deists with a probability argument. He argued that nature and religion have many of the same problems with respect to human knowledge; therefore God is probably responsible for both. Neither of these approaches turned the tide of deism or dampened its spirit, but the evangelical revival associated with John Wesley (1703-1791), his brother Charles Wesley (1707-1788) and their friend George Whitfield (1714-1770) did. The Wesley-Whitfield revival with its union of head and heart mitigated against the Cartesian dichotomy of mind and body. With its emphasis on religious experience through the abiding presence of the Holy Spirit, the revival avoided the anthropomorphic error of conceiving God as only a distant King. With its emphasis on the incarnation of God in Christ, the revival stressed God's involvement in the world and God's concern for individual people and social problems.

At the same time that deism gained ground in Britain, unitarianism became popular among the Calvinist dissenters. In a world in which God exercised his sovereignty by decrees issued before the foundations of the earth, the incarnation of God in Christ seemed to be unnecessary. In fact, this is one of the problems with Perkins's revisions of Calvin's theology that became the norm among the English and Dutch. Joseph Hallett (d. 1744), James Peirce (d. 1726) and Nathaniel Lardner (1684-1768) led in the movement that now regarded Jesus through Arian eyes. The Arian movement had developed shortly after the legalization of Christianity in the fourth century when Arius argued against the divine nature of Christ. Arianism has reappeared in different forms up to the present day. Jesus was a man who stood faithful to God's moral law, even unto death. But he added nothing to the dignity, majesty and sovereignty of God. Unitarianism would cut a huge swath through the Calvinist churches of New England into the nineteenth century as entire congregations accepted the new Arianism, which was perfectly consistent with the philosophical model of God they had adopted.

By the end of the eighteenth century, William Perkins's model of reducing issues to two alternatives had become the dominant way of thinking in the English-speaking world. Popular aphorisms reinforce this way of thinking, such as, "There are two sides to every question." Of course, a question may have many sides, but in Perkins's method questions only have two sides. This deeply ingrained pattern of thought in the English-speaking world is reflected in the politics of representative democracy that has always tended to have only two major political parties, which represent the two ways of looking at an issue. Within the intellectual climate of the Enlightenment, the English-speaking world had great influence because of the development of representative government and the limitations placed on kings. In the natural world observed by scientific investigation, scientists were faced by the two alternatives that their worldview allowed them: (1) phe-

nomena occurred by the direct action of God, or (2) phenomena occurred as the result of the laws of nature. The idea that God could be
active within nature was not an alternative allowed to them by their
prevailing worldview.

Charles Darwin (1809-1882) demonstrates the problem of worldview
as well as anyone in the nineteenth century. Darwin was an evangelical
theologian trained in theology at Cambridge. Darwin and his wife
were both members of the wealthy Wedgewood family, long supporters
of evangelical causes in England, and Darwin was not obliged to work
to earn his living. His family's wealth left him free to pursue his hobby
of collecting bugs and shells. The theology that Darwin was trained in
taught him that God created all life forms by fiat. The immutability of
the species was accepted as theological fact, not because it was taught
by the Bible but because it had been laid down by Aristotle as an aspect
of the unchanging nature of the forms. Theology accepted the immutability of the species because it was solid science that had stood the test
of time. This holdover from the medieval worldview was represented in
Renaissance painting, most notably in *The Birth of Venus* by Botticelli,
in which Venus emerges from her shell fully mature. It is quite a different image than the biblical picture of God urging the earth and the
seas to continually bring forth life (Gen 1:11, 20, 24), but Aristotle's
view became the basis for interpreting the Genesis creation story because it offered the scientific view current at the time.

When Darwin came to realize that organisms change over time, he
was placed in the jaws of the Perkins's dilemma. God either created all
species unchangeable by fiat or God had nothing to do with the development of life at all. Within this worldview Darwin could not think in
terms of a third or fourth or fifth option. In *On the Origin of Species*,
Darwin presents the alternative over and over: either "each species has
been independently created" by a "special act of creation" or nature produced the species without any involvement by God.[12] Darwin belonged

---

[12]Charles Darwin, *The Origin of Species* (New York: Gramercy Books, 1979), pp. 69, 110. Originally published as *On the Origin of Species by Means of Natural Selection*, this edition is a reproduction of the first edition of 1859 with the historical sketch of Darwin and glossary added
from the sixth edition. Throughout his book Darwin restates his philosophical assumption
that God either created all species immutably by a special act of creation or he was not involved

to that stream of intellectual development that conceived of God as a King who issues decrees from his throne, far removed from events. Once the decree has been issued, matters take their own course in fulfillment of the decree. Darwin concluded, "To my mind it accords better with what we know of the laws impressed upon matter by the Creator, that the production and extinction of the past and present inhabitants of the world should have been due to secondary causes, like those determining the birth and death of the individual."[13] With Darwin we find the full-blown assumption that if someone can describe a phenomenon, then God is not involved in the phenomenon. Newton had been careful to distinguish between description and explanation. The explanation is the path of Plato and Aristotle.

SCIENTIFIC THEOLOGY

From the time of Archbishop Ussher (d. 1656) during the reign of James I and Charles I, theologians wanted to develop the scientific way to do theology because of its certainty. Ussher dated the creation of the world by calculating the genealogies of the Bible, in spite of the biblical prohibition against developing beliefs based on genealogies (1 Tim 1:4; Tit 3:9). In terms of his influence on modern theology, however, Ussher was a pioneer for what eventually became biblical criticism. As part of the Reformation tradition of ridding theology of tradition, Ussher ironically played the pivotal role in developing the tradition of the scientific investigation of the Bible. Until the time of Darwin the scientific approach meant demonstrating that the Bible is a book of science. Under the Perkins view, if the Bible is not a book of science, then it is not true. Within the English-speaking world, the prevailing attitude toward the Bible continues in this Perkinsian vein.

With the ever-expanding scientific understanding of the world after the seventeenth century, God had a smaller and smaller sphere in which to act, as the deistic view concluded. In this context, German rationalism produced a new scientific approach to theology in the

---

in the development of life at all. See, for example, pages 113, 189, 192, 195, 198, 201, 216, 219, 223, 399, 415-17, 432, 444-48, 450, 452-54, 457, 458.
[13]Ibid., p. 458.

nineteenth century. The emphasis shifted away from attempting to understand God's will for the world toward an attempt to understand the phenomenon of religion. The focus shifted from God to people. This new approach allowed for a more scientific method of study in which people and human artifacts became the object of study rather than God. A world in which God had no place to act did not allow for revelation in the view of many of the new biblical critics; therefore, the Bible came to be viewed as a human artifact reflecting the beliefs and practices of people in ancient cultures. Among the many flaws of the nineteenth-century German scientific critics was the view that present understanding of the world is the standard by which the Bible should be judged. Cultural anthropology had not yet developed as a discipline to provide a means of self-understanding, and European hubris was at its zenith. This approach to the Bible came to be identified with "liberal" theology in the English-speaking world. But the liberals were not the only ones to attempt a scientific approach to the Bible.

The scientific approach to the Bible began within the English Puritan movement, with people like Ussher, and it spread in the late seventeenth century to Germany through the Pietism associated with Philip Jacob Spener (1635-1705) and his disciple August Hermann Francke (1663-1727). Francke's approach to biblical studies involved familiarity with other ancient texts to provide a basis for understanding the biblical message. He even went so far as to criticize Luther's translation of the Bible and to call for revisions based on modern scholarship.

In North America, popular Christianity embraced a scientific approach to religion in the nineteenth century. Charles Grandison Finney (1792-1875), popular revival preacher, compiled "the laws of revival." Part of the success of the Scofield Reference Bible (1909) in its promotion of a dispensational interpretation of the Bible lies in the claim made by C. I. Scofield (1843-1921) that earlier reference editions of the Bible were "unscientific."[14] The Scofield Reference

[14]C. I. Scofield, ed., Introduction to *The Scofield Reference Bible* (New York: Oxford University Press, 1945), p. iii.

Bible incorporated Archbishop Ussher's dating of events in the Bible at the top of each page. His notes on the first chapter of Genesis attempt to give a scientific framework for the creation of the world. Widely appreciated by conservative Presbyterians, Scofield's Bible became an early icon of the fundamentalist movement following the adoption of "The Five Fundamentals" by the General Assembly of the Presbyterian Church in the U.S.A. in 1910. One of Scofield's contemporaries would exhibit the rare ability to step outside the weight of his received theological tradition and return to the source of his tradition.

B. B. Warfield (1851-1921) taught at Princeton Theological Seminary, where he advocated an inerrant understanding of the Bible and accepted the probability of an evolutionary understanding of life. What Warfield did not accept was the simple dichotomy between the Bible and evolution. He recognized that the scientific view of evolution was a different idea than the philosophical view of natural selection.[15] Natural selection as Darwin presented it is both a primary and final cause. Darwin discusses the efficient cause of the development of the species in terms of the slight mutations that occur from one generation to another in an organism over time that give an organism an advantage over its competition for survival. Darwin also discusses a final cause or teleological dimension of evolution that attributes the mutations exclusively to chance. Whereas Darwin had concluded that if a phenomenon had an observable efficient cause that could be described scientifically, then God could not be involved with it in any way. Warfield concluded that nature can be described scientifically and that God can be involved with it. Warfield did not simply reflect on Darwin's work from his study. Warfield was a cattle breeder who understood the principles at work.

The fundamentalist-modernist controversy that erupted in the Presbyterian Church in the U.S.A. in 1922 represented a defeat for Warfield's reasoning and a victory for the old Perkins logic followed by the liberal and conservative Presbyterian factions. The controversy helped

---

[15]For an excellent presentation of Warfield's understanding, see Mark A. Noll and David N. Livingstone, *B. B. Warfield: Evolution, Science, and Scripture* (Grand Rapids: Baker, 2000).

push the wings of the Presbyterian Church farther apart as liberals grew disinclined to accept the miraculous and conservatives grew more suspicious of modern science. For the liberals, there seemed to be no place for an interventionist God in a world governed by the laws of nature. For the conservatives, if scientific ideas about the age of the earth and the development of life were true, then the Bible was not true. Both conclusions are based on the conception of God as a distant King who intervenes from time to time in the world to arbitrarily "violate" the laws of nature. As Lewis A. Drummond used to say, the fundamentalists and the liberals are two peas in the same rationalistic pod. The choice seemed clear: one could either believe the Bible or believe modern science. The Presbyterians had a classic Perkins dichotomy on their hands. In the end, the Presbyterian Church in the U.S.A. would split as J. Gresham Machen and others left to form the Orthodox Presbyterian Church in 1936.

Another theological stream of thought emerged from Darwin's argument for evolution by natural selection. This is known as process theology, which began in the philosophical world outside of theological circles and was gradually taken up by theologians in search of a new philosophical basis for theology. We will examine its approach in chapter three, but we should take note of it in this survey. Contributors to process thought include the mathematician and philosopher Alfred North Whitehead (1861-1964), the philosopher W. E. Hocking (1873-1966) and the philosopher Charles Hartshorne (1897-2000). Theologians who built on the philosophical foundation of process thought include the archbishop of Canterbury William Temple (1881-1944), the French Jesuit paleontologist and theologian Pierre Teilhard de Chardin (1881-1955) and the Methodist theologian John B. Cobb Jr. (1925-).

American Christianity has deep roots in the Perkins stream of English Puritans. The methodology, if not the theology, was appropriated by John Wesley in the "method" of his spirituality. Leading Arminian revivalists like Charles Grandison Finney followed Perkins's tradition of drawing dichotomies in his arguments. It is little wonder then that American Christianity suffered a number of devastating disruptions based on the Perkins dichotomizing tendency. In addition to the fracture between science and faith, American Christians made a divide in other areas of faith which the Bible does not divide. The social gospel controversy pitted evangelism against social concern, as though Christians had to choose one or the other.

Following the exhaustion of the fundamentalist-modernist controversy, many mainstream American and British theologians and pastors fell under the influence of the neo-orthodoxy movement in Europe. Neo-orthodoxy began with the Swiss theologians Karl Barth (1886-1968) and Emil Brunner (1889-1966), who sought to return to a more solidly Reformed approach to religion with a more positive view of the Bible following the disaster of World War I. Other leaders in the movement included Paul Tillich (1886-1965), Rudolf Bultmann (1884-1976) and Reinhold Niebuhr (1892-1971). While Bultmann, Tillich and Niebuhr developed philosophical theology systems based on either existentialism or ontology, Barth and Brunner placed their emphasis on a more biblical approach. Barth had no place for philosophy within his system and criticized Brunner's willingness to consider the possibility that natural theology might have any value. Neo-orthodoxy is odd as a movement because it did not have a common approach or body of tenets like most other movements. What these theologians and their followers had in common was a desire to find a way to have faith in the face of a world system that had no place for the activity of God. To a great extent they accepted the dichotomy between science and faith. If anything, they widened the breach to emphasize the qualitative distance between people and God. Barth and neo-orthodox theologians in general accepted the findings of modern science, but for the most part neo-orthodoxy had no place for discussions of the relationship between a scientific explanation of the world and the activity of God.

Bultmann accepted the philosophical position that God does not interact, interfere or intervene in the world. He had no place for an objective incarnation of God in the flesh through the virginal conception of Jesus. Likewise, he had no place for a resurrection of Jesus from the dead. Bultmann believed in the time-space continuum of cause and effect that had no place for God. As an existentialist, therefore, Bultmann argued for faith as faith. Barth, on the other hand, stressed the incarnation of God in Christ as the ultimate revelation of God to the world. In so doing, however, he laid the foundations for a trend to think of the Bible as a witness to the revelation of God rather than as the revelation of God. Though the strongest influence of neo-orthodoxy was felt by Presbyterians, many mainline theologians and pastors were swept up in the movement. In terms of impact on how American Christian theologians and pastors thought and preached about God's activity in the world, Barth's theology encouraged the generation following World War II not to think about how science and religion related to each other. Contemplation of such issues would necessarily involve philosophy and reason. As a Reformed theologian Barth believed that human reason was much too flawed to reach any constructive insights about such things. Of course, some theologians in the mainline denominations would dabble in science and religion in the mid-twentieth century, but for the most part neo-orthodoxy represented a retreat from theological engagement with science. For some the field of science and religion was not regarded as a priority, but for others it had even lost intellectual respectability.

While neo-orthodoxy swept through mainline seminaries and theological schools, a new approach to science and religion emerged with the Seventh-day Adventists. In their desire to be faithful to the Bible in matters of practice as well as belief, the Seventh-day Adventists continue to practice aspects of the Old Covenant, including worship on the sabbath day rather than on the Lord's day. The seventh day as the day of rest has a special place in Adventist understanding of creation. George McCready Price, a geologist writing in the early twentieth century, proposed a "catastrophe" to account for the appearance of age in the geological record. This argument was renewed by Henry M. Morris and John C. Whitcomb, who were not Adventists, in their 1961 book *The Genesis Flood*. Since then, the creation science movement has involved a number of people from different academic fields who argue for a literal interpretation of the Genesis account of creation based on an alternative interpretation of the scientific evidence. The creation science approach assumes that faithfulness to the Bible means faithfulness to a literal understanding of the text as a series of scientific statements of fact. The creation science movement has had wide influence among Christians in the fundamentalist tradition far beyond the Seventh-day Adventists.

One of the main features of the literalist interpretation of the first chapter of Genesis involves determining what the text literally says. In an odd twist, most of those who want to preserve the literal meaning of the text are actually trying to preserve the medieval Aristotelian meaning of the text without knowing it. Aristotle believed in the unchanging forms, and his view became incorporated into the traditional reading of the text that many people have taken for granted for centuries. By this reading, God must have created all forms of life by fiat. This tradition, rather than the text, represents the primary concern of literalists. The text says something quite different, though it is never translated into English, because it violates the traditional understanding of the text.

Hebrew does not have temporal verb tenses that denote past, present and future, as does English. The verbs in the Hebrew text are in the imperfect tense, which denote ongoing or incomplete action. The English translation tradition puts Hebrew into a temporal mode when the language actually emphasizes the quality rather than the time of action. Thus the first act of creation might be translated, "And then God begins to say and continues to keep on saying, 'Let there begin to be and continue to keep on being light'" (Gen 1:3). In other words, the text indicates God's continuing involvement in the existence of light.

When we come to the creation of life, something else happens. Though God creates light by fiat, he does something different in creating life. According to the text, "And then God begins to say and continues to say, 'Let the earth begin and continue to keep on putting forth vegetation, plants yielding seed, fruit trees bearing fruit, each according to its kind in which is their seed upon the earth'" (Gen 1:11).[16]

---

[16]Those interested in a word by word analysis of the Hebrew text may consult John Joseph Owens, *Analytical Key to the Old Testament: Genesis* (New York: Harper & Row, 1978).

In the case of plants and animals God calls upon the elements to produce life. The time frame is also significant because the text indicates that God has continued his involvement in creation since he began. This continual time frame for creation is intensified by the way the text describes the days of creation. The traditional English way of translation places the days in a consecutive sequence with a time frame of one week. The traditional reading refers to "the" first day, "the" second day, "the" third day and so forth. The text does not actually have the definite article. Hebrew has a definite article that would normally be used to indicate consecutive sequence. The text deliberately does not speak of consecutive days. Instead it speaks of "one" day, "a" second day, "a" third day and so forth. In other words, the literal reading of the text does not allow for a creation that took place in the span of six consecutive twenty-four-hour days. Instead, it describes the creative activity of God spread over a timeless span.

This kind of misinterpretation of the text occurs when people accommodate the Bible to a culture and its values. Several centuries ago the Christian community incorporated the best science of its day into the reading of the text. To abandon the Hebrew text for a chronological reading of the text seemed more scientific to Archbishop Ussher. But what do we do when the science changes? And the science always changes.

MODELS AND THE DEATH OF POETRY

Modern Western culture is unique in world history for having lost its poetry. All cultures, except modern Western culture, appreciate poetry. At the beginning of the twentieth century, Americans enjoyed poetry as a form of popular entertainment. (People still read poetry for fun.) Poetry belonged to the masses. People devoured poetry in the popular press. Before radio and television the magazine industry flourished, and every issue of magazines included poetry. The old characterization of Protestant preaching was "three points and a poem." With World War I, however, America lost its poetry. T. S. Eliot introduced a new kind of poem that ignored meter, rhythm and rhyme, while avoiding any obvious objective meaning. Poetry ceased to communicate to a broad public as poetry had done through countless centuries in cultures around the world.

The other art forms joined poetry in its embrace of brute fact and visceral experience. With poetry, we also lost painting, sculpture, opera, ballet and classical music. Some still train artists in all these fields, and artists still perform in all these fields. Unfortunately, these art forms no longer belong to or are embraced by the broad culture. They belong only to a small elite. The arts became academic after World War I. They grew introspective and are used by artists searching for meaning. They became obsessed with realism. They died to the culture. The novel almost died at the hands of James Joyce and his ilk, but enough artists still had a story to tell to keep the novel alive. This shift in poetry and the arts left little room for the place of symbol, simile or metaphor as vehicles for truth and meaning.

During the modern period and especially after World War I, a mindset characterized by literalism grew to prominence within both the religious and scientific communities. We often think of literalism with respect to primitive societies, but it might be more helpful to think of primitive societies as concerned with concrete thought instead of literalistic thought. Within primitive societies that do not have a highly developed sense of abstract thought, even the concrete is observed, experienced, described and understood in poetic terms. Poetry precedes science, for without poetry the kind of symbolic thought necessary for scientific theory may have never developed. Theology also relies on poetic models for thinking about God. In Christian theology, the poetic models come from the Bible.

From the time of Augustine, Western Christianity has preferred the model of God as King. This model became fixed with the English interpretation of Calvin. With its emphasis on the sovereignty of God as King, the system that came to be called Calvinism reduced the deity to the office of a king. Calvin's theology was much broader, but in *A Golden Chain*, William Perkins explained God in terms of his "main" office. The idea of a king became more than a way of talking about an aspect of God; it took on the burden of presenting the essential nature of God in the common mind. Theologians would continue to elaborate the fine points of the doctrine of God, but even meticulous theologians fall prey to their systems. By its nature, philosophical theology constructs a framework for organizing the Christian faith. Perkins developed one way of organizing the Christian faith. Thomas Aquinas developed another way. Augustine developed a third way. The impulse of Western society since the Puritan revolution has conceived of God as a King who rules the world through his decrees. This model worked for religion and science. When God's involvement with the world no longer fit the model, society did not say, "Our model must be wrong." Instead, the intellectual stream concluded that God is not involved with anything that science can describe. This situation illustrates a problem with models in all fields when people forget that models are only models. The actual phenomenon is always bigger and more complex than its metaphor or model, which only provides an intimation of reality.

When we take a biblical approach to faith rather than a philosophical approach, we find numerous models for how God relates to the world. Surprisingly, the model of king is not the most prominent. Yes, the model of God as King is clearly present throughout Scripture. Heaven is his throne and the earth is his footstool (Is 66:1). This model describes the authority and dignity of God, but it is not the model the Bible uses for describing how God relates to the world on a continuing basis. When Jesus described the kingdom of God, it had little to do with decrees. The kingdom of God is like a shepherd who goes out into the darkness looking for a lost sheep (Lk 15:3-7). The kingdom of God is like a woman who turns her house upside down looking for a lost (marriage) coin (Lk 15:8-10). The kingdom of God is like a distraught father who rejoices when a good-for-nothing son comes home (Lk 15:11-24). The kingdom of God is like a pearl merchant who is willing to sacrifice everything he has to obtain a pearl that he highly prizes (Mt 13:45-46). The kingdom of God is like a man who sells everything he has to acquire a field where a treasure is hidden (Mt 13:44). The kingdom of God is like a net that catches both good and bad fish that must eventually be separated (Mt 13:47-50). The kingdom of God is many things, but it is not anything like a king who issues decrees. On those few occasions when Jesus spoke of the kingdom in terms of a king, it was to point out that people do not follow the decrees of the king (Mt 22:1-14).

As King, God has the power to do anything he pleases. How God exercises that power involves models other than that of king. From the time of the establishment of the kingdom of Israel, the Bible presents God as exercising his power like a shepherd. The psalms of David, the great king who had been a shepherd, reflect this preference. Jesus also preferred this model of divine involvement with the world. Jesus referred to himself as the good shepherd who lays down his life for his sheep (Jn 10:11) and referred to the kingdom as a sheepfold (Jn 10:1-2). The shepherd does not drive the sheep but calls to them, and they follow because they know and trust their shepherd (Jn 10:3-5). The shepherd allows his flock to range within a given parameter, but he constantly interacts with his flock when it is preoccupied with its own business of eating and drinking.

Beyond the model of a shepherd, however, the Bible likens God's activity in the world to a variety of images. God is like a potter working with the clay as it revolves in his hands (Jer 18:1-11). The image of a potter is one of intimate interaction with the clay. Turning the pot takes time. The clay gradually changes in the hands of the potter and assumes a variety of shapes before it is finished. God compares himself with everything from a mother hen to a cuckolded husband. What the modern mind since the Reformation has lost is the meaning of the biblical text. Whenever God compares himself with anything in the physical world, we may be sure that he is not that thing—not even a king. God speaks to humans by analogies. The language of the Bible is the language of comparison because humans have no frame of reference for comprehending God. Unfortunately, the modern world has lost its poetry.

In this climate, when poetry no longer spoke for or to the culture, people lost their understanding of poetic language. The modern world is concerned with brute fact. In a modern way of logical thinking, the formula God = X pleads for a single value for X. God cannot be both King and Shepherd. The modern world cannot deal with scientific laws and an involved God at the same time. Without a sense of poetry and the way analogies work, people lose the ability to use models, whether in theology or in science. The model, whether scientific or theological, is not the reality. A theological system is never more than a human-constructed model of God. It may be useful for understanding an aspect of God that it affirms, but it is always woefully inadequate as a total understanding of God.

3

THE PROCESS
THEOLOGY OPTION

◆◇◆

In the last decade of the twentieth century two schools of theology long thought dead or dying reappeared on the scene. One school revived the design argument of natural theology in the form of the intelligent design movement. The other revived the sinking fortunes of process theology. Both schools involved the relation of science and religion focused on how God relates to the physical world, but from radically different perspectives. Both were encouraged in their revitalization by massive sums of money made available to science and religion discussions by the John Templeton Foundation. Templeton supported research from a variety of perspectives without prejudice in hopes that the law of large numbers would prevail and some substantive work would emerge. The fervent activity in science and religion provided the climate in which a forum on intelligent design emerged. Likewise, the Zygon Center under the leadership of Philip Hefner, professor emeritus at Lutheran School of Theology at Chicago, provided a friendly atmosphere for the pursuit of process approaches to science and religion. John Cobb and Ian Barbour became enthusiastic proponents of the process approach. The intelligent design movement is a modern expression of a very old idea, but process theology represents a new way of thinking about God based largely on Darwin's evolutionary model.

With the rise of geology and paleontology as discrete sciences in the

nineteenth century, Aristotle's old view of the fixed species began to
erode as Comte de Buffon (1707-1788), Erasmus Darwin (1731-1802)
and Jean-Baptiste Lamarck (1744-1829) began to speculate about a developmental process of life forms. This speculation began to spill over
into other branches of philosophy and theology as the evolutionary
model gained popularity.[1]

EVOLUTIONARY PHILOSOPHY

Evolutionary thought already had a well-established beachhead in European intellectual circles when Charles Darwin took his famous cruise.
While the new sciences experimented with evolutionary theories, philosophers made these theories respectable in the mainstream of intellectual life.

Hegel. Georg Wilhem Friedrich Hegel's idealistic philosophy that focused on rationality or "spirit" dominated nineteenth-century philosophy.
Hegel set rational spirit against the objects of which spirit was aware. In
his speculations about the self-consciousness of all thinking spirits,
Hegel arrived at a concept of universal spirit. In this regard, individual
persons and the totality of nature represent the manifestations of the
universal spirit. Because of the relationship of rational spirit to physical
objects, Hegel argued that reason is both "substance" and "infinite
power."[2] In order to exercise its power, reason expresses itself through
individual objects. Thus Hegel rejected a dualism that would set rational
objects against phenomenal objects. In nature and history the Absolute
Spirit moves to self-consciousness and self-realization. Hegel used
human consciousness as his model for understanding Universal Spirit in
dialectic rationality as it progresses from thesis to antithesis to synthesis.
In this approach logic and being are equivalent. Spirit is only fully realized as it expresses itself through nature. Thus, nature and history are

---

[1] I am indebted to Eric C. Rust, who first introduced me to philosophy and the questions related
to science and religion when I was a master of divinity student. Twenty-five years later as I
turned to this topic, I also turned to Rust's insightful treatment of this subject, *Evolutionary
Philosophies and Contemporary Theology* (Philadelphia: Westminster Press, 1967). Because Rust
had a different theological perspective than I, his critique has proven particularly valuable.
[2] Georg W. F. Hegel, *The Philosophy of History*, trans. J. Sibree, Great Books in Philosophy (Buf-
falo, N.Y.: Prometheus Books, 1991), p. 9.

"necessary" for the self-fulfillment of Spirit.[3]

Hegel disagreed with the theistic understanding of God that drew a distinction between finite spirit and Absolute Spirit. He rejected the idea of a personal God, which he regarded as an inadequate description of Absolute Spirit. Rather than a traditional trinitarian understanding of God, Hegel's saw the Spirit begetting the World, which is the Son, as a matter of necessity for its own development. The estrangement from Absolute Spirit that finite spirits experience constitutes Hegel's version of the Fall, but it is merely a necessary aspect of the dialectic of the Spirit. Hegel universalized the gospel story metaphorically to argue that the theistic God of religion must die in order for the Absolute Spirit of philosophy to rise.[4]

Hegel's disciples. Hegel's philosophy has continued to influence Western thought down to the present day, but his followers would take his thought in a variety of directions. Hegel's student Ludwig Feuerbach saw no need for the Absolute Spirit as he explored human reason as absolute—man as the only true God. The march of man to self-realization lies not through reason but through the total corporeal experience of material existence—not the mind but the stomach! Karl Marx and Friedrich Engels retained Hegel's dialectic, but they followed Feuerbach's lead and regarded the process as materialistic. Nature is in tension with itself, and out of this struggle new forms appear that then struggle with each other as nature unfolds into history. This movement has both a dynamic quality and a deterministic quality that inevitably and necessarily leads to its goal of utopian society.[5]

Evolution as a metaphysical model was proposed in Gifford Lectures by Lloyd Morgan and Samuel Alexander, who introduced the concept of

---

[3]G. W. F. Hegel, *The Phenomenology of Mind*, trans. J. B. Baillie (New York: Harper Torchbook, 1967), p. 808.

[4]Hegel develops these ideas of Fall, reconciliation and death of the theistic notion of God in his treatment of revealed religion in *Phenomenology of Mind*, pp. 750-85.

[5]Rust, *Evolutionary Philosophies and Contemporary Theology*, pp. 60-61. Rust argues that "Hegel's philosophy can offer no satisfactory basis for a Christian natural theology or a Christian apologetic." In support of this conclusion he cites the following faults: (1) minimizes the individual, (2) ignores human freedom, (3) rationalizes sin as a necessary stage of the dialectic, (4) reduces reconciliation to rationality, (5) emphasis on being rather than ethics, (6) evades personal transcendence.

"emergence" in their interpretations of the universe.[6] Morgan distinguished between a "resultant" that can be explained on the basis of its antecedents, and an "emergent" that represents a novelty. An emergent cannot be explained or predicted from what went before; neither can it be reduced to a lower level. For example, if someone happened to have been around during the quantum fluxes following the big bang, could they have predicted from the current state the formation of atoms? Some would say that the formation of atoms represents an emergent rather than a resultant. On the other hand, a chemical reaction would be considered a resultant. Emergence will be discussed at greater length in chapter five.

Because of the continuity of progress across the discontinuity of levels, Morgan suggested a cosmic drive within the process that produced emergents from matter to life to mind. Morgan identified this cosmic drive, present throughout the process, as God. Alexander suggested that Einstein's "space-time" is the stuff from which the universe evolves. Alexander recognized no transcendent quality other than the interdependent space-time, out of which all later emergents must evolve. Both mind and matter emerge from space-time. God does not provide the driving force of the process. Rather, God is the next level to emerge beyond mind. To the extent that one would speak of deity as actually present, one might speak of the totality of space-time as God.[7]

Henri Bergson's evolutionary philosophy began with life rather than matter.[8] He argued that matter emerged from life and that a life force, the *élan vital*, ran throughout the process. Like the ancient Greeks, Bergson considered change to be the basic fact of experience; therefore, reality is a process best described as evolutionary. The process stresses dynamic becoming rather than static being. The process of "becoming" experiences time as irreversible, unidirectional, continuous and indi-

---

[6]See A. Lloyd Morgan, *Emergent Evolution* (London: Williams & Norgate, 1927), and Samuel Alexander, *Space, Time, and Deity* (London: Macmillan, 1920).

[7]Rust, *Evolutionary Philosophies and Contemporary Theology*, p. 87. Rust argues that these views result in a naturalistic pantheism characterized by determinism, a lack of human freedom and the absence of transcendence.

[8]Henri Bergson's basic ideas may be found in *Matter and Memory*, trans. Nancy Margaret Paul and W. Scott Palmer (New York: Humanities Press, 1970); *Creative Evolution*, trans. A. Mitchell (New York: Modern Library, 1944); and *The Two Sources of Morality and Religion*, trans. R. A. Audra and C. Brereton (London: Macmillan, 1935).

visible in duration rather than as discrete points or instants of time.[9] For Bergson God is the immanent life force that permeates the whole of reality, and matter is the cast-off residue of the advance of the life force. Bergson, Morgan and Alexander focus on nature in their exploration of process, but they have no place for God's involvement in human history.

Organic models. Jan Smuts described the universe as an organism in which the various parts are integrally related in a complex pattern that Smuts called "holistic."[10] Holism runs through the entire structure of the universe to bring about wholeness. No object within the universe is discrete or detached. Rather, every object forms a "field" in relationship with other "fields" throughout the universe and in the historical relationship of past, present and future. Each organism is the product of its past and the preparation for its future or successors. The holistic factor creates ever more complex wholes as the process advances from physicochemical structures to life to mind. Mechanistic causation operates at the earlier stages but is gradually rendered redundant as holism assumes the dominant role in structures. Smuts does not identify holism with God. Neither does his system address the problem of evil.

Like Smuts, Alfred North Whitehead assumed that the model of an organism must serve to explain the universe. In taking this model Whitehead rejected the scientific notion of "simple location" or the practice of describing a thing as particular or discrete without reference to other regions of space and time.[11] In his critique of modern science Whitehead argued that the focus on mechanism and materialism led to a confusion of abstract models with reality. In applying his critique to evolution, Whitehead argued that a materialistic or naturalistic explanation of evolution was inconsistent with the process of evolution.[12] Science has the challenge to explain the increasing complexity of material toward organisms rather than the meaningless change or inter-

---

[9]It is interesting to note that by the beginning of the twenty-first century, a growing number of physicists have abandoned the view of flowing time as an illusion.

[10]For his position, see Jan C. Smuts, *Holism and Evolution* (New York: Viking Press, 1961).

[11]Alfred North Whitehead, *Science and the Modern World* (New York: Free Press, 1967), pp. 49-50, 91. In this discussion, Whitehead explains his famous "fallacy of misplaced concreteness."

[12]Ibid., p. 107.

action of lumps of matter that one would expect. There also appears to be a degree of flexibility in the environment of organisms as community rather than as individual, isolated objects. While science had tended to view objects in terms of "simple location," Whitehead suggested a more interrelated universe. Instead of a naturalistic, mechanistic universe, he proposed an organic process.[13]

In describing the organic process, Whitehead proposed that the grouping of parts of the process that influence one another constitutes a "nexus."[14] The nexus or "actual occasion" has both a physical and mental dimension. All the parts "prehend" or have a feeling for one another, which brings unity to the whole. Whitehead rejected the idea of "enduring substance" in favor of successive actual occasions that are related over time as a nexus in which the actual occasions achieve self-attainment before passing away. Though this moment passes away, it is prehended by its successors in the nexus, surviving as "memory."

Eternal objects are the potentialities that could become a part of the process as actual entities.[15] Whitehead's conception of God selects those potentialities that become actual entities. God does not create the eternal objects but exercises creativity with the eternal objects, which need God as much as God needs them. God has both a mental and a physical dimension by which he relates to potentialities and actual entities. Through this interrelationship, God shares in the "becoming" of the world and moves toward full self-realization. As God creatively confronts actuality with potentiality, the world creates itself as the incarnation of God.[16]

---

[13]Ibid., p. 119.

[14]Whitehead gives his definitions and explanations of *nexus, actual occasions* and *prehension* in *Process and Reality: An Essay in Cosmology* (New York: Macmillan, 1960), pp. 27-30. This book came from Whitehead's Gifford Lectures of 1927-1928.

[15]Ibid., pp. 159-60.

[16]Rust, *Evolutionary Philosophies and Contemporary Theology*, p. 113. According to Rust, Whitehead's God is a pantheistic deity of the Spinozoistic variety that evolves with nature to develop consciousness. In addition, Rust cites other problems with Whitehead's approach: (1) his empirical approach provides no basis for his conception of reality, (2) his concept of actuality and potentiality provides no basis for God's continuing identity, and (3) the organism model does not provide a basis for understanding human and divine personal being. William Temple observed that Whitehead "leaves us with a totality of God + World, wherein each explains the other but

EVOLUTIONARY THEOLOGY

As scientific naturalism and materialism captured the imagination of the academy and broad sections of the intellectual community, evolutionary theory was taken up as an approach to natural theology. In many ways this venture represents the same sort of concession to naturalistic assumptions that Bultmann and others of the neo-orthodox movement were making in Germany at the same time.

William Temple. William Temple was influenced by the whole stream of evolutionary thought before him. His approach to the topic of process begins with mind and its relationship to the objects it apprehends in the world. Mind is at home in the world but transcends the world, bringing unity and rational coherence to the whole. While he accepted the reality of the material world as described by science, he also believed that naturalism could not explain the universe. Personal being was the key to Temple's understanding of the universe and its process. Temple found mind all the way through the evolutionary process, even in rudimentary form at the atomic level.

In the long, upward movement from mineral to vegetable to animal, a progression develops from experience to response to learning to self-consciousness to cognition. The very idea that mind can comprehend a process in which it emerged at the end suggests that it has been a part of the process throughout. Temple argued that *"the more completely we include Mind within Nature, the more inexplicable must Nature become except by reference to Mind."*[17] Mind is concerned with the facts of existence but also with values of goodness, truth and beauty, which add a transcendent quality to the immanence of Mind. Especially with goodness comes the obligation of duty, and this sense of duty requires some personal explanation for the universe. A materialistic explanation will not do.

Temple's God is both immanent within the process and transcendent as personal being. This deity is not pantheistic, for Temple does not identify God with the world. Instead, the world is the medium for

---

the totality itself is unexplained" (see William Temple, *Nature, God, and Man* [London: Macmillan, 1934], p. 263). One might say that Whitehead's totality is more a tautology.

[17]Temple, *Nature, God, and Man*, p. 133 (italics original).

God's expression. As such, Temple does not allow for a distinction between natural events and miraculous events since all events are subject to the will of God. Even the indeterminacy of the quantum world is contingent on the will of God, for God is not merely a fellow traveler within the world. God is the Creator. The presence of mind throughout creation provides a philosophical basis for both general revelation and special revelation. Again, Temple makes no radical distinction between the two because both are guided by God.[18]

Temple must account for the problem of evil in a world created and guided by a personal God who values goodness, truth and beauty. At the dawn of moral consciousness, biological self-centeredness results in a fall rather than an ascent. Here, Temple speaks of sin as a great probability for which God made provision in his plan rather than regarding sin as part of the plan. So, grace is introduced to the process beyond the mere introduction of values. Temple makes clear that this personal, Creator God is as much concerned with history as with the process of nature. History does not change God or bring about God's self-realization, but God cares about the affairs of people and the course of creation within history. God is immanent in history as well as in nature, bringing his purpose to fulfillment. Yet Temple affirms a degree of human freedom, such that God in his immanence does not know beforehand how people will respond. This view of God's immanent knowledge is held alongside Temple's affirmation that in the eternality of God's transcendence, God grasps the totality of history as a completed whole.[19] Temple insists on both aspects of God's knowledge and resists collapsing the paradox into either position.[20]

Eric Rust's primary complaint against Temple is that he set out to produce natural theology but ended with Christian philosophy as he comes to the brink of expounding the necessity of the incarnation. The implications of Temple's view, which takes Augustine and Einstein as seriously as quantum mechanics, for the contemporary discussion of God's foreknowledge is pertinent. It would seem by Temple's account

---

[18]Ibid., p. 314.
[19]Ibid., p. 444.
[20]Rust, *Evolutionary Philosophies and Contemporary Theology*, p. 146.

that God knows the future by virtue of his transcendence rather than through his immanence, just as we know music from hearing rather than from seeing. The immanence of God relates to creation from the inside, which means temporal experience of creation, while the transcendence of God relates to creation from the perspective of eternity. This paradox would seem to be consistent with the nature of the three-in-one God.

Teilhard de Chardin. Pierre Teilhard de Chardin accepted evolution as an all-embracing fact that can be applied to all of the universe, from the origin of the universe to the origin of life to the origin of the human species.[21] In his approach Teilhard gives the phenomenon of thought equal footing with the material phenomena of nature. This approach makes the human observer the center and goal of the evolutionary process from the beginning and throughout the process.[22] This approach necessarily steps outside the bounds of scientific empiricist orthodoxy. His metaphysical bias allows Teilhard to conceive of a mental aspect to matter. Teilhard's approach, as with others, does not arrive at mind as the conclusion of his study. Rather, he assumes the mental nature of the universe and proceeds from that perspective.

Teilhard does not explore the actual beginning of the universe but focuses on the "law of complexification," whereby the basic stuff of the universe is organized from energy to atoms to elements to molecules.[23] The amount of energy from which all matter emerges is fixed, resulting in scientific pessimism about the future of the universe as all energy is used up and a stagnant equilibrium results throughout the entire universe. Teilhard says that the pessimism arises because science only considers the "without" of matter while ignoring the "within" or consciousness.[24] This psychic energy "within" matter drives the complexification of the universe. Teilhard assumes that all energy is psychic in nature with a *tangential energy* that links an element with elements of the same

---

[21]Teilhard sets forth his convictions about evolution as the grand theory in Pierre Teilhard de Chardin, *The Vision of the Past*, trans. J. M. Cohen (New York: Harper & Row, 1967).

[22]Teilhard expounds this view in Pierre Teilhard de Chardin, *The Phenomenon of Man*, trans. Bernard Wall (New York: Harper & Row, 1965).

[23]Ibid., p. 48.

[24]Ibid., pp. 53-66.

order, and a *radial energy* that draws it toward complexity.[25]

In spite of the evolutionary model Teilhard sees certain points of radical change that burst forth. Complexification results in the basic matter of the universe forming the globe of our planet with a variety of layers or zones that include the barysphere, lithosphere, hydrosphere, atmosphere and stratosphere.[26] Teilhard proposes that in addition to these spheres, a *biosphere* appeared as "the temperate zone of polymerization" in which "the *within* of the earth" would bring forth life.[27] He insisted that the change from inorganic to organic molecules "could not be the result of a simple continuous process."[28] Once life appeared, complexification driven from within resulted in more complex life forms, but always any radical change was drawn forth.

Through successive stages of complexification, Teilhard traces how the "within" drives the process until the next great break—the *noosphere*, the realm of the mind. This realm burst forth "when for the first time in a living creature instinct perceived itself in its own mirror."[29] The world of developed humanity in the noosphere, however, is a world filled with problems that require action. Choices must be made for the good of all in order for all to survive. Like Prefect Renault in *Casablanca*, Teilhard argues that isolationism is not a practical policy. He argues that complexification moves the thinking world to collective unity. The noosphere, with its enormous layers, "must somewhere ahead become involuted to a point which we might call *Omega*, which fuses and consumes them integrally in itself."[30] At Omega point, the tangential and radial arms of energy, the Universal and the Personal, converge as Hyper-Personal.[31] This level of complexification involves greater unity and a greater depth of personal consciousness made possible by love.

God is Teilhard's Omega point. In order to attract all of the universe, Omega point must not be only a future aspiration but a present

---

[25]Ibid., pp. 63-66.
[26]Ibid., p. 68.
[27]Ibid., pp. 71, 78.
[28]Ibid., p. 79.
[29]Ibid., p. 181.
[30]Ibid., p. 259.
[31]Ibid., p. 260.

reality through all time. Omega is not subject to the forces of evolution but is independent of them. Omega point does not emerge from the rise of consciousness. It has already emerged, otherwise it could not draw all things to itself. Teilhard observes that "Autonomy, actuality, irreversibility, and thus finally transcendence are the four attributes of Omega."[32] Omega point is Teilhard's *"Prime Mover."*[33]

In the epilogue to *The Phenomenon of Man*, Teilhard asserts that the Omega point may be known today in Christianity that makes "the uncompromising affirmation of a personal God: God as providence, directing the universe with loving, watchful care; and God the revealer, communicating himself to man on the level of and through the ways of intelligence."[34] He also insists that Christianity focuses on "a prodigious biological operation—that of Redeeming Incarnation."[35] Teilhard describes the incarnation as "partially immersing himself in things, by becoming 'element,' and then, from this point of vantage in the heart of matter, assuming the control and leadership of what we now call evolution."[36] When Christ has gathered everything to himself and transformed it, "he will close in upon himself and his conquests" to rejoin "the divine focus he has never left."[37] Teilhard calls this final act in which St. Paul tells us "God shall be all in all," "a superior form of 'pantheism' without a trace of the poison of adulteration or annihilation."[38]

In his critique of Teilhard, Rust observes that Teilhard begins with natural theology before moving to "Christian philosophy to Christian theology and increasingly to mystical vision."[39] He identifies Teilhard's primary weaknesses as a "tendency to immanentism" and a "shallow treatment of the issue of evil."[40] Concerning the latter point, Rust elaborates:

> Teilhard's treatment of evil is patchy. He treats sin too statically and does not take the challenge seriously enough. The Incarnation, the

---

[32]Ibid., p. 271.
[33]Ibid.
[34]Ibid., pp. 292-93.
[35]Ibid., p. 293.
[36]Ibid., p. 294.
[37]Ibid.
[38]Ibid.
[39]Rust, *Evolutionary Philosophies*, p. 174.
[40]Ibid., p. 175.

Cross, and the Resurrection would have to be dealt with at a deeper level if the mystery of evil is to be treated adequately. Actually the surd nature of evil would raise very serious questions for the kind of system Teilhard offers with its tendencies to monism and immanentism. This is not, however, a theological investigation, and we shall leave the criticism at this point.[41]

Hartshorne. Charles Hartshorne is representative of the American school of process theology. As a student he was Whitehead's assistant at Harvard. Hartshorne taught at the University of Chicago, where many of the leading voices of process theology studied, including John Cobb, Bernard Loomer, Bernard Meland, Schubert Ogden and Daniel Day Williams.[42] The process theologians have widely followed Whitehead's approach to evolutionary philosophy rather than the more Christian approaches of Teilhard and Temple.

Like Whitehead and Teilhard, Hartshorne viewed the universe as psychic in nature, with a mental dimension to matter. He also shared Whitehead's organismic view of the universe and its constituent parts. This nature allows all matter to experience social relationships and shared experience. At some level all of nature has feelings. Everything above the electronic level has a social dimension. Even electrons are social beings, though disembodied spirits, that interact with other particles by virtue of the radius. He allowed for no dualism between mind and matter, though he allowed that a limited dualism may appear in the form of the social relationships. The parts of a tree operate as a democracy. Within vertebrates, however, the animal acts as a whole with a master mind that governs the organism.

Social reality involves change as much as enduring identity. Social reality involves a temporal succession of experiences whereby the unchanged factors from experience to experience provide the basis for identity. Memory of experience forms an important aspect of the social relationship. Human pleasure is a social experience because it involves

[41]Ibid.
[42]The guiding light after Hartshorne is probably John Cobb, who, with David Ray Griffin, founded the Center for Process Studies at Claremont in 1973, which "seeks to promote a new way of thinking based on the work of philosophers Alfred North Whitehead (1861-1947) and Charles Hartshorne (1897-2000)," www.ctr4process.org/about/general.shtml.

the shared experience of a multitude of bodily cells. In this sense the human mind is a "group mind" since it embraces the feelings of the constituent psychic members that make up the human body. Human society, however, lacks the integration necessary for "group mind" to occur. Where the pleasure or enjoyment of a human society occurs, it results from love.

The pan-psychic process that Hartshorne describes involves a monarchical deity who brings all of the universe into "organismic" wholeness. Without some central organizing and guiding principle the chaos operating at the individual level would make science impossible. The initiative for order does not come from the freedom of the individual entity but from the guiding principle it responds to. Hartshorne conceives of a universe that is open to the future. Not all logically possible futures are actually possible because of the limitations of circumstances, but whatever actually happens is determined by the past it came out of. God fulfills a necessary function in providing the cosmic memory that provides the continuity of the universe.

Hartshorne's God is a dipolar deity that involves both being, in the classical theistic and pantheistic sense, but also becoming. He breaks with both theism and pantheism in proposing a *panentheistic* deity. God is not the world, yet God includes the world within himself. God changes as the universe changes, but his identity continues from moment to moment by that aspect that does not change.[43] Here Hartshorne applies to God analogically the enduring model of other entities. God's essence is love, which does not change. Otherwise, God is in the process of becoming, because the universe and its changes are included in God. Hartshorne's God is not immutable, but God's individual being is preserved through the great sweep of change by his abstract essence.[44]

This view of God does not lead to the Absolute, but to the Supreme Relative.[45] Though the universe is included within God, the universe

---

[43]Charles Hartshorne, *Man's Vision of God and the Logic of Theism* (Hamden, Conn.: Archon, 1964), p. 107.

[44]Ibid., p. 237.

[45]Rust, *Evolutionary Philosophies and Contemporary Theology*, p. 191.

does not exhaust God. There is something else that represents the being of God that can allow for any possible future for the universe. Hartshorne conceives the perfection of God as that "than which no *other individual* being could *conceivably* be greater, but which *itself*, in another 'state,' could become greater."[46] Since God includes all the past of the universe, he is always surpassing himself. Because all of the universe is included in God, God experiences the suffering and the joy of the world through his sympathetic love.[47] Though God is the monarchical mind, God is not an autocrat. God neither coerces nor determines the future, leaving the universe free to develop as it will, though always with the "persuasion" of love, which weights the possible responses.[48]

The omnipotence of God has to do with his immediate knowledge relative to the feelings and actions of the universe. God's knowledge is always growing. The absolute dimension of the knowledge of God concerns his "cognitive adequacy."[49] In Hartshorne's system sin involves an absence of concern rather than a positive experience. Thus, God knows about the sin but does not participate in it since it is an exclusion. Nonetheless, God shares in the positive or concrete results of any such exclusion. In this way God experiences the suffering of the universe.[50] In his critique of Hartshorne, Rust focuses on the neglect of the Christian understanding of *creatio ex nihilo*. Hartshorne's universe appears to be derived from God. Many problems proceed from this beginning, which Rust does not explore, though he does discuss the problem of defining personal identity within the organic model, a problem Hartshorne shares with Whitehead, Cobb and others.

Cobb. John Cobb (1925-), a Methodist theologian who followed Hartshorne and Whitehead, has reinterpreted Christian faith in terms of process thought. He reinterpreted the history of Christological doctrine to think of the Logos as present in Jesus, which is to say "in-

---

[46]Charles Hartshorne, *The Divine Relativity: A Social Conception of God* (New Haven, Conn.: Yale University Press, 1976), p. 20.

[47]Hartshorne, *Man's Vision of God*, p. 114.

[48]Hartshorne, *Divine Relativity*, p. 142. Hartshorne credits Whitehead with discovering the metaphysical concept of the persuasion of God.

[49]Rust, *Evolutionary Philosophies and Contemporary Theology*, p. 196.

[50]Ibid., pp. 198-200.

carnate," yet at the same time distinct from Jesus. Cobb explained that "In such presence the distinction of what is present and that in which it is present remains."[51] Cobb criticized the assumption of classical Christianity that "Jesus' relation to God was different from ours."[52] Cobb affirmed a "concrete particularity of the divine presence" in Jesus, but added that this same presence "is in each of us."[53]

Cobb explained his approach to Christian faith in terms of his philosophical commitments to Whitehead's scheme:

> Whitehead has enabled me to renew my faith in Jesus Christ. But of course I am not enabled to believe in Jesus Christ as he appears in other perspectives. Hence, when I explain who Jesus Christ is, I do so from my Whiteheadian perspective. I believe this perspective illuminates and clarifies, and if I did not believe that, I would grow dissatisfied with the perspective. But as long as it *is* my perspective, I have no choice but to understand Jesus Christ in it.[54]

Cobb expresses an unusual honesty in his recognition that his commitment to a philosophical system takes priority in his understanding of both science and theology.[55] It takes a remarkably self-aware person to understand this dynamic about their own theological method. This commitment to his philosophical system allows Cobb to give a new meaning to the word *Jesus*, and to challenge the prevailing understanding of quantum mechanics. He rejects the assumptions of mainstream physicists that differ from those of Whitehead. Cobb asks, "What would happen if one approached the quantum world as a field of Whiteheadian interpenetrating events in which there were neither particles nor waves?"[56]

While we may disagree with Cobb's method and his conclusions, Cobb helps in recognizing the extent to which the philosophical commitments of a scientist or a theologian may color the way they understand the workings of the universe or the workings of God. Cobb hon-

---

[51]John B. Cobb Jr., *Christ in a Pluralistic Age* (Philadelphia: Westminster Press, 1975), p. 170.
[52]Ibid., p. 131.
[53]Ibid., pp. 130-31.
[54]John B. Cobb Jr., "A Personal Appreciation," *Zygon* 31, no. 1 (1996): 48.
[55]Ibid., p. 47.
[56]Ibid., p. 49.

estly acknowledges his commitments, while too many scientists and theologians remain unaware of their own.

CONCLUSION

On the positive side the number and variety of evolutionary philosophies and theologies underscores the problem with the idea of natural selection. Natural selection does not provide an intellectually satisfying answer to the problem of why organisms should evolve at all, especially considering the problem of entropy at the macro level and chaos at the micro level. The problems of entropy and chaos will be discussed in later chapters, but these forces would seem to mitigate against any growing complexity. While these approaches may concede that some form of evolution has taken place, their very existence cries out that the emperor has no clothes.

The process approach also stresses the dynamic relationship of God to the physical world. It is not necessary, however, to move in the direction that many within this tradition have taken in order to affirm God's involvement in the world. The process tradition seems largely to react against the static model of God presented by the deists and carried forward by the British tradition of natural theology. Despite the organic model of the process school, however, elements of the old Aristotelian universe remain. The universe appears always to have been here, as Aristotle claimed. Arthur Peacocke criticized process theology for its rejection of *creation from nothing:*

> First, the theology denies *creation ex nihilo*, which is essential to the notion of God as Creator. I also disagree with its exclusive metaphysics of event and its panpsychism. This panpsychism—now re-labeled "pan-experimentalism"—is a dead end, misconceiving both epistemologically and ontologically the relation between the sciences of different levels of complexity and the emergence of genuine realities at higher levels.[57]

In his assessment of process theology, John Polkinghorne has de-

[57]See "The Significance of Alfred North Whitehead," *Research News & Opportunities* 3, no. 6 (February 2003): 23-24.

scribed the rise of process theology in America and the significance of Ian Barbour in its renewed form:

> Out of the fabric of religious tradition and community experience arises a vocabulary of faith which some people have adopted to new ways of conceiving the Christian faith in light of scientific thought. Ian Barbour's approach stands within the Christian intellectual tradition, but expresses ancient doctrine in ways compatible with methodological naturalism. Barbour describes the uniqueness of Jesus as a matter of degree in which the relationship of Jesus to God represents a continuation and intensification of what had preceded him in evolutionary development.[58]

Polkinghorne rejects process theology on two grounds. First, its emphasis on "event" as discontinuous change does not give adequate place to the role of continuous development seen in quantum theory. Second, process theology limits God's freedom of action to persuasion alone. Polkinghorne argues that "Such a conception of deity falls short of describing a being who could be the basis for an everlasting hope."[59] The God of the process can make no offer of hope or of salvation because the God of the process neither overcomes evil nor bestows grace. The process approach tends to concede the field to a philosophical system by which the Christian faith is reinterpreted. A pantheistic God of philosophers like Spinoza or any other source "will not do for Christianity. Its God is not a World Principle, embodied in the cosmos and so both coming into being with the origin of the universe and also fading away into nothingness when that universe eventually draws to its dying close."[60] Polkinghorne observes that panentheism implies "a considerable degree of effective detachment of creation from the God who exercises persuasion but possesses no direct power."[61] At the same time that process thought detaches God from any exercise of power within the universe, it also tends to identify God with the universe within

---

[58]John Polkinghorne, *Science and the Trinity* (New Haven, Conn.: Yale University Press, 2004), p. 17.
[59]Ibid., p. 19.
[60]Ibid., pp. 93-94.
[61]Ibid., p. 96.

which God is impotent. Polkinghorne argues that a panentheist model does not lessen the problem of evil but heightens it because "The more closely God is identified with creation, the more acute become the problems posed by the existence of evil within that creation."[62]

In dealing with the problem of suffering, Ian Barbour has argued that "by accepting the limitations of divine power we avoid blaming God for particular forms of evil and suffering."[63] This approach to deity certainly gets God off the hook, but it also denies God any credit for the development of the universe and the human race. If God is impotent to do anything, then humans can take the credit. God is a good friend along for the ride, wishing us all the best, but no real help. We are on our own.

The response of the universe to the love of God sounds remarkably like the account Aristotle gave for the development of the universe. By Aristotle's account the divine did not create the universe or set it in motion, but the stuff of the universe began to move in response to the beauty of divinity. In an effort to make the organic model seem respectable to Darwinians, process thinkers have made their theology incompatible with the physics of cosmology current today. In this way they expose the basic problem with developing a theological system based on the prevailing theories of science. What happens when the science changes? We commit what C. S. Lewis called "chronological snobbery" if we believe that the current science is the final science.

In many ways process theology represents an elaborate form of God-of-the-gaps reasoning. The process theologians have found a place for God where he will not get in the way. For the most part, process theology has nothing to say about God's involvement with people in history at the cognitive self-conscious level. There is little place for cognitive revelation in the process. Process theology appropriates much of the vocabulary of orthodox Christianity, but frequently ascribes new meaning to terms and doctrines long accepted as normative of faith.

Methodologically, we see that the tradition of process theology does not discover metaphysical realities; rather, it assumes enormous meta-

---

[62]Ibid., p. 97.
[63]Ian Barbour, *Religion and Science* (New York: HarperSanFrancisco, 1997), p. 323.

physical realities and develops a system to exploit them as Marx did. In this way they commit the fallacy of analogy for which Hume criticized the natural theologians of the eighteenth century with their mechanical model of the universe. Not terribly dissimilar from the mindset of the eighteenth-century determinists, the process school of thought, Polkinghorne argues, insists upon "a Humean dismissal of anything that suggests a happening out of the ordinary."[64]

Perhaps the greatest theological strength of process theology resides in its reaction to a deterministic monarchical model of God that approached modalism and made the Holy Spirit logically unnecessary or at least unimportant. Ian Barbour has asserted that "it is in the biblical idea of *the Spirit* that we find the closest fit to the process understanding of God's presence in the world."[65] Unfortunately, in affirming the presence of "Spirit" (Barbour usually avoids the more doctrinally firm term "Holy Spirit," which designates the third person of the Trinity),[66] Barbour continues the either-or reductionist method of the modern period laid down by the Puritans and shared by too many other schools of modern theological thought.

Process theology has responded to the death of the old deterministic universe with an emphasis on freedom. Though inspired by Darwin, process theology does not engage science so much as it imposes a set of values on science on which its system is based. In explaining that human freedom is the foundation for process theology, Ian Barbour wrote, "Human experience is the starting point from which process thought generalizes and extrapolates to develop a set of metaphysical categories that are exemplified by all entities."[67] This emphasis may explain in part why process theology has largely remained an American phenomenon that few outside the United States take seriously. In many ways process theology represents a projection of American idealism on the universe. At the same time it endows matter with a quasi-human nature, for surely matter does not have freedom of choice about its

---

[64]Ibid., p. 36.

[65]Ian Barbour, *When Science Meets Religion* (London: HarperCollins, 2000), p. 176.

[66]In his conclusion to *Religion and Science*, Barbour refers "to the biblical concept of the Holy Spirit" and continues by discussing his concept of *the Spirit* (see *Religion and Science*, p. 332).

[67]Barbour, *Religion and Science*, p. 323.

destiny if it has no self-conscious decision-making ability. Yet the strongest emotional appeal that process thinkers bring to the table against the involvement of God in the universe with a purpose or plan to direct its outcome is that such a situation would deny to the universe its freedom to become. At the quantum level, electrons have no opinion or preference for what they do. Electrons have a notorious reputation for not planning ahead. Their future is not determined, which is to say that their future is open and may be affected by a variety of future conditions, as experimental physicists have discovered. From a quantum perspective electrons do not have a determined future that would be denied to them if God acted on them as any other condition might act on them.

Process theology makes the same error as the reductionist monarchical model makes when it assumes that God must always act in only one way. Rather than think that God must always do the same thing, we may think of God relating differently but appropriately to every level of organization of the universe. He may operate in a deterministic way at some points and in an indeterminate way at other points. Like Calvinism and Arminianism, process theology would have God always do it the same way, which leaves God much less free than the people who think about God.

Evangelicals have only lately begun to enter the discussion of the relation of science to Christian faith. Any successful engagement, however, must use biblical categories, for the great issues depend on a sober discussion of how scientific discoveries relate to biblical revelation about the nature of reality. As Alister McGrath has argued, "the best dialogue possibilities exist between orthodox Christian theology and the natural sciences, rather than process thought."[68] The only unique contribution Christians have to make comes from their understanding of special revelation. The continuing attention to hermeneutics that grapple with the ever-changing questions of technological society will be uppermost in the discussion. It will be of critical importance to speak to the issues of the day without altering fundamental

---

[68]"Significance of Alfred North Whitehead," pp. 23-24.

Christian doctrines to make them acceptable to the prejudices of the day. To make a helpful contribution, however, we must deal with the biblical message of God's continuous activity and involvement with creation and history.

4

BEYOND THE GOD
OF THE GAPS

✦✧✦

AT ONE TIME, PEOPLE IN the West took for granted that God
was involved in the world. People credited or blamed God for everything that happened. This view prevailed for a thousand years, from
the rise of Christendom to the rise of modern science. In his literary
criticism of medieval literature, C. S. Lewis argued that the Middle
Ages developed a syncretistic model of the universe that combined and
harmonized Platonic, Aristotelian, Stoical, pagan and Christian elements. This model would not grow obsolete until the end of the seventeenth century.[1] Much has been made of the "medieval synthesis," but
Lewis contended that the model was never an easy synthesis or one in
which the great minds took delight. According to Lewis,

> The Pagan elements embedded in it involved a conception of God, and
> of man's place in the universe, which, if not in logical contradiction to
> Christianity, were subtly out of harmony with it. There was no direct
> "conflict between religion and science" of the nineteenth-century type;
> but there was an incompatibility of temperament.[2]

The medieval mind believed that events could be correlated with
their causes, thus producing a hope for discovering the secrets of nature.
But why does this conviction set the West apart from the rest of the

---

[1]C. S. Lewis, *The Discarded Image: An Introduction to Medieval and Renaissance Literature* (Cambridge: Cambridge University Press, 2000), pp. 12-13.
[2]Ibid, pp. 18-19.

world in the development of the scientific method? Whitehead offers this answer:

> When we compare this tone of thought in Europe with the attitude of other civilizations when left to themselves, there seems but one source for its origin. It must come from the medieval insistence on the rationality of God, conceived as with the personal energy of Jehovah and with the rationality of a Greek philosopher. Every detail was supervised and ordered: the search into nature could only result in the vindication of the faith in rationality. . . .
>
> In Asia, the conceptions of God were of a being who was either too arbitrary or too impersonal for such ideas to have much effect on instinctive habits of mind. Any definite occurrence might be due to the fiat of an irrational despot, or might issue from some impersonal, inscrutable origin of things. There was not the same confidence as in the intelligible rationality of a personal being. I am not arguing that the European trust in the scrutability of nature was logically justified even by its own theology. My only point is to understand how it arose. My explanation is that faith in the possibility of science, generated antecedently to the development of modern scientific theory, is an unconscious derivative from medieval theology.[3]

THE ADVENT OF MODERN SCIENCE

With the development of the scientific method, however, people began to wonder in what sense God was involved with the world. Much of the mystery of the world had been explained simply in the past by pointing to God. Beginning with the Copernican revolution, people began to find explanations for many of the mysteries that they had attributed to God. Little by little, men of learning began to describe more and more of the mysteries of the world. In the process, the world ceased to be called *creation* and began to be called *nature*.

Bacon. Oddly enough, the distancing of God from the world did not happen as the result of an effort to distance God from the world. Neither did it happen as a result of separating science and faith. Science, as

---

[3]Alfred North Whitehead, *Science and the Modern World* (New York: Free Press, 1967), pp. 12-13. This book formed the Lowell Lectures of 1925.

such, did not yet exist as a discipline separate from philosophy, and philosophy belonged to the faith. Nor did it happen as a result of eliminating theological affirmations from the assumptions of those who attempted to understand the operations of their world. Instead, the distancing of God from the world came as an unintended consequence of the effort to free the quest for knowledge (*scientia* or science) from the stranglehold of the affirmations of Greek philosophy and the philosophical tradition. Francis Bacon (1561-1626) proposed a method of rigorous experimental investigation whereby general laws of nature could be construed and future behavior of nature predicted. His method jettisoned the metaphysical forms of Aristotelian philosophy that had dominated Western thinking since the high Middle Ages and replaced it with the reliance on observable phenomena or *empiricism*.

Galileo. Unfortunately for Galileo Galilei (1564-1642), the scientific method espoused by the Protestant Bacon clashed with the entrenched Aristotelian academic establishment of Catholic Italy. It is always dangerous for an academic to go against the academic power structure, but doubly so for Galileo, who came into his own as the bitter continental conflict had commenced between Catholics and Protestants, known as the Thirty Years' War. The historical situation clouds the dynamics involved and perpetuates the modern myth that Galileo's troubles involved a conflict between science and faith. Galileo had not questioned God or the Bible. He had done something much more seditious to the academy. He had questioned Aristotle's understanding of nature.

While Galileo is remembered for his descriptions of falling bodies and his observations of the heavenly bodies, some of his notions helped to ease God out of his corner of the world. Galileo distinguished between primary qualities and secondary qualities. Primary qualities involved extension and motion, and applied to the fundamental particles of matter as objective qualities. Secondary qualities involved experiences like sound, color, odor and taste, and were considered subjective bodily experiences of the observer. Galileo limited legitimate investigation to the primary qualities. In other words, Galileo rejected the old Aristotelian metaphysic, but he replaced it with a new metaphysic grounded in his own presuppositions about physics. Later generations of physicists, chemists and biologists would ground Galileo's secondary qualities firmly in the realm of empirical investigation, but the tradition of a new metaphysic had unintentionally begun. It would grow and spread even as its initial foundations would be cast aside. Such is the power of tradition. As Eric Rust observed, "Already nature was being reduced to the status of an extended order of purely physical bodies in motion."[4] Descartes would press the issue further.

Descartes. While Copernicus, Kepler, Bacon and Galileo established empiricism as the foundation of the scientific method, René Descartes established rationalism as the mistress of empiricism. The practical outcome of Descartes' famous dictum, *"Cogito ergo sum,"* was that mind and God were removed from nature. Rationality observed nature from the outside. Descartes followed Galileo in his view that secondary qualities were irrelevant since they could not be measured, and Descartes' universe was a mechanical one that could be described geometrically. An advocate of radical skepticism, Descartes grounded the legitimacy of empiricism in the existence of God, who guaranteed that sensory perception was reliable. Descartes conceived of the universe as a vast continuum of moving matter operating through a continuous system of vortices through which the planets moved. Descartes believed that God had established the laws to run this vast machine and had set it in motion. Most of Descartes' notions about the actual nature of nature were wrong, but the basis for his ideas became an essential feature of the new tradition. His dichotomy of mind and matter became a persistent aspect of the new philosophical metaphysic that guided the development of Western culture. Still, Descartes could locate the soul in the pineal gland because it seemed to have no other purpose![5]

Newton. Isaac Newton provided a basis for understanding the laws of motion that had escaped Descartes. Through the use of his newly invented calculus, Newton devised a system for explaining mathematically the motions of the vast machine. The new mechanical universe obeyed absolute laws in a deterministic fashion such that Newton

---

[4]Eric C. Rust, *Science and Faith* (Oxford: Oxford University Press, 1967), p. 16.
[5]C. A. Coulson, *Science and Christian Belief* (Chapel Hill: University of North Carolina Press, 1955), p. 20.

felt confident of absolute certainty in his calculations. Newton's universe was one of absolute time and absolute space. Newton rejected the Cartesian view of continuous matter, accepting instead the growing view of solid atoms moving in empty space. Neither did he accept Descartes' method of offering hypotheses based on rationalism without empirical data. Though he rejected the fruit of Descartes' philosophical speculation, he retained Descartes' dichotomy of mind and matter, and made it a standard feature of the intellectual climate of the day. While he did not engage in the metaphysical explanations of Descartes, he did not hesitate to ascribe to God what his calculations and data could not explain. He credited God with establishing the orbital paths of the planets, for "repairing" the orbits where irregularities existed for which he could not otherwise account, and for maintaining the stars in their fixed positions. C. A. Coulson observed that when Newton could not explain the spinning of the earth on its axis by his law of gravity, he declared, "the diurnal rotations of the planets could not be derived from gravity, but required a divine arm to impress it on them."[6]

Laplace. With his nebular hypothesis, Pierre Simon de Laplace (1749-1827) provided an explanation for the orbital paths of the planets around the sun without resorting to Newton's recourse to God. The condensing of nebular gases to form the planets could account for the orbital patterns in the model proposed by Laplace. Furthermore, Laplace proposed a mathematical model to account for the self-correction of planetary motion over time, making intervention by God unnecessary. Ian Barbour observed of this critical episode in intellectual history: "The world was no longer seen as the purposeful divine drama of the Middle Ages or even as the continuing object of providential supervision, as for Newton, but as a set of interacting natural forces."[7] With Laplace, the new metaphysic of *determinism* comes to full flower. He envisioned a closed universe of matter in motion that could be completely and accurately described with certainty according to an absolute

---

[6]Isaac Newton, quoted in ibid. Coulson cites Newton's letter to the master of Trinity College, Cambridge.
[7]Ibid.

mechanical system of cause-and-effect. In such a universe Laplace reasoned that it would be possible to know the previous and future state of all matter with certainty.

Ray. With physics and astronomy on the ascendancy, offering explanations for the mechanical nature of the universe, there seemed little for naturalists who observed living organisms to do. John Ray (1627-1705) did not accept such a mechanical view of nature and argued along with Ralph Cudworth for a more organic understanding of nature. Ray introduced a system for the classification of organisms and proposed that a "plastic" model of the universe lent itself more to the overriding divine purpose than a mechanical model.[8] Ray saw in an organism's ability to adapt to its environment the working out of the divine plan. While Ray marveled at the changes that might take place within a species, he argued that the species themselves were fixed. He understood these as "created by God at first, and by him conserved to this day in the same state and condition in which they were first made."[9] Ray saw the designing hand of God in the living things he observed and became a great advocate of the design argument. No other explanation for the intricacies of life seemed possible.

Linnaeus. Carolus Linnaeus (1707-1778), the Swedish naturalist, improved upon Ray's classification system of organisms and developed the binomial nomenclature (genus and species) still in use today. Linnaeus shared Ray's sense of awe at the wonder of life and shared the view that organisms demonstrated the work of a Designer. The idea for his classification system, in fact, came from the Genesis account of creation that described God making "kinds." At first Linnaeus believed the fixed "kinds" to be the *species* level, but later thought of "kinds" as the *genus* and finally the *order*.[10] Linnaeus firmly believed that the "kinds" did not change. They had been "fixed" by God. It remained for the naturalist to describe what God had done, as he remarked, "*Deus*

---

[8]Rust, *Science and Faith*, p. 22.

[9]John Ray, *The Wisdom of God Manifested in the Work of Creation*, 11th ed. (London, 1743), pp. 287-88, as cited in Rust, *Science and Faith*, p. 23.

[10]Harry L. Poe and Jimmy H. Davis, *Science and Faith: An Evangelical Dialogue* (Nashville: Broadman & Holman, 2000), p. 112. I acknowledge my debt to my colleague Dr. Davis, who wrote this section of our book.

creavit. Linnaeus disposuit" (God creates. Linnaeus arranges.).[11]

Darwin. Charles Darwin (1809-1882) proposed that the variety of species had come about as a result of small changes over time that eventually resulted in new species. Instead of species "fixed" by God in an original act of creation, the theory of natural selection offered an explanation for the development of life that did not require the involvement of God. As Kenneth Miller has observed, "Charles Darwin had established the mutability of species, and severed forever Linnaeus's direct connection between each living thing and the hand of God."[12] Rather than the result of a grand design, the Darwinian theory attributed the appearance of life as the result of chance. Natural selection provided a new metaphysic as a first cause.

THE GOD OF THE GAPS

Almost one hundred years after Darwin published *The Origin of the Species by Natural Selection*, C. A. Coulson delivered the McNair Lectures at the University of North Carolina, where he coined the term *God of the gaps* to describe the approach to science and religion that had relegated God's activity to the gaps in scientific knowledge. Coulson warned, "There is no 'God of the gaps' to take over at those strategic places where science fails; and the reason is that gaps of this sort have the unpreventable habit of shrinking."[13] The God-of-the-gaps approach that accompanied much of the development of modern science by Christians tended to view God as involved in part of nature. The inexplicable was the realm of God. Once something could be explained rationally as a result of empirical observation, there seemed no place left for God to inhabit.

Coulson's phrase became a standard feature of discussions of science and religion. Whereas Coulson had employed the phrase to argue for the involvement of God throughout nature, the phrase is commonly employed to castigate any effort to give God a place in the physical

[11]Carolus Linnaeus, quoted in Kenneth R. Miller, *Finding Darwin's God: A Scientist's Search for Common Ground Between God and Evolution* (New York: Perennial, 2002), p. 196.
[12]Ibid., p. 197.
[13]Coulson, *Science and Christian Belief*, p. 20. Coulson delivered his lectures in 1954.

world. Coulson insisted, "Either God is in the whole of Nature, with no gaps, or He's not there at all."[14] In this sentence Coulson presents the primary alternatives: (1) God is in the whole of nature, (2) God is in the gaps that science cannot explain, or (3) God is not in nature at all. Each of these alternatives, however, allows for a variety of positions.[15]

The God-of-the-gaps dilemma arises in retrospect because since the beginning of the rise of modern science, a new metaphysic has risen with it to provide an underlying basis for science. Aristotle's metaphysic of forms provided that foundation for the late medieval period. Certain features of Aristotle's metaphysic persisted into the twentieth century. Newton retained a view of absolute time and space that did not finally fall until Einstein's work. Aristotle's static universe persisted until the big bang theory made it no longer tenable. Bit by bit, however, a new metaphysic developed as a part of the unspoken culture assumed by the scientific community. Materialism and naturalism grew through the partial contributions of thinkers as varied as Descartes and Pascal to Hume and Darwin.

Metaphysics is concerned with existence and reality. Metaphysics involves a prior "speculation on questions that cannot be answered by scientific observation and experiment."[16] The oddity of materialism and naturalism is that they appear to be scientific conclusions when, in fact, they are metaphysical speculations. They assert that only the physical world of observable phenomena exists and that all phenomena can be explained by natural causes within the physical world. Descartes and Pascal did not believe in this metaphysic, but they contributed to its development. They believed in God, but this belief does not necessarily supply people with a functional metaphysic of the nature of existence

---

[14]Ibid., p. 22.

[15]Process theology presents one such option for how God might be in the whole of nature. By the whole of nature, however, process theology means that God is a part of the process of nature. Some forms of process thought would go so far as to identify God with the process of nature. While striving to make God at one with the whole of nature, however, even process theology suffers from the God-of-the-gaps syndrome. By its identification of God with the natural process, it removes God from the realm of history where other concerns and their explanations dominate.

[16]Roger Hancock, "History of Metaphysics," in *The Encyclopedia of Philosophy*, ed. Paul Edwards (New York: Macmillan, 1972), 5:289.

and reality. Different questions are involved. Belief in God provided the founders of modern science with confidence that a rational, knowable world exists. This belief, however, did not supply them with knowledge of how it works. They had profound confidence in the Bible as revelation from God, but they did not find in Scripture an explanation of how the blood circulates or how the heavenly bodies move in relation to one another. Like a child taking apart a toy, they wanted to know how it works. But they knew who had made it.

Descartes' dualism of mind and body led to the twin brothers of naturalism and materialism that have had a metaphysical heyday in the modern world. For some reason these twins seem to have a scientific respectability about them, yet modern health care has given the lie to Descartes' misconception. The old alchemy that understood medicine in terms of the "humors" had nothing to say on the subject. Modern health care, however, has realized the unity of mind and body as well as their impact on one another. Until recently, the medical community thought of health as a purely physical issue involving the condition of the body. In recent years, however, health has come to be seen as a multidimensional issue that involves body, mind and external relationships at a distance. New texts stress that health involves physical, emotional, social, intellectual, spiritual, occupational and environmental dimensions.[17] This intimate psychosomatic unity encompasses the ancient Hebrew idea of the soul—not a ghost but the totality of a person. Naturalism and materialism continue to wield enormous influence as aspects of the new metaphysics even though the intellectual foundations for them have disappeared. People have emotional as well as intellectual reasons for holding their beliefs.

Bacon had urged men of learning to abandon the philosophical traditions of the ancient Greeks that prevented them from acquiring new knowledge. As the natural philosophers gradually shed themselves of the constraints of Aristotelian forms and their accompanying presuppositional baggage, modern science began to emerge. While people of faith developed the scientific method and laid the foundations for

---

[17]Wayne A. Payne, Dale B. Hahn and Ellen B. Lucas, *Understanding Your Health* (New York: McGraw-Hill, 2011), pp. 14-18.

modern science, they failed to lay a metaphysical foundation consistent with their faith. They proceeded as though the abandonment of Aristotle was enough. Pascal's vacuum was not the only one produced in the seventeenth century. Without a commonly shared metaphysic, the common culture of the inquiring minds slowly developed attitudes that formed the presuppositions about existence and reality. Those who performed experiments with nature could not avoid metaphysical speculations because of the very nature of experimentation.

Metaphysical speculation arises in the midst of observations. The natural philosophers and later the scientists who specialized in particular areas of natural philosophy observed that the appearance of things often misrepresents them. Why should this be so? As soon as people shift from asking the "how" question to asking the "why" question, they have moved from science to metaphysics. We have seen how Descartes introduced the metaphysical distinction between mind and matter. Hegel's metaphysic would declare that the world of matter exists in order for spirit or mind to express its purpose. Because of the speculative nature of metaphysics, however, it is just as easy to imagine an alternative reality. Because metaphysics also asks what kind of real things actually exist, it is possible to dispense with mind or spirit altogether, as Marx did, leaving only the material world as the totality of all that actually exists. On the other hand, we may imagine a metaphysic which does not allow the reality of matter. Science has operated with the presupposition of a rational, knowable universe since the Middle Ages. Without the Creator God, however, other alternatives are not only conceivable but are presently under discussion. Quantum theory in particular has raised metaphysical questions that suggest that all of physical reality and the world of phenomena is an illusion, especially when viewed from a Hindu or Buddhist point of view.

A metaphysic provides a conceptual framework for considering questions. It provides a filter for understanding the world and making sense of experience. A metaphysic devoted to causality in a material world conceives of real questions with real answers as those which extend the presupposition further. In this way a metaphysic affects epistemology, or what it is possible to know. The God-of-the-gaps phenomenon arises as people try to fix the place in nature where God may be found to act. This understanding of divine activity is consistent with every other kind of real event in a closed material world. If the activity of God cannot be shown to be of the same kind as other events in the material world, then it cannot be understood as real. Of course, if the activity of God can be described within nature, then it must be a natural event rather than a divine action!

Newton could not conceive of how gravity operated on an object at a distance. A new way of thinking was necessary before someone could conceive of how it might work. The problem of how God might operate in the physical world is a similar problem. The God-of-the-gaps phenomenon is an example of the attempt to think of divine causality in the same way one thinks of physical causality. With a materialistic/naturalistic metaphysic, if one can provide a physical description of a phenomenon that might be thought of as its cause, then God must not have been involved after all. J. P. Moreland and John Mark Reynolds have identified the problem with this conclusion, for "it makes the false assumption that theories about God's actions are rendered false by the mere existence of . . . naturalistic accounts dealing with the same events."[18] To a great extent the problem lies with people who believe in God while at the same time holding a metaphysic that does not permit God to act in the physical realm. At the heart of the Christian faith lies the ultimate expression of this conflict: the incarnation. Was Jesus fully man or fully God? We ask God to show himself in ways we can perceive, but when he does, we say he is just a man. The central event of Christian faith demands that Christians employ a metaphysic that allows for multiple levels of experience. Any activity of God in the physical world that can be observed can necessarily be described according to the categories of nature. Does this make divine activity and natural laws mutually exclusive?

A term has arisen to describe the approach of the person who believes in God yet who has appropriated the metaphysic of the scientific community: *methodological naturalism*. It is an intriguing term because

---

[18]J. P. Moreland and John Mark Reynolds, eds., *Three Views on Creation and Evolution* (Grand Rapids: Zondervan, 1999), p. 22.

it allows one to continue to believe in God while behaving as though naturalism were a part of the scientific method. Those who developed and perfected the scientific method did not espouse naturalism. They were concerned with discovering what happens in nature, but they never presumed to think that what happens in nature is all that happens. Instead of naturalism, they espoused objectivity as much as it is possible. The new metaphysic, however, identifies naturalism with science. The case for methodological naturalism relates to a fear that science will suffer if scientists believe in God. The fear seems to be that a scientist will introduce God into the middle of an equation rather than leaving him in one of the gaps. Tenaciously holding to the existence of a Creator God did not inhibit the advance of science in the seventeenth, eighteenth and nineteenth centuries. On the other hand, tenaciously holding to a metaphysic has always been dangerous for the advance of science. Consider two cases in point. Galileo was not punished by the academic authorities because his belief in God was in question. He was punished because he rejected the Aristotelian metaphysic. Einstein fudged his data to introduce the cosmological constant to his theory not because of his theology but because of his metaphysic. Staying with Einstein, we could identify a third case when he rejected the implications of quantum theory with the terse remark that God does not play dice. How did he arrive at this view? An inner voice told him so![19] More often than not it is one's metaphysic, rather than one's view of God, that threatens science.

Another intriguing feature of the new metaphysics is that it imposes a "naturalism of the gaps" at those points where science cannot speak. Science has nothing to say about what it has nothing to say, but philosophy rushes in and speaks freely. While objectivity and a focus on describing what may be observed of the physical world lie at the heart of the method of the sciences, we cannot make the same statement about naturalism. It would be much more accurate to say of the development of modern science over the last five hundred years that it is the result of methodological theism. The assumptions of belief in a Creator

---

[19]Abraham Pais, *"Subtle Is the Lord . . .": The Science and Life of Albert Einstein* (New York: Oxford University Press, 1982), p. 443.

who established a stable universe that may be known are implicit in the research and discoveries of the founders of modern science. Methodological naturalism provides no methodological assumptions that advance knowledge. Once theists discovered the basic patterns of what they called the laws of nature which were established by their God, then naturalists offered a philosophical theory of the universe. Naturalism, however, did not lead to the development of modern science. Naturalism arose as a philosophical meditation on modern science.

A Noninterventionist God

The discussion of how God relates to the universe or how God acts on the physical world has tended to involve how God "intervenes" in the world. The discussion is framed with the assumption of a deistic God who lives far away and drops in from time to time. This absentee landowner fits with the deterministic absolutism of eighteenth-century philosophy, but it neither fits modern science nor the ancient Bible. Rather than conceiving of God as puttering about in the gaps or intervening in the universe from far off, the Bible describes God as ever present. Can such a view be consistent with what modern science tells us about the kind of universe in which we live and of which we ourselves are a part?

We live in a universe that appears to be perfectly suited for interaction. If this were not so, science would be impossible. Without the openness to interaction, observation of the universe at all levels would not be possible. But the universe is not only open to observation, it is also open to interruption and alteration. The "laws of nature" do not bar intervention, interruption and alteration; they permit it and make it possible. The direction of human history is the story of the interaction with the universe by self-conscious beings who observe, imagine, interrupt and alter nature.

- We alter the effects of temperature with clothes.
- We alter the effects of rain and wind by constructing shelter.
- We stop the flow of rivers and alter currents with dams and canals.
- We harness electricity and channel its current.
- We fly with heavier than air vehicles.

We have learned to mitigate the laws of nature. Humans enforce their will on the universe, regardless of the laws of nature, as we optimistically follow our scientific research to find the "ways around" what appears to be a barrier. Science does not halt to ponder whether human intervention in nature might somehow limit nature's freedom to express itself. The prehistoric development of farming and the domestication of animals both constitute a violation of the natural order. Plants do not grow in neat little rows in nature. Wild animals do not stand still to allow a human to remove their milk in nature. Yet the process of domestication alters the natural behavior of animals. The storage of food in clay jars and grass baskets interferes with the natural process of biological decay. Curing meat and drying fruit to eat months later represents an intervention in the natural process of rot and putrification.

Mind operates on matter every day in human experience. All of us do it. We operate on matter at a distance without violating any of the natural laws. The children's game of rock-paper-scissors illustrates how one law of nature may trump another. In the game the three elements have static properties until they interact. Paper covers rock. Rock breaks scissors. Scissors cut paper. One property trumps another property. The charm of the game lies in the fact that each object can be defeated by an object that is weaker than an object it can defeat. The strengths and weaknesses of the objects depend on specific circumstances. The "laws" of nature also have the relative quality of the children's game. Humans can trump the laws of nature. Hot air balloons are heavy and should fall, but hot air rising trumps gravity. An object the size and weight of a 747 jet should not fly, but fast-moving air creating less pressure trumps gravity. The laws of aerodynamics trump the laws of gravity, but we do not normally think of flight as a violation of the laws of nature. Light should spread out as it travels, but light amplification by stimulation through emissions of radiation (laser) trumps the normal behavior of light and causes it to travel in a narrow, focused beam. The laws never stop being what they are, but they combine in unique ways to produce different effects.

We live in a universe designed for interaction. God's involvement in such a universe would not constitute the "suspension" of the laws of nature or a "violation" of the natural order. God has the same freedom of interaction with the universe as every other sentient being, though he has far greater skill: no hands! If God is as smart as humans, then God does not violate the laws of nature by interacting with nature anymore than humans do. John Polkinghorne has fairly reasoned that "if creatures can act as agents in the world (a capacity that human beings directly experience but which itself is not, as yet, well understood in terms of a scientific account of detailed process), it would not seem reasonable to deny the possibility of some analogous capacity in the Creator."[20]

Darwin's theory, oddly enough, is based on the poetic analogy of human interaction with the normal reproduction process of animals and plants. Animal breeding and the development of hybrid plants involves human interference with a natural process while not breaking any of the laws of nature. Darwin recognized that a process similar to human-directed breeding programs takes place with all life at large. With the same data, however, we may conclude that God actively selects and that death is a feature of selection.

For a long time human interference with the natural state of humans took modest steps. We used a stick to help us walk when our legs grew weak. We invented glasses to help us see when our eyes grew dim. We invented hearing aids to help us hear when we began to grow deaf. But we became more invasive. We put braces on our teeth to straighten them. We put braces on legs to straighten them. We cut open our bodies and altered our physical condition to repair hearts and remove damaged organs. Now we have grown bolder and have within our grasp the ability to alter our genetic makeup. Genetic engineering constitutes a radical intervention in the natural process, but we can do it. We have the freedom to interact with the physical world in profound ways. What Darwin demonstrated by his research is that life is open to interference, intervention and alteration. Genetic engineering, nuclear fission, aeronautics, vaccinations and the synthesis of chemicals all involve interventions and alterations of the course of nature. Science and technology deal with the violation, alteration and manipulation of nature. The

---

[20]John Polkinghorne, *Science and the Trinity* (New Haven, Conn.: Yale University Press, 2004), p. 5.

more we probe, however, the more we realize that nature is arranged to make it friendly to interference or interaction by intelligent life. The more intelligent we become, the more we realize just how open the universe really is. As Polkinghorne has observed, "science's description of physical process is not drawn so tight as to condemn God to the non-interactive role of a deistic spectator."[21] God is at least as free and able as humans to interact with the universe.

A TRINITARIAN GOD

The Christian faith understands God to exist as a relational being who is Father, Son and Holy Spirit.[22] The theological term for this relationship is *Trinity*. In the science and religion conversations in the West since Bacon, different thinkers and groups have tended to choose one of the three persons of the Trinity as their God. The monarchical model of God utilized by Calvinists and deists tends to have a functional view of God as the Father. The panentheist God of process theology conceives of God essentially as Holy Spirit. Pietists tend to gravitate toward the more intimate and approachable Son as their God. Theological systems from classical theology to Calvinism to process theology have in common the tendency to conceive of God as acting in the same way at all times, a view unsustainable from Scripture but perfectly consistent with a philosophical approach to faith. Polkinghorne has argued that "God's utter perfection lies in the total appropriateness at all times of the Creator's relationship with creation, whether that creation is a quark soup or the home of humanity."[23]

---

[21]Ibid., p. 84.

[22]This section on the Trinity comes in large part from an essay contributed to an edited volume that came from papers presented at the 2002 C. S. Lewis Summer Institute in Oxford and Cambridge that dealt with the theme of time and eternity (see Harry Lee Poe, "Conclusion," *What God Knows: Time and the Question of Divine Knowledge*, ed. Harry Lee Poe and J. Stanley Mattson [Waco, Tex.: Baylor University Press, 2005], pp. 161-75). This material builds on a discussion of the Trinity in our earlier book: Harry L. Poe and Jimmy H. Davis, *Science and Faith: An Evangelical Dialogue* (Nashville: Broadman & Holman, 2000), pp. 175-87. Since beginning this discussion, John Polkinghorne has written an important book on this subject that also stresses that a Christian view of science must take into consideration a trinitarian understanding of God (see John Polkinghorne, *Science and the Trinity* [New Haven, Conn.: Yale University Press, 2004]).

[23]Polkinghorne, *Science and the Trinity*, p. 107.

While the issues for theists differ from those of Buddhists and Hindus, the issues for trinitarians may provide a solution for how God relates to time and space. William Lane Craig helps us recognize that the creation of time and space introduces a radical new experience for God in terms of relating to something other than God.[24] This experience of relating to time and space rivals the incarnation in terms of relating to something radically different from God. Philosophical discussions about God and time, however, rarely involve a discussion of the trinitarian God who exists as Father, Son and Holy Spirit. Christians affirm a single Creator God who exists in three persons. At the same time, they affirm both the complete transcendence of God, who is totally other than the physical world, and the true incarnation of God for thirty-three years on earth as fully God and fully human forever joined by his resurrection and exaltation. The incarnation suggests that the persons of the Godhead relate to time and space in different ways. In time and space the Son of God experiences the full effects of physical existence unless ameliorated by God the Father, including limited knowledge of the future. God the Holy Spirit continues the divine involvement in creation and mediates God's will over creation. John Polkinghorne has recognized that a Christian view of science must grapple with a trinitarian God in which "The Father is the fundamental ground of creation's being, while the Word is the source of creation's deep order and the Spirit is ceaselessly at work within the contingencies of open history."[25] This mediating role of the Holy Spirit involves the intercession between God and the physical order.

The problem of the Trinity involves, among other things, the problem of divine knowledge. Just as God's knowledge concerns time as an aspect of physical reality, the Trinity relates to space as a physical reality. Christians understand God to consist of three persons in a nonphysical, nonspatial, nontemporal state of being. The problem of the Trinity exists from the perspective of a spatial and temporal world in

---

[24]William Lane Craig, "God, Time, and Eternity," in *What God Knows: Time and the Question of Divine Knowledge*, ed. Harry Lee Poe and J. Stanley Mattson (Waco, Tex.: Baylor University Press, 2005), pp. 75-93.

[25]Polkinghorne, *Science and the Trinity*, p. 81.

which we would tend to conceive of three persons as discrete beings.

The attributes of God apply to all three persons of the Godhead eternally—attributes such as love, holiness and goodness. Distinguished from the attributes, however, are the properties of the persons of the Godhead. Millard Erickson suggests that though omniscience, omnipotence and omnipresence are properties ascribed to God, they do not necessarily apply to all three persons of the Godhead *in time*.[26] For instance, the Son did not possess these properties during the incarnation, but that thirty-three-year temporal experience does not preclude these properties before or after the incarnation. We might argue that the Holy Spirit possesses the property of omnipresence in relating to the entire physical realm. On the other hand, we might argue that the Father does not exist everywhere, for "everywhere" would suggest physical location. Instead, the Father might be said to exist "no *where*." As the exalted Lord who governs the universe, the Son functions in a relationship to the physical world distinct from that of the Father, who does not step into this relationship until the new creation. The Son mediates between the world of humans and the transcendent Father, while the Holy Spirit mediates the world to the Son.

Father. In the Hebrew and Christian Scriptures, God does not appear to anyone except "the innocents" in Genesis, which suggests an experience out of time. Otherwise, Yahweh reveals himself and acts through angelic messengers and through the Spirit of the Lord, and the Father acts and speaks through angels and through the Holy Spirit. The Godhead, Yahweh, the Father, the Ancient of Days, remains constantly aware yet forever removed from the world of time and space. The Father is completely transcendent, eternal in being, complete in perfection, absolute in holiness and all other attributes. As such the Father does not relate directly to the immanent, the temporal, the in-

---

[26]Millard Erickson has given the most lucid explanation of the distinction between divine attributes, shared by all three persons of the Trinity, and divine properties. Erickson states, "The attributes are the qualities of the entire Godhead. They should not be confused with *properties*, which, technically speaking, are the distinctive characteristics of the various persons of the Trinity. Properties are functions (general), activities (more specific), or acts (most specific) of the individual members of the Godhead" (see Millard Erickson, *Christian Theology* [Grand Rapids: Baker, 1985], p. 265).

complete or the tentative. Does this understanding of God suggest a form of modalism, as Jehovah's Witnesses have affirmed, such that the manifestations of God vary from time to time, but God is never more than one person at a time? The eternal, dynamic relationship of Father, Son and Spirit across the divide—of heaven and earth, eternal and temporal, spiritual and physical, transcendent and immanent—would mitigate against any form of modalism.

Son. Process theologians have argued that a divine plan or goal for the universe and humanity would destroy free will. Even more, many have argued that divine knowledge would destroy free will. The incarnation provides a case study for how God's knowledge does not destroy human free will. In the complex dynamics of the cross, the Father knew and experienced the decisions of the Son, who could not see beyond the moment in time of the flesh, except when the Father parted the veil of eternity and made things known to him. The incarnation meant captivity to the time-space continuum or no real incarnation would have taken place: Jesus could not know the future and could be killed, but the Father raised him from the dead and made the future known to him.

The Son not only entered into space in the incarnation, he entered into space-time. Even if the Father experiences time in some way or some form of time, the Father would not experience it as space-time. To do so, the Father would also have to take on physical form and experience incarnation into the space-time continuum. As Dorothy L. Sayers observed, "It may be more fruitful to consider Time as a part of creation, or perhaps that Time is necessarily associated with Being in Activity—that is, not with God the Father but with God the Son; with the Energy and not with the Idea."[27]

The Son declared that no one knows the day or the hour of the events that lead up to the end of time itself (Mt 24:36), except the Father. On the other hand, the Son did know what was in the human heart (Mk 2:8; Lk 5:22), which involved knowledge of the present moment contemporary with the incarnation. Though the Son emptied

---

[27]Dorothy L. Sayers, *The Mind of the Maker* (New York: Living Age, 1956), p. 101.

himself of his divine omnipotence at the incarnation, such that he could be nailed to a cross and die, still he did not empty himself of deity (Phil 2:6-8). The incarnation involved spiritual knowledge that Jesus perceived because the incarnation did not impose limits on the divine nature; he enjoyed full holiness, love, joy, peace and the plethora of the divine nature not limited by time and space.

In God's incarnation, however, God comes to grips with a fundamental problem posed by a universe in which people can have freedom: theodicy, or the problem of suffering. A trinitarian God experiences this problem from the inside and not merely from the vantage point of ultimate wisdom and knowledge. As Father, Son and Spirit, the trinitarian God becomes a part of his own physical creation as the Son while never ceasing to be distinct from it as the Father. God experiences the pain and suffering through participation in the cosmos. John Polkinghorne has noted the uniqueness of the Trinity to engage the problem of suffering: "The depth of the problem posed by the demands of theodicy is only adequately met in Christian thinking by a Trinitarian understanding of the cross of Christ, seen as the event in which the incarnate God truly shares to the uttermost in the travail of creation."[28]

Holy Spirit. The Holy Spirit of God proceeds from, but is not separate from, God the Father, the Ancient of Days. The Holy Spirit extends into time and space and exercises the power of God in time and space. In the first mention of the Spirit in Genesis, the Spirit of God moves upon chaotic creation before it is ordered. The Holy Spirit is not a servant or lesser being, like an angel. Neither is the Holy Spirit another spiritual being, like the demiurge of Platonism. The Holy Spirit is God involved in the space-time continuum, while the Father is God who remains in eternity. While the Holy Spirit exercises the power of God and shares all attributes of God, the Holy Spirit never acts or speaks in Hebrew or Christian Scriptures apart from the Father or the Son. Whereas the incarnation of the Son has a particular character, coming to a particular place and point in space-time, the Holy Spirit always has an extended character, like a wave.

---

[28]Polkinghorne, *Science and the Trinity*, pp. 72-73.

The Holy Spirit animates the four fundamental forces of the universe and the derivative laws of nature by analogy as the human brain animates the central nervous system or the cardiovascular system of the human body. As an analogy based on the human body, however, this model suffers from the problem of all anthropomorphic projections on deity. The world is not the body of God. Nonetheless, this model illustrates the normal, uninterrupted flow of events in nature that may yet be interrupted by an exercise of the will. Our breathing continues without taking time to think about it. It continues in an uninterrupted flow, unless I exercise my will and hold my breath. Buddhism, Hinduism, deism and process theology have no divine "will" that can do anything other than the automatic function. The Son of God, the exalted Christ, represents the active, concerned, involved aspect of deity that has the capacity to exercise will.

Much of modern theology in its attempt to relate to or respond to Darwin presses for a choice between an immanent God identified with nature and a transcendent God removed from nature.[29] This modern reductionist, either-or approach of theology corresponds to Heisenberg's uncertainty principle[30] and the collapse of the wave function, only in the case of theology it leads to the collapse of the fullness of God. The modern theological approach that involves choosing a single preferred model for God corresponds to the idea in physics that the act of observation affects the data. In observing the location of a particle, we lose the sense of its velocity, and when we observe the velocity of a particle, we lose the sense of its location. Even so, in looking for the immanence of God we lose God's transcendence, and in looking for the transcendence of God we lose God's immanence.

The relationship of the Father, Son and Holy Spirit suggests a solution to how God relates to the physical world of time and space. The Holy Spirit interacts with the world of phenomenal experience

---

[29]We are indebted to Ted Davis, professor of the history of science at Messiah College, for this insight from his study of the history of science in the twentieth century.

[30]In pondering the phenomenon of an electron behaving like a discrete particle and a continuous wave, Heisenberg's uncertainty principle refers to the inability of an observer to know the location and the velocity of an electron at the same time. This principle resulted in the end of Enlightenment science that believed in absolute certainty.

on a temporal basis and mediates the physical world to the Son who guides the cosmos. The Holy Spirit is free to interact with an open universe from the simplest to the most complex structures of the physical world which do not have a determined future in a world of quantum mechanics and mutating DNA. The Son in turn interacts personally with humans through the Holy Spirit and mediates with the Father, who exists beyond time and space. Polkinghorne has explained that "Christ is to be recognized precisely as the One who, in the two natures, human and divine, constitutes the bridge between the infinite life of the Creator and the finite lives of creatures."[31] As the exalted Christ, the Son reigns over the universe and the unfolding of history. The Son guides the process of redemption to its conclusion: "When he has done this, then the Son himself will be made subject to him who put everything under him, so that God may be all in all" (1 Cor 15:28). At the new creation the nature of reality changes, but God does not change. In the dazzling imagery of Revelation, the Father and the Son sit on a single throne, and the Holy Spirit (the river of the water of life) proceeds from them (Rev 22:1). The apparent contradictions of the triune God disappear as the nature of space-time changes in the new creation.

Eschaton. Robert Russell's speculations about eschatology and its implications for both science and Christian theology suggest the possibility of "reverse causality" from future to present, rather than the unidirectional causality of past to present we have grown accustomed to. Such an experience as "reverse causality" might also be construed as coming from outside time rather than from the future.[32] Russell rightly associates the event of the resurrection of Christ with eschatology and the new creation. The resurrection involves continuity with the present experience of the world, yet it involves a radical transformation of the old into something amazingly new. Do we have grounds to expect a "new physics" of the resurrection?

---

[31]Polkinghorne, *Science and the Trinity*, p. 114.
[32]Robert John Russell, "Eschatology and Scientific Cosmology: From Conflict to Interaction," in *What God Knows: Time and the Question of Divine Knowledge*, ed. Harry Lee Poe and J. Stanley Mattson (Waco, Tex.: Baylor University Press, 2005), pp. 95-120.

The experience of the universe is a story of changing physics. The gradual emergence of the four forces (did they emerge or did they separate?) as energy begets matter suggests that the models of physics have changed and may change again. It does no good to say that the four forces (weak nuclear force, strong nuclear force, electromagnetism and gravity) emerged quickly in scant moments of time. Whether the four fundamental forces began as a unified field or gradually emerged does not matter for purposes of illustrating that something about the physics of the universe has changed. From our perspective the individuality of the four forces took place so long ago that it is rather easy psychologically to dismiss their significance for a universe whose physics may change again.

By recent reckoning, gravity emerged as an individual force at 10^{-43} seconds after the big bang. For those not used to dealing with large and small numbers, this number represents a fraction of the first second of time with a decimal followed by 42 zeros and a one:

.000000000000000000000000000000000000000001

At 10^{-35} seconds the strong nuclear force emerged and the great inflation occurred, dramatically increasing the size of the universe from the size of an atom to the size of a pumpkin. The number of zeroes is less, but still it is a tiny fraction of our time:

.00000000000000000000000000000000001

From our perspective the passage of time between the two events is as insignificant as the miniscule size of the new universe. If we go back in time to the emergence of gravity, however, then the universe would have been around since the beginning of time! It was not a short amount of time then. If we take relativity seriously, it was a huge amount of time. Likewise, the space of the universe, though only the size of a pumpkin, had suddenly enlarged enormously. We speak of the passage of time in terms of tiny fractions of a second, but there were no seconds, days or years then, only the passage of time and the expansion of space up to that point. The universe had always been the same up to that point, but then the physics changed. From our perspective it would be

the equivalent of the universe behaving the same way from the stabili-
zation of the four fundamental forces at one hundred billionth of the
first second until now. At least, it would seem logical that the relative
nature of time would work that way at the beginning, except that before
the four fundamental forces operated as discrete forces, the physics of
relativity did not exist as it does now. It is neither logically nor scientifically unreasonable to expect that our universe will have another
physics in its future. What sort of situation might cause such a change?
It is hard to say since we do not know what sort of scientific situation
caused the previous great change.

PART TWO

What Kind of World Allows God to Interact?

The issue of how God might interact with the world arises in the context of understanding what kind of universe exists. Modern science became possible in the context of a theological climate in which people believed that God governed the universe by law as King. Science developed as an act of devotion in which the believer sought to know the laws of God. God as King is a theological model. The behavior of the universe according to discernible laws is a theological model that became a scientific model.

The observability of the patterns of nature that we call laws has raised the issue of how God relates to such a universe. If the universe normally operates according to God's laws and then God does something in the universe apart from the normal operation of the laws, has God violated his own laws? The problem of the violation of the laws of nature by God comes to us primarily as a philosophical problem. Most issues in science and religion are philosophical in nature rather than either scientific or theological.

Often the great philosophical problems we raise emerge because of the assumptions we have before we even notice a problem. In using a poetic analogy like "law" to describe how the universe works, we borrow a term from government to talk about atoms, cells and energy. This poetic metaphor had become the established model for talking about science before the great parliamentary revolution that followed the English Civil War. More importantly, how the pioneers of science in the seventeenth century understood the laws of nature differs dramatically from how scientists understand the world after Einstein and Niels Bohr.

From a deterministic universe to one of contingency, probability and emergence, our universe is not the same place in which the old philosophical problems of the eighteenth-century philosophers arose. In light of the way we now understand the universe to operate and behave, we must reconsider in what sense the laws of nature keep God out and the extent to which the laws of nature create corridors through which God may actively and continually participate in the world.

In considering what kind of universe God has to interact with, we will follow the trajectory of the organization of the universe according to Arthur Peacocke's scheme that moves from simplicity to complexity. Major components of the universe will be grouped by the disciplines of physics, chemistry, biology and history as we consider what openings the universe has within its structure to allow for God's interaction.

5

COSMOLOGY AND THE
EMERGENCE OF EVERYTHING

✦◇✦

THE FIRST TIME SOMEONE SEES the night sky away from city lights, he or she is amazed with the number and brilliance of the stars. Although some old starry friends are brighter than usual, others are hidden by the thousands of points of light in the night sky. This starry view takes us back to the awe of the psalmist when he wrote, "The heavens declare the glory of God; / the skies proclaim the work of his hands" (Ps 19:1).

As the ancients observed the day and night skies, they saw patterns and cycles that convinced them that the heavens were a giant timepiece. People speculate that the rising and setting of the sun led to the concept of the day; the behavior of the sun, moon and the five planets gave rise to the seven-day week; the phases of the moon to the month; and the procession of the constellations to the year. Great archaeological finds, for example Stonehenge in England and the observatory at the Mayan city of Chichén Itzá, appear to be constructed to aid in recording these seasonal regularities.

OBSERVATIONS

Originally, observations were made with one's eyes using visible light. In the twentieth century scientists discovered that they could observe the universe using the entire electromagnetic spectrum: radio waves, microwaves, infrared, visible, ultraviolet, x-rays and gamma rays.[1] A "ruler" used to measure distances in the universe is the light year (9,460,730,472,580.9 kilometers or about 5,879,000,000,000 miles) or the distance that light travels in one year.[2] Observations reveal that the universe contains planets, stars, black holes, dust clouds, galaxies, clusters of galaxies, dark matter and dark energy. Observations reveal a very large universe and an expanding universe.

A very large universe. Starting with our home star, the sun, we discover that the earth is 98,000,000 miles from the sun; light travels this distance in only eight minutes. It takes sun light about 4.2 hours to reach Neptune.[3] The closest star to the sun is Proxima Centauri which is 4.2 light years away. The sun is located in the Milky Way galaxy, which is about 100,000 light years in diameter and about 1,000 light years thick. The Milky Way galaxy contains about 200 billion stars. The closest galaxies, visible in the Southern Hemisphere, are the Large Magellanic Cloud and Small Magellanic Cloud, which are about 169,000 light years and 210,000 light years away, respectively. The closest galaxy, visible in the Northern Hemisphere, is the Andromeda galaxy, which is two million light years away.

Just as stars are organized into galaxies, galaxies form clusters and superclusters separated by great voids. The Milky Way galaxy is part of the Local Group cluster, which consists of thirty galaxies with a 10-million-light-year diameter. The Local Group is part of the Virgo Supercluster, with a diameter of about 200 million light years, and contains about one hundred groups and clusters of galaxies arranged in thin sheets. Great holes are interspersed among the sheets; the holes

---

[1]All electromagnetic radiation travels at the same speed, called the speed of light: 299,792,458 meters per second or 186,282.397 miles per second. The different parts of electromagnetic radiation differ from each other in their wavelength and energy. Radio waves have the longest wavelengths (1 mm to greater than 100,000 km) and have the smallest energy while gamma rays have the shortest wavelength (less than 0.03 nm) and the largest energy. The different parts of the electromagnetic spectrum allow astronomers to "see" through dust clouds and observe energetic events that would be opaque in the visible spectrum.

[2]Another "ruler" is the megaparsec (Mpc) which is approximately 3,262,000 light years. Distances between galaxies are typically measured in megaparsecs.

[3]Since August 24, 2006, astronomers have stated that the solar system consists of eight planets (Mercury, Venus, Earth, Mars, Jupiter, Saturn, Uranus and Neptune) and three dwarf planets (Ceres, Pluto and Eris).

have diameters ranging between 100 million to 400 million light years. Observations from the Hubble Space Telescope suggest that there are at least eight billion galaxies arranged into several hundred thousand clusters.[4]

An expanding universe. During the early part of the twentieth century, astronomers discovered that the wavelength of light from other galaxies was shifted toward the red end of the electromagnetic spectrum. This phenomenon is called redshift. The American astronomer Edwin Hubble discovered that the redshift of distant galaxies increases in proportion to their distance from the earth. The Hubble observations indicated an expanding universe. The whole universe is expanding, which results in the space between the galaxies getting larger rather than one galaxy moving away from another. A visual image of this process is represented by the baking of raisin bread with the raisins representing the galaxies and the bread dough representing the fabric of space. Initially, the raisins are close together. As the bread is baked, the dough expands, taking each raisin farther from every other raisin. The raisins (galaxies) have not traveled away from each other in the dough (space) but rather have been carried by the dough (space) as it has expanded. Recent studies imply that the rate of expansion is increasing, and it appears that the expansion will continue indefinitely.

MODELS

As soon as people began collecting measurements of the heavens, they began trying to understand how all the parts fit together. In science, models are mental pictures that represent things that are difficult to observe, such as objects or processes that are too small to be seen (atoms), too slow to be observed (coal formation) or too vast and far away to be observed at once (universe).

Geocentric model. Model building of the heavens began with the ancients. From the ancient Greeks we received the geocentric model. Building on the ideas of Eudoxus of Cnidus (c. 408-c. 355 B.C.), Aris-

---

[4]Corey Powell, "A Discover Field Guide: The Exotic New Universe," *Discover* 26 (2005): 34.

totle (384-322 B.C.) proposed a universe in which a stationary earth is surrounded by fifty-five concentric crystalline spheres to which the

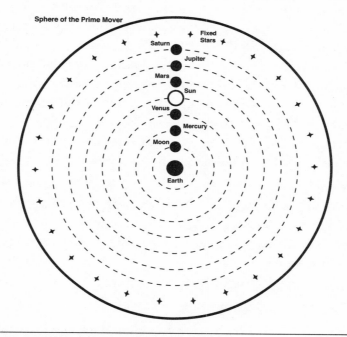

Figure 5.1. Aristotle's earth-centered universe

heavenly objects were attached (see fig. 5.1).

Figure 5.1 is not drawn to scale and does not include the "buffering" spheres between the spheres containing the celestial objects. The Prime Mover caused the outermost sphere to rotate, and this motion was imparted from sphere to sphere. Aristotle further divided the universe into two regions: the earth (sublunary region) and the heavens (superlunary region). Each region was composed of different elements and behaved differently. The earth or sublunary region was the abode of change. Aristotle's cosmology was composed of four elements—earth, water, air and fire. The element earth was the heaviest, with its natural place being the center of the universe, thus, the earth was located at the center of the universe. Objects moved until they reached their natural place. Rocks (being composed of mostly the element earth) move downward, while flames (being lighter) move upward. Everything moved until it found its place in nature. In Aristotle's cosmology the heavens, or superlunary region, were perfect and unchanging being made of a fifth element, aether or quintessence. Thus the moon, planets (Mercury, Venus, Mars, Jupiter and Saturn), the sun, and the fixed stars were all made of this fifth element and were entirely different from the massive, heavy earth. Unlike the objects on earth, the heavenly objects were in constant motion; their motion resulted from the movement of the spheres they were attached to. Aristotle's cosmology provided a complete picture of the universe and fit well into people's everyday observations.

Although Aristotle's scheme could explain many features of planetary motion, it could not explain two observations:

- *Retrograde motion.* The planets, like the stars, travel from east to west through the night sky. However, the motion of some planets, like Mars, occasionally seems to stop and then begin moving west to east to be followed by another stop to be followed by a resumption of the east to west motion.

- *Brightness of planets.* The same planet will appear brighter at one time of the year than at another time of the year.

Ptolemy (A.D. c. 85-165) proposed a technical solution that explained these observations by using the mathematical concepts of deferent, epicycle and equant. In figure 5.2, the earth (E) is placed slightly from the center (C) of the sphere (deferent or eccentric circle) to which is attached a circle (epicycle) which carries the planet (P). By carefully choosing the speeds for the deferent and epicycle, the retrograde motion of the planets could be accounted for. To achieve closer agreement with the observed motions, Ptolemy added the equant (Q), which is directly opposite the earth from the center of the deferent. A point on the deferent (F) moved through equal angles around the equant in equal times so that it speeds up as it gets further from the equant (Q). Each planet required a different combination of deferent, epicycle and equant to reproduce the planet's motions. Although this *ad hoc* model violated the aesthetic sensibilities of Aristotle's model, Ptolemy's model lasted for over a thousand years because it did account for the motions of the heavenly bodies and allowed accurate calculations of phenomena such as eclipses.

One final note on the Ptolemaic model of the universe may prove helpful. Although today we envision a large universe, the ancients envisioned a much more diminutive abode. A stationary earth requires that the sphere containing the stars complete one rotation around the earth in one day. Using today's measurements, the Ptolemaic geocentric universe is estimated to have a radius of about fifty million miles, which is less than the distance from the sun to the planet Venus.[5] Although this seems like a small universe to us today, it was about as large as a

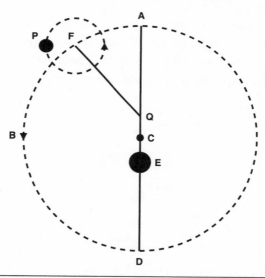

Figure 5.2. Ptolemy's cosmology. E is the earth, C is the geometric center of the deferent, Q is the equant, F is the center of the epicycle and P is the planet.

geocentric universe can be. The reason for this restriction is the speed with which the outer sphere of stars has to move to complete a revolution in twenty-four hours. The stellar sphere with a radius of about fifty million miles would have to travel at a speed of thirteen million miles per hour to complete its twenty-four-hour revolution. If the radius of the stellar sphere were as large as our understanding of the solar system (about five trillion miles), the speed of the sphere would have to

[5]Timothy Ferris, *Coming of Age in the Milky Way* (New York: Perennial, 1988), p. 34.

be about 1.3 trillion miles per hour, which is faster than the speed of light. Thus, the Ptolemaic geocentric universe was diminutive but very complicated with its deferents, epicycles and equants.

Heliocentric model. In 1543, the Polish astronomer Nicolaus Copernicus (1473-1543) stated in his great work *De Revolutionibus* that one of his inspirations was to get rid of the monstrous idea of the equant, which violated circular motion. Copernicus proposed what to him was a more aesthetically pleasing idea: that the sun was at the center of the universe.[6] Figure 5.3 illustrates the Copernican heliocentric model of the universe with the sun in the center and the earth and the five known planets orbiting the sun in circular orbits, while the stars are very distant objects. Copernicus proposed a twenty-four-hour rotation of the earth to explain the apparent motion of the sun and stars. This model also

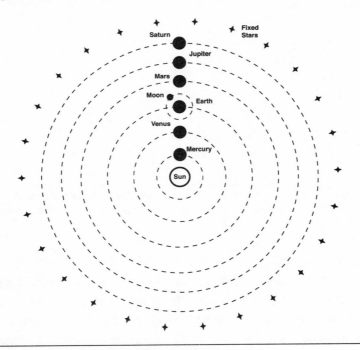

Figure 5.3. Copernican heliocentric universe

[6]The Greek astronomer and mathematician Aristarchus (310-230 B.C.) was probably the first person to propose the heliocentric model. His model was rejected in favor of the geocentric model.

gave a much simpler explanation for the varying brightness and retrograde motion of the planets, both of which depend on the relative relationships between the earth and a planet as both orbit the sun. Because Copernicus assumed uniform circular motion for the planets, his model required epicycles to explain all the details of planetary motion. Although Copernicus's model did not contain the equant, it contained about as many epicycles as Ptolemy's and was not any more aesthetically pleasing (fig. 5.4).

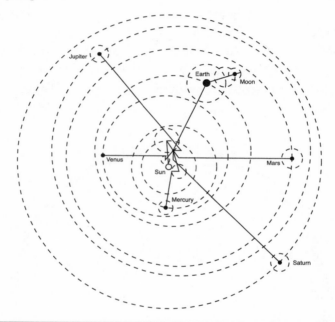

Figure 5.4. The complexity of the Copernican model. Note that none of the planetary orbits are centered on the sun and the use of epicycles. (Adapted from Alexandre Koyre, *The Astronomical Revolution* [Ithaca, N.Y.: Cornell University Press, 1973].)

Previously, we saw that the size of the Ptolemaic model stretched out to our current concept of the orbit of the planet Venus. So how large was the originally proposed Copernican model of the universe? Since the stellar parallax (see fig. 5.6) was not observable in Copernicus's time, the stars had to be at a minimum of about six trillion miles or one light year away, which would make the Copernican model more than a hundred thousand times larger than the Ptolemaic model.[7] This vast space between Saturn, the last known planet, and the stars caused many conceptual problems. For example, what is in all that space? According to Aristotelian cosmology, something had to be there because there was no such thing as a vacuum.

Geoheliocentric model. The Danish astronomer Tycho Brahe (1546-1601) had made the most accurate astronomical observations of his time. Tycho liked the mathematics of the Copernican system but believed that the earth was too sluggish to be continually in motion and also believed that if the earth orbited the sun annually there should be an observable stellar parallax. In 1587, he proposed a geoheliocentric model, with the earth at the center and the sun and moon orbiting the earth. The other five planets revolved around the sun (fig. 5.5).

How to judge between models. With the publication of Copernicus's

Figure 5.5. Tychonic system

[7]Ferris, *Coming of Age in the Milky Way*, p. 38.

De Revolutionibus Orbium Coelestium (On the Revolutions of the Celestial Spheres) in 1543, natural philosophers (scientists) now had two competing models of the universe. How would they choose between them? At one level medieval astronomers viewed the work of Ptolemy and Copernicus as a mathematical device that "saved the appearances" by correctly predicting the movement of the planets but conceptually had no connection with the actual physical reality of the heavens. Almost a hundred years later, Galileo and his critics would still be debating whether these models reflected the true structure of the universe or whether these models just "saved the appearances." Copernicus and Galileo believed that certain models did reflect the structure of the universe, and a model was much more than just a calculation device. Regarding this, John Polkinghorne wrote, "After all, if we did not believe that what we know about the physical world is telling us what it is like, why should we bother to do pure science at all?"[8] As discussed in the introduction, even though we might believe that the model is telling us something about the physical world, we must be careful not to assume that the model tells us everything about the physical world.

Ignoring the mathematical devices such as epicycles, at their very heart the proposals of Aristotle and Copernicus envisioned two different universes. In the Aristotelian universe the earth was stationary and the sun moved, while in the Copernican universe the earth moved and the sun was stationary. At this most basic level, how do we distinguish between two competing models? Throughout history many criteria have been used to judge between models. The most common criteria include:

- agreement with data
- coherence with other accepted theories
- elegance and simplicity (in terms of mathematics)
- scope—links to other disciplines
- fruitfulness—what kind of predictions can it make[9]

---

[8]John Polkinghorne, "Science and Theology in the Twenty-First Century," *Zygon* 35 (2000): 941-53.

[9]Ian G. Barbour, *Religion and Science: Historical and Contemporary Issues* (New York: HarperCollins, 1997), pp. 106-36.

In 1543 the Aristotelian/Ptolemaic model would have seemed more likely than the Copernican model. Looking backward with 20/20 hindsight, we find that mindset hard to believe, but consider the following. Both models calculated the positions of the heavenly bodies with the same degree of accuracy. Although the Copernican model gave a less contrived explanation for retrograde motion and the order of the planets, the Copernican model was in complete conflict with the prevailing physics of the day, which had no way of explaining how the earth in the Copernican system could have three types of motion (rotation on its axis, revolution around the sun and precession around its rotation axis). Neither could the physics explain how a massive body like the earth could stay in orbit or why we do not detect the alleged motion of the earth. Both models were not very aesthetically pleasing, with the Copernican model having an expansive void beyond Saturn. Both models agreed that if the earth orbited the sun, then a stellar parallax should be observed. A stellar parallax is the apparent change of the observed position of a nearby star in regard to the background of stars due to the motion of the earth around the sun (fig. 5.6).

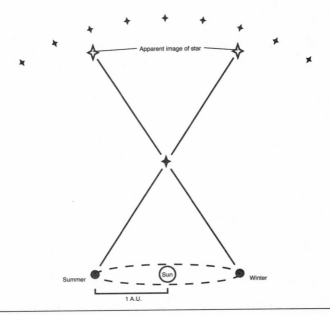

Figure 5.6. Stellar parallax

Since the time of the ancient Greeks, the stellar parallax had not been observed; in fact Galileo had not been able to observe the stellar parallax with his telescope. To many scientists of the day the lack of an observation of the stellar parallax proved the geocentric model. To others, who believed in the heliocentric model, the lack of an observation of the stellar parallax implied that the stars were too far away for it to be observed. Although to their contemporaries this latter explanation seemed contrived, it proved correct when the stellar parallax was observed in 1838.[10]

In 1610, Galileo Galilei used the telescope to observe that the planet Venus had phases similar to the moon. Since the phases of Venus cannot be explained by the Ptolemaic system, many astronomers settled on the Tychonic system because it fit commonsense notions of the relative motions of the sun and earth, and agreed with the nonobservation of the stellar parallax.

By the latter part of the seventeenth century the Copernican heliocentric model had replaced other models. One reason for this shift was the publication in 1687 by the English mathematician Isaac Newton of *Philosophiæ Naturalis Principia Mathematica*, which provided a new physics that showed that earthly and heavenly motions could be explained by one set of laws (the law of universal gravitation and three laws of motion). As more and more observations were made, it was soon realized that the sun was one star of many. In 1785 the German-English musician and astronomer William Herschel (1738-1822) proposed that the universe consisted of the Milky Way galaxy, which he proposed was a disk of stars with the sun at its center. This model persisted until the early part of the twentieth century. All these models, whether ancient Greek or nineteenth century, were static models that implied an eternal universe. All this changed with the observations of Edwin Hubble, which revealed a dynamic, expanding universe.

Big bang model: Background. In the late nineteenth and early twentieth centuries, several scientific observations caused some scientists to contemplate a finite and dynamic model for the universe:

---

[10]Friedrich Wilhelm Bessel (1784-1846), a German mathematician and astronomer, first observed in 1838 that 61 Cygni has a parallax.

- *Radioactivity.* In 1896 the French physicist Antoine Henri Becquerel (1852-1908)[11] discovered radioactivity.[12] This discovery revealed that certain elements like uranium spontaneously decayed into other elements. Scientists realized that some elements do not last forever and questioned whether the universe can be eternal if samples of these elements still exist.

- *Redshift of galaxies.* In 1912 the American astronomer Vesto Slipher (1875-1969) observed a shift in the spectral lines of galaxies and thus discovered what is today called the redshift. Although the Doppler Effect (change in frequency depending upon whether an object is approaching or receding) has been used to explain the redshift, the resulting change in the wavelength of the light from the stars is due to a different physical process. Scientists explain the cosmological redshift as arising from the light photons increasing in wavelength as the result of space itself expanding. Since in the visible spectrum blue light has the shorter wavelength, the term *blueshift* is used when the light from the moving object is at shorter wavelengths. Additionally, in the visible spectrum, red light has the longer wavelength, which led to the term *redshift* for light shifted to longer wavelengths. What is actually being measured is the shift in the spectral lines of an element such as hydrogen that is in the star or galaxy. A redshift is observed as the spectral lines have been shifted to the red end of the spectrum. By measuring stellar spectra, Slipher observed that the spectra of the galaxies were redshifted and thus moving away from earth. These observations raised the question of whether the universe could have this type of motion and still be static.

- *The general theory of relativity.* In 1916 the German-American physicist Albert Einstein (1879-1955) published "The Foundation of the General Theory of Relativity,"[13] which proposed a theory of gravity

---

[11]Becquerel won the 1903 Nobel Prize in physics for discovering radioactivity.

[12]The word *radioactivity* was coined by the Polish-French physicist-chemist Marie Curie (1867-1934), who shared the 1903 Nobel Prize in physics with her husband, French physicist Pierre Curie (1859-1906), and Becquerel.

[13]Albert Einstein, "Die Grundlagen der allegemeinen Relativätstheorie," *Annalen der Physik* 49 (1916).

in terms of masses warping the space-time fabric of the universe. Einstein realized that his equation predicted an expanding universe. Because he believed in a static universe, Einstein modified his equations to remove the expansion prediction. Einstein would later say that this modification was one of the greatest mistakes of his career.

Big bang model: Current understanding. We are now ready to review the current scientific thinking on the origin (cosmogony) and structure (cosmology) of the universe.[14] The following narrative comes from both astronomical observations and high-energy experiments and theoretical physics calculations. As one gets closer and closer to the big bang event, there is more uncertainty in the proposed events since these theoretical calculations have not yet been confirmed by high-energy physics experiments.[15] According to this theory the universe began about 13.7 billion years ago, infinitely small and infinitely hot (possibly an infinitely dense gravitational singularity) (fig. 5.7).[16] The big bang is not an explosion but the simultaneous appearance of space and time (the universe), which has been expanding every since. The raisin-bread model for this expansion was discussed previously.

All that we observe today was included in this initial appearance of space-time. This tiny universe contained the four fundamental forces that regulate the structures of the nucleus (strong and weak nuclear forces), atoms (electromagnetic force) and clumps of matter (gravity). Since that beginning the universe has been expanding and cooling.

Very little is known about the time between the appearance of space-time (big bang) and about 10^{-43} seconds after the big bang. At the initial temperatures of the big bang the four fundamental forces should have been of equal strength and should have been united as one force, and all

---

[14]For a more detailed discussion of this topic, please see Harry L. Poe and Jimmy H. Davis, *Science and Faith: An Evangelical Dialogue* (Nashville: Broadman & Holman, 2000), pp. 65-69, as well as the NASA website, "Cosmology: The Study of the Universe," http://map.gsfc.nasa .gov/universe/WMAP_Universe.pdf.

[15]In 2008, CERN, the European Organization for Nuclear Research, with headquarters in Geneva, began the startup of the Large Hadron Collider instrument. Scientists hope to use the Large Hadron Collider to recreate the conditions just after the big bang.

[16]The latest estimate of the age of the universe from the Wilkinson Microwave Anisotropy Probe (WMAP) is 13.73 ± 0.12 billion years, as reported at the NASA website on May 30, 2011, http://map.gsfc.nasa.gov.

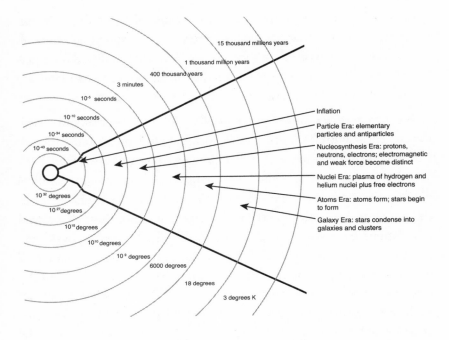

Figure 5.7. Big bang model

probably existed as high-energy radiation (photons) comparable to gamma rays. There is no single theory to explain this early period. General relativity predicts that the beginning was a gravitational singularity. However, because of the extremely small size of the universe, quantum mechanical effects should have dominated this early universe. A quantum gravitation theory is needed that would combine general relativity (gravity) with quantum mechanics (the other three forces) into a unified whole. One possibility is the attempt to explain all particles and forces in nature as vibrations of extremely tiny energy strings through string theory, superstring theory or M theory.[17] Although popular in certain sections of physics, there are currently no experimental ways to falsify any of these theories.

At the extremely high initial temperatures, when two photons col-

---

[17]For further information about string theory, see "The Official String Theory Web Site," http://superstringtheory.com.

lided a particle and antiparticle would be created, with the particle and antiparticle immediately colliding with each other to produce two more photons. Since no particles would be stable at these temperatures, the particle creation and annihilation would be repeated over and over.

As the universe expanded, the temperature of the universe decreased. At about 10^{-39} seconds, the temperature was cool enough for gravity to separate from the other three forces followed by the separation of the strong force at 10^{-35} seconds, leaving the electroweak combined force. It is thought that separation of the strong force released enough energy for a sudden inflation in the size of the universe.[18] The volume of the universe increased by a factor of 10^{80}, increasing from the volume less than that of an atom to the volume of a pumpkin (2.4 feet or 0.73 meters).[19] The electroweak era lasted until approximately 10^{-10} seconds after the big bang.

Beginning with 10^{-10} seconds and onward, physicists and astronomers have experimental evidence to collaborate their theoretical calculations.[20] During the particle era, the electromagnetic force and the weak nuclear force separate. At the beginning of this era there was the continuous swirl between matter, antimatter and light. Somehow, there was one extra matter particle for every 10 billion antimatter particles.[21] By the end of the era only matter and a lot of light were left.

At approximately 0.001 seconds after the big bang, the era of nucleosynthesis begins. Elementary particles begin to combine to form protons and neutrons.[22] During this era, matter would have consisted of

[18]Inflation was not part of the original big bang theory. It was proposed in 1980 by theoretical physicist and astronomer Alan Guth to explain the observed flat, homogenous and isotropic appearance of the universe. The Wilkinson Microwave Anisotropy Probe (WMAP) data is in agreement with the predictions that the inflationary theory makes, as reported on May 30, 2011, at the NASA website, http://map.gsfc.nasa.gov.

[19]Bradley W. Carroll and Dale A. Ostlie, *An Introduction to Modern Astrophysics*, 2nd ed. (New York: Pearson/Addison-Wesley, 2007), pp. 1242-43.

[20]Experimental data has been obtained at accelerator sites, such as Fermi Lab in the United States and CERN in Europe.

[21]The 2008 Nobel Prize in physics was awarded to Yoichiro Nambu (United States), Makoto Kobayahsi (Japan), and Toshihide Maskawa (Japan) for theoretical work on broken symmetries, including the amount of matter and antimatter created in the big bang.

[22]Two types of elementary particles are quarks and leptons. Quarks combine to form protons and neutrons and are found in atomic nuclei. Electrons are elementary particles and are an example of leptons.

a sea of protons, neutrons and electrons. The temperature was too large for protons and neutrons to bind to form nuclei or for electrons to bind to protons to form atoms.

At approximately three minutes after the big bang the universe has expanded and cooled enough to allow the combination of protons and neutrons to form nuclei. Thus, the era of nuclei began. During this era, helium nuclei form, consisting of two protons and two neutrons. This era would appear as a plasma of hydrogen nuclei, helium nuclei and electrons.

At approximately 400,000 years after the big bang, the universe had expanded and cooled enough to allow the combination of electrons with nuclei to form atoms, beginning the era of atoms. Matter as we know it has appeared. The big bang had enough energy to form the first three atoms on the periodic table: hydrogen, helium and lithium. With the formation of atoms, photons of light only weakly interacted with matter and the universe became transparent. Before this time the elementary particles and ionized atoms scattered light similar to the way water droplets in a fog scatter light.

The photons of light that decoupled from matter approximately 400,000 years after the big bang have been traveling through space-time ever since. After being cooled and having their wavelength stretched by the expansion of the universe, these photons can now be observed as cosmic microwave background (CMB) radiation.[23] By studying the physical properties of the CMB, scientists can learn about the distribution of matter in the early universe. The most striking feature of the CMB is its uniformity, which indicates that the distribution of matter approximately 400,000 years after the big bang was uniform and homogeneous.[24]

Philosophers of science connect this homogeneous distribution of matter to the temporal bias of the second law of thermodynamics. Most laws of physics work equally well for processes that happen in one di-

---

[23]The existence of the CMB is one of the evidences supporting the big bang theory. Part of the "snow" seen on a TV set comes from the CMB.

[24]The CMB radiation is very cold (2.725 K) and is uniform to better than one part in a thousand, as reported at the NASA website on May 30, 2011, http://map.gsfc.nasa.gov.

rection as well as in the reverse direction. There is no time bias. But we all observe irreversible processes in nature: water flows spontaneously downhill but never flows spontaneously uphill. One law of physics, the second law of thermodynamics has a temporal bias. This law states that closed systems only move from nonequilibrium states to equilibrium states, or from useful energy to less-useful energy, or from order to disorder, or from low entropy to high entropy. To some, the big bang narrative seems to violate the second law of thermodynamics in that it goes from matter evenly distributed to matter organized into stars, planets and galaxies. Actually, matter evenly distributed is a low entropy state, while matter clumped together is a high entropy state. How can that be? As the Australian philosopher of science Huw Price states,

> It all depends upon what forces are in charge. A normal gas tends to spread out, but that's because the dominant force—pressure—is repulsive. In a system dominated by an attractive force, such as gravity, a uniform distribution of matter is highly unstable. The natural behavior of such matter is to clump together.[25]

Once atoms formed, gravity began acting on this matter, gradually collecting matter into denser and denser areas that ultimately resulted in stars. Since the initial state of the universe was very homogeneous and since gravity needs variations in the distribution of matter to be effective, it can be surprising that we observe clumps of matter (stars) in today's universe. How did this nonhomogeneity arise? It arose from the particle-antiparticle-light fluctuations in the early universe plus inflation. In the early universe at any instance there would be elementary particles in one area and nothing in another. In the next instance the elementary particles would be in another area and so forth. The average of all these fluctuations would be a homogeneous distribution of particles. These fluctuations of the particles are at the quantum or subatomic level. With inflation the quantum fluctuations inflated from the subatomic level to a macroscopic level, resulting in tiny variations in

---

[25]Huw Price, "On the Origins of the Arrow of Time: Why There Is Still a Puzzle About the Low-Entropy Past," in *Contemporary Debates in Philosophy of Science*, ed. Christopher Hitchcock (Oxford: Blackwell, 2004), pp. 219-39.

the distribution of matter. This tiny variation in matter is all it takes for gravity to begin further concentrating the matter.

As the concentration of matter increased, friction would begin heating up the gas cloud of hydrogen that formed. Finally, the temperature would become large enough for fusion of hydrogen into helium to begin, and a star is born.

At about one billion years after the big bang, gravity has had time to collect the stars into galaxies, beginning the era of galaxies. Gradually galaxies collected into clusters resulting in the universe that we see today. Since first generation stars are thought to contain only hydrogen and helium, no rocky planets existed in the first galaxies. Throughout the different star life cycles, elements such as carbon and iron were synthesized by nuclear fusion. Upon the death of the first stars through supernova explosions, elements beyond iron were synthesized. About ten billion years after the big bang, gravity began organizing this star dust into second-generation stars. This dust had a complicated composition consisting not only of hydrogen and helium gases but also solid materials such as minerals and rocks. As the second-generation stars formed, gravity distributed some of this star dust into a disk orbiting at right angles to the rotation of the star. This material in the disk gradually condensed into rocky planets, gaseous planets, asteroids and comets; a solar system was born. On one of these rocky planets, life appeared about ten billion years after the big bang.

It appears that about nine billion years after the big bang an interesting thing happened to the universe's expansion rate. Since the inflationary period there was a gradual deceleration in the expansion rate. Approximately five billion years ago the expansion rate began to accelerate again, and the rate has been gradually increasing ever since.[26] A recently postulated form of matter/energy called dark energy has been postulated as the source of this expansion. Further research is needed to understand dark energy and its effect on the expansion rate.

Composition of the universe. You and I, dogs and cats, flowers and trees, planets and stars are made of atoms. Atoms are what we see and

[26]Adam G. Riess et al., "Observational Evidence from Supernovae for an Accelerating Universe and a Cosmological Constant," *Astronomical Journal* 116 (1998): 1009-38

feel, and what we think of when we think of the universe. (Physicists and cosmologists label atoms as baryonic matter. Baryons are particles such as protons and neutrons, which are made of three quarks.) But only 5 percent of the matter/energy in the universe is made of atoms, with dark matter making up 23 percent and dark energy making up 72 percent of the total.[27] Dark matter exerts a gravitational pull but does not absorb or emit light. Dark matter has been proposed as the explanation for the rotational rate of galaxies. Candidates for dark matter include MACHOs and WIMPs. MACHOs (Massive Compact Halo Objects) could be dim neutron stars or brown dwarf stars. If dark matter is mostly MACHOs, then the amount of baryonic matter would be greatly increased. WIMPs (Weakly Interacting Massive Particles) are nonbaryonic particles that could have been produced shortly after the big bang. Unlike the other forms of matter/energy, dark energy is postulated to permeate all of space. As we have seen, dark energy also has been proposed to explain the recent increase in the universe's expansion rate. In addition, the inclusion of dark energy in cosmological calculations results in better estimates of the age of the universe as well as the large-scale distribution of galaxies and clusters.

DIRECTIONAL UNIVERSE: SIMPLICITY TO COMPLEXITY

The big bang saga deals with level one of Peacocke's levels of complexity (fig 5.8), which were presented in the introduction. The universe developed in ever-increasing complexity from elementary particles to atoms to first-generation stars to second-generation stars and planets with their minerals, rocks and molecules (water, oxygen, nitrogen and so forth) to galaxies to galaxy clusters. On the planets more and more complex molecules developed followed by the appearance of life, which leads us to another chapter and another level of complexity

How did we get from the beginning of the universe with its homogeneous sea of elementary particles and photons to the heterogeneous universe of today? What we observe is the emergence of complex systems from simple interactions. Each level of complexity

---

[27]The term *matter/energy* is used since matter and energy are interchangeable according to Einstein's equation.

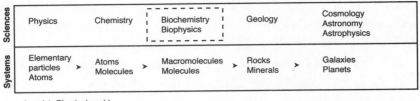

Level 1: Physical world

Figure 5.8. Level 1: Physical world of Peacocke's levels of complexity

has new properties that are irreducible to the previous system's constituent parts. The new whole is greater than the sum of its parts. The study of emergence is in its infancy. Although one of the pioneers of modern emergence, American theoretical biologist Stuart Kauffman, argued that complexity emerged from self-organization especially at the biological level, a well-defined epistemological criterion for studying emergences is lacking.[28] In spite of these epistemological problems, as biologist Harold J. Morowitz states, "we can follow the evolutionary unfolding of the world in terms of significant emergences, even though we lack exact predictions and precise understanding of what is taking place."[29] In general we can observe the following. At the point of emergence of complexity the system has an inconceivably vast array of possible configurations. Some force or law prunes or eliminates most of these configurations, resulting in a new, more complex whole containing properties not present before the emergence. In this and the following chapters we will examine the simple states that existed, what pruned these states and what new properties emerged.

In this chapter we will focus on Peacocke's first level of complexity, "physical world." In later chapters we will focus on other levels of complexity. Following the work of Morowitz, seven different emergences of complexes can be seen in Peacocke's physical world level.[30] The first

---

[28]Stuart Kauffman, *At Home in the Universe: The Search for the Laws of Self-Organization and Complexity* (Oxford: Oxford University Press, 1995).

[29]Harold J. Morowitz, *The Emergence of Everything: How the World Became Complex* (Oxford: Oxford University Press, 2002), p. 20.

[30]Morowitz proposes twenty-eight emergences ranging from the emergence of the universe to the emergence of the spiritual.

emergence is the appearance of the universe, or as philosophers have asked, Why is there something rather than nothing? Current scientific theory deals with the development of the universe after its beginning, but current theory cannot deal with the very beginning. In the future a "theory of everything" may allow a scientific insight into this emergence, or this emergence may forever remain a mystery.

The emergence of large-scale structure or a heterogeneous universe. As discussed earlier, right after the big bang the universe was a homogeneous fog of elementary particles and photons of light that were expanding. With the separation of gravity and the strong force from the other forces, the universe underwent a rapid inflation, which resulted in mass density gradients. There is a vast array of possible ways these density gradients could be distributed. Gravity became the pruning agent that distributed these density gradients into the large-scale structure of the universe that we observe today. Under the dynamics of gravity, regions of high density are attractive centers pulling regions of lower density toward them. Over time the large-scale structure of the universe resulted. Stars are organized into galaxies, which are collected into clusters (fifty to one thousand galaxies) and superclusters (collection of clusters containing over 100,000 galaxies). Superclusters are organized into filaments, which are the largest known structures that are thread-like in shape and up to 262 billion light years in length. A subtype of filament is called a great wall. Filaments surround immense voids.

The emergence of matter and stars. Initially the density gradients were composed of elementary particles of quarks and leptons. As the universe cooled, the quarks combined to form nuclei of hydrogen and helium, resulting in a universe of nuclei and electrons. Finally the universe cooled enough for electrons to bind to the nuclei, resulting in atoms and the emergence of matter. With the binding of the electrons to the nuclei, a new "pruning principle," the Pauli exclusion principle, arose restricting how the electrons relate to the nuclei. The interaction of free electrons and free nuclei is governed by electrostatics: like charges repel, and unlike charges attract. Once an electron and nucleus combine to form an atom, the Pauli exclusion principle of quantum mechanics restricts the distance that an electron can be from the nucleus, as well as how many electrons can be at that distance. The Pauli exclusion principle is a nondynamic selection rule that emerges when electrons bind to nuclei. The whole (an atom) is really different from its parts (nucleus and individual electrons). The emergence of matter is the beginning of chemistry, which impacts future emergences such as biology and neurology. The Pauli exclusion principle will be discussed at greater length in chapter six.

Initially, all the matter was hydrogen and helium atoms, but the dynamics of gravity organized this matter into stars. With the formation of stars a new phenomenon arose, nucleosynthesis. Nucleosynthesis, either in the burning or death of a star, generates all the rest of the elements of the chemist's periodic table. The electronic configuration of each of these new atoms is also controlled by the Pauli exclusion principle. The number of protons in the nucleus determine the identity of matter; for example, all hydrogen atoms have one proton, all oxygen atoms have eight protons, and all uranium atoms have ninety-two protons.

The emergence of planets and solar systems. With the death of the first stars, matter was scattered into the neighboring space. Gravity began recollecting this matter into new, second-generation stars. Because the matter exploded off in various directions, not all of it condensed into a new star. Some of the matter collected into an accretion disk that orbits the developing star. Within the disk, gravity collected the matter into rocky planets, gaseous planets, comets, asteroids and so forth. Gravity, temperature and chemistry determines whether the matter exists as gases, liquids or solids, and whether the solids exist as minerals or rocks.

When atoms bond to one another through metallic, ionic or covalent bonds, new propreties emerge. We cannot say that a single atom of iron is mallable and ductile, but a collection of iron atoms is indeed mallable and ductile. We can say a collection of water molecules is wet, but we cannot say that a single water molecule is wet.

Emergence of planetary structure. The material making up the earth is distributed by density into a series of shells. The innermost shell is the inner core, which is followed by the outer core, lower mantle, upper mantle and crust. The crust plus upper mantle is called the lithosphere, which rests on a molten layer called the asthenosphere (fig 5.9).

The lithosphere is broken into pieces called plates, which float on the asthenosphere. Although the general structure can be explained in

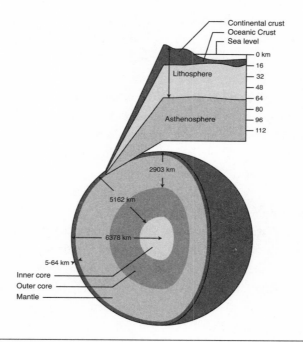

Figure 5.9. Shell structure of the earth and location of the lithosphere

terms of physical and chemical principles, the overall structure of the earth is very complex and many questions about its composition remain, such as whether there is an ideal concentration of radioactive elements within the planets

Emergence of the earth systems. In addition to the shell structure of the earth, there emerged three zones or systems at the earth's surface: lithosphere (solid), hydrosphere (liquid) and atmosphere (gas). The pruning principle for the earth systems appears to be the fact that there are only three phases of matter on the earth.[31] The lithosphere

---

[31]There is a fourth state of matter called the plasma, which is a partially ionized gas that occurs at high temperatures. Since stars are so hot, most of the matter in the universe is in the plasma state.

consists of three types of rock: igneous (formed by melting and are the most common type), sedimentary (formed by weathering and deposition) and metamorphic (formed by heat and pressure without melting). The rock cycle is a dynamic process that converts one type of rock into another type.

The waters in the hydrosphere are distributed between oceans, lakes, rivers, clouds, groundwater, glaciers and permafrost. The water cycle through evaporation, condensation and precipitation relates all the water sources in the hydrosphere.

The atmosphere consists of a mixture of gases comprising primarily nitrogen, oxygen, carbon dioxide and water vapor. Some of the layers of the atmosphere are troposphere, stratosphere, mesosphere, thermosphere and exosphere. The troposphere is closest to the earth's surface and is the location of the earth's weather.

A Universe Teaming with Life?

Although speculation about other stars having planets can be traced back to sixteenth-century Italian philosopher Giordano Bruno, it was not until the twentieth century that technology developed that allowed the detection of planets outside the Solar System. This type of planet is called an extrasolar planet or exoplanet. The two most common methods for detecting exoplanets are the Doppler method and the transit method. The Doppler method is based on the fact that as a planet orbits its star, the star moves around the center of the star system's center of mass. The star's movement causes displacements in the spectral lines of the star (the Doppler effect). The transit method uses the fact that when a planet crosses the parent star's disk, the brightness of the star drops. The amount of change in both methods can be related to the size of the planet. Other methods are used to detect exoplanets, but these two are the most common methods.

The first confirmed discovery of an exoplanet was made in 1988 by Canadian astronomers using the Doppler method. An exoplanet was found in a binary star system, Gamma Cephei, about forty-five light years away, and has a mass about 1.6 times that of Jupiter. The first confirmed discovery of an exoplanet orbiting a sun-like star (51 Pegasi, about fifty-one light years away) took place in 1995. This exoplanet has a mass of about 0.5 that of Jupiter and orbits very close to the star. Most of the earth-bound exoplanet discoveries were of planets that were like Jupiter either in elliptical orbits far from the star or in circular orbits very close to the star. To escape the limiting effects of the earth's atmosphere, NASA designed the Kepler satellite to detect earth-size planets in the habitable zone around other stars. Kepler was launched on March 7, 2009, on a three-and-one-half-year mission to observe more than 156,000 stars simultaneously in the Cygnus-Lyra region of the northern sky. After a year of searching, on February 2, 2011, the Kepler team announced the discovery of 1,235 planet candidates, with 68 of these being approximately earth-size, 288 superearth-size, 662 Neptune-size, 165 Jupiter-size, and 19 larger than Jupiter. In addition, 54 planetary candidates were found in their star's habitable zone, with five of these being near earth-sized. Of the 1,235 planet candidates, 408 of these are multiples in 170 planetary systems.[32] Since Kepler's field of view covers only 1/400 of the sky, Kepler scientists estimate that the Milky Way contains at least 50 billion planets with at least 500 million of these planets in their star's habitable zone.[33]

Do these Kepler estimates mean that the universe is teaming with life on all these planets? And are there other civilizations? Those involved with the Search for Extraterrestrial Intelligence (SETI) project would argue that these Kepler planetary candidates have life, and thousands of them have communicative civilizations. Others are more cautious on the number of possible candidates for life and other civilizations. Leaders of the more cautious approach include geologist Peter D. Ward and astronomer Donald Brownlee in their book *Rare Earth: Why*

---

[32]The NASA Kepler probe has accelerated the discovery of planet candidates. Although the European Union site, The Extrasolar Planets Encyclopaedia (http://exoplanet.eu/catalog .php), lists 552 confirmed exoplanets, as of May 30, 2011, it acknowledged the 1,235 planet candidates proposed by the Kepler scientists.

[33]Michael Mewhinney and Rachel Hoover, "NASA Finds Earth-Sized Planet Candidates in Habitable Zone, 6-Planet System," *NASA Ames Research Center*, February 1, 2011, http:// kepler.nasa.gov/news/nasakeplernews/index.cfm?FuseAction=ShowNews&NewsID=98; Seth Borenstein, "Cosmic Census Finds Crowd of Planets in Our Galaxy," *Seattle Sun Times*, February 19, 2011, http://seattletimes.nwsource.com/html/businesstechnology/2014276945_ apusscicosmiccensus.html.

Complex Life Is Uncommon in the Universe, and evolutionary paleobiologist Simon Conway Morris in his book *Life's Solution: Inevitable Humans in a Lonely Universe.*[34]

One limiting factor is the type of host star for the planet. A suitable star system is one that is made up of a single star; this avoids all the gravitational instabilities that a planet would experience in a binary star system. As reported by the Harvard-Smithsonian Center for Astrophysics, upwards of two-thirds of all the star systems in the Milky Way galaxy are single stars.[35] In addition the star should have a lifetime long enough for not only life to occur but for a civilization to develop. Three types of stars have lifetimes over ten billion years and make up 91.5 percent of all stars. However, 80 percent of these stars are red dwarfs: because of the small size of red dwarfs, a planet would have to orbit so close to the star that its rotation would become tidally coupled to the star. This coupling would keep one side of the planet toward the sun, resulting in one side of the planet freezing and the other "boiling." The other two types of stars with long lifetimes only make up 11.5 percent of star types; the sun is one of these.

Once a planet orbits one of these stars, there are further restrictions. Not only does the planet need to be in the habitable zone (having liquid water), but apparently it also needs a satellite as large as the moon to reduce fluctuations in the planet's tilt axis. This stable axis also results in a more consistent distribution of stellar radiation onto the planet. In addition the composition of the planet should have abundant amounts of carbon, oxygen, heavier elements and water, with a large enough size for plate tectonics to rebuild and replenish the planet. It will be interesting to observe on which side of this argument the data falls in the coming decades.

No matter which side of the debate over the distribution of life one falls on, it appears that the universe is fine-tuned for life to exist. Let us

---

[34]Peter D. Ward and Donald Brownlee, *Rare Earth: Why Complex Life Is Uncommon in the Universe* (New York: Copernicus, 2000); Simon Conway Morris, *Life's Solution: Inevitable Humans in a Lonely Universe* (Cambridge: Cambridge University Press, 2003).

[35]David A. Aguilar and Christine Pulliam, "Most Milky Way Stars Are Single," Harvard-Smithsonian Center for Astrophysics, January 30, 2006, www.cfa.harvard.edu/news/2006/pr200611.html.

consider the following variables: having enough time, having the right subatomic particles and having the right atoms.

Having enough time. As discussed previously, life is thought to have appeared on earth about ten billion years after the big bang. This amount of time is thought to be needed for first-generation stars to form, live and die. This process would produce the elements needed to make second-generation stars and their planets on which life can appear.

The life span of the universe results from the interaction between the size of the big bang and the size of gravity. The size of the big bang causes the fabric of the universe to expand. At the same time, the force of gravity exerts a "breaking effect" on the expansion. Calculations show that if the force of the big bang were slightly larger (one part in a million), the expansion rate for the universe would be too large for gravity to condense matter into stars. If the force of the big bang were slightly smaller (one part in a billion billion), the force of gravity would be large enough to stop the expansion of the universe and recompact it (the "big crunch") in less time than it took for life to appear. In both cases, the size of the big bang and gravity seem to be fine-tuned to provide enough time for life to appear.

Having the right subatomic particles. Even if the universe hangs around long enough for second-generation stars to form, the right building blocks are needed for life to exist. Atoms are made of electrons orbiting a nucleus composed of protons and neutrons. Even though both proton and neutrons are composed of three quarks, the neutron outweighs the proton by 0.138 percent. This small mass difference is critical. "There seems no fundamental reason why the neutron should be the more massive of the two. Furthermore, the mass difference is quite small, a mere tenth of a percent. One might think it would make no difference. But it does make a difference. Indeed it is crucial."[36] The slightly larger neutron decays while the proton does not. The stable proton results in the existence of hydrogen atoms, the major component of stars as well as living organisms.

Another factor in the stability of atoms is the charge ratio between

---

[36]George Greenstein, *The Symbiotic Universe: Life and Mind in the Cosmos* (New York: William Morrow, 1988), p. 93.

the proton and electron. The proton has a positive charge while the electron has a negative charge, with the two charges being equal in value. This equality in charge value is surprising because the proton and electron are very different in composition and mass. Protons are not elemental particles but are made of three elemental quarks. In contrast electrons are elemental particles which belong to the lepton family. Protons are 1,836 times more massive than electrons. One might expect the charge difference between the proton and electron to be more like their mass difference. Yet if their charge difference was one part in a billion, electrostatics would cause an object the size of a person to fly apart. An object as large as the earth would fly apart if the difference in electrical charge was only one part in a billion billion. Thus, the electron-proton charge equality must be finely tuned for the universe to exist.

Having the right atoms. The most common atoms needed by living organisms, in order of relative abundance, are oxygen, carbon, hydrogen and nitrogen. We will examine the magnitudes that the strong force and gravity have on obtaining these elements through nucleosynthesis. The strong force governs the degree to which protons and neutrons stick together in the nucleus. If the strong force was stronger by just 0.3 percent, then the attraction between the proton and neutron becomes so great that protons are always bound to neutrons. Under these conditions the most common form of hydrogen would not exist; the most common form of hydrogen has only one proton in its nucleus. If the strong force was weaker by 2 percent, protons and neutrons would not bind in the nucleus, resulting in a universe of only hydrogen atoms.

Gravity compacts a cloud of hydrogen gas until the gas reaches a temperature high enough for nucleosynthesis to begin. If the force of gravity was slightly weaker, the gas cloud would not be compressed enough for nucleosynthesis to occur, resulting in a starless universe of hydrogen gas. If the force of gravity was slightly stronger, only stars much larger than the sun would form. This type of star has a very short life span and would die before life had time to appear.

In addition to these three fine-tuning examples, there are approximately sixty-seven more examples for the fine-tuning of the universe and the earth.[37] English astronomer Fred Hoyle (1915-2001) comments, "A common sense interpretation of the facts suggests that a super-intellect has monkeyed with physics, as well as with chemistry and biology, and that there are no blind forces worth speaking about in nature. The numbers one calculates from the facts seem to me so overwhelming as to put this conclusion almost beyond question."[38] This data caused Hoyle, an atheist, to begin suggesting that there was intelligence behind the universe. In response to the fine-tuning, American astronomer Robert Jastrow (1925-2008) remarked,

> For the scientist who has lived by his faith in the power of reason, the story ends like a bad dream. He has scaled the mountain of ignorance; he is about to conquer the highest peak; as he pulls himself over the final rock, he is greeted by a band of theologians who have been sitting there for centuries.[39]

The fine-tuning of the universe not only reflects purpose but also reflects some of the characteristics of God. Great care is reflected in the amount of matter and energy that was needed for the universe to become habitable for life. A huge home is needed for life (about fourteen billion light years across) with vast amounts of matter and energy (about 100 billion trillion stars). As the Canadian astronomer Hugh Ross (1945-) stated, "God invested heavily in living creatures. He constructed all these stars and carefully crafted them throughout the age of the universe so that at this brief moment in the history of the cosmos humans could exist and have a pleasant place to live."[40] This planning and commitment of resources suggests a very caring Creator.

Summary

The universe has had many instances of the emergence of complexity followed by long periods of no novelty occuring. In many instances the

---

[37]Hugh Ross, "Big Bang Model Refined by Fire," in *Mere Creation: Science, Faith and Intelligent Design*, ed. William A. Dembski (Downers Grove, Ill.: InterVarsity Press, 1998), pp. 372-80.

[38]Fred Hoyle, "The Universe: Past and Present Reflections," *Engineering and Science*, November 1981, pp. 8-12.

[39]Robert Jastrow, *God and the Astronomers* (New York: W. W. Norton, 1978), p. 116.

[40]Hugh Ross, *The Creator and the Cosmos* (Colorado Springs: NavPress, 1993), p. 125.

pruning mechanism involved existing agents such as gravity and the large-scale structure of the universe, or physics and chemistry principles and the shell structure of the earth. In some cases the pruning mechanism involved the emergence of a new agent such as the Pauli exclusion principle and the electronic configurations of atoms. Underlying all the observed emergences is an apparent fine-tuning of the universe for the development of life. This fine-tuning points to a purpose and provides clues to the nature of the Creator.

This book does not attempt to prove the existence of God. It assumes God's existence and explores how God might interact with the kind of universe we have without violating its physical laws. In chapters six and seven we will explore some of the avenues through which God may be interacting with his universe.

6

GOD, UNCERTAINTY
AND OPENNESS

✦✧✦

IN CHAPTER FIVE WE EXAMINED the emergence of complexity within the big bang model of the universe. In this chapter and the next, we examine whether there is any room for God's activity in this emerging universe. As we discussed in the introduction, it is very hard to picture God's activity in mundane, everyday activities. Through *cursus communis naturae* thinking, closed machine/clockwork models and methodological naturalism usage, it is easy to exclude God's activity from all thoughts about nature. Is nature hermetically sealed with God on the outside? Or is nature open to activity by God without having to invoke miracles?

A century after Einstein proposed his two theories of relativity, the average person has not yet moved into his universe. Most of us still live in a universe in which the shortest distance between two points is a straight line. In Einstein's universe, however, the shortest distance between two points is a curved line, because the universe is curved. By the rules of Euclidean geometry we live in a universe in which two straight lines cannot enclose a space. If we draw two straight lines around the surface of a basketball, however, we begin to grasp Einstein's notion of the curvature of space. A straight line around a basketball will create an "equator." Two straight lines drawn on the curvature of space, like a basketball, will intersect twice. Two straight lines drawn around a basketball will enclose four spaces. At the macro level Euclid's geometry has been replaced by non-Euclidean geometry. This simple example of the implications of Einstein's physics veils the extent to which old thought patterns born of old philosophy and science continue to dominate our thinking and our theology. The old mechanical model for the universe has no place for God to act. Einstein's curved universe simply provides an example of how the conceptual thought of people determines what kinds of ideas they might be able to consider. The idea that God cannot operate in a universe in which physical laws operate represents a kind of logic that is internally consistent and conformed to the realities of Isaac Newton's universe. The old view that God cannot operate in a universe with physical laws no longer conforms to the new realities of modern science.

In these two chapters we will examine what type of universe (both inanimate and animate) exists—closed or open. Further, we will examine whether there is any room for God's activity in the inanimate and animate aspects of the universe, and we will propose possible ways God could interact. In these two chapters we will examine three areas (quantum mechanics, chaos and genetics). By examining these three areas we are not saying that God's activity is limited to these three areas, but rather we have examined these areas because they give us clues about the openness of the universe at many different levels. In this chapter we examine phenomena involving quantum mechanics and chaos theory. In chapter seven, we will present an overview of the current scientific thinking in regard to living organisms as we use genetics to focus on how God's activity is facilitated by this aspect of life. In other words, these features of the universe not only account for how the universe operates, they also provide the means for God's operation within the universe.

Why quantum mechanics? Quantum mechanics deals with the behavior of objects as small as or smaller than atoms. As was discussed in chapter five, for the first 10^{-35} seconds after the big bang, the universe was smaller than an atom. It was during this period that the fundamental particles and fundamental forces began to emerge. All that emerged after this period can be envisioned as the interaction of these particles and forces. Thus, an overview of quantum mechanics will suggest the degree of openness of the universe at this critical stage of its development. At this early stage, was the universe a blind machine moving forward, or was it a combination of openness and order that allowed God's guidance? In addition, quantum mechanics is at the heart of all the atoms that make up every object in the physical universe—from galaxies to the biochemistry of living organisms.

Chaos deals with large collections of objects that become unpredictable because of their extreme sensitivity to initial conditions. After first-generation stars died, large clouds of gas and dust formed. These interstellar clouds were "nurseries" in which second-generation stars and their planets formed. The relationship between the particles in these clouds was very chaotic; thus, chaos was involved in the processes that led directly to the earth, to life and ultimately to us. Was there openness to the activity of God in these processes? On earth, flowing streams and weather have chaotic properties. In the Bible, God controls these processes; is there openness to the activity of God here?

A CLOCKWORK UNIVERSE?

In the Renaissance, natural philosophers began having success in applying mathematical models to their observations of nature.[1] The German astronomer Johannes Kepler (1571-1630) used mathematics to show that the planets move around the sun in elliptical orbits.[2] The Italian astronomer Galileo Galilei (1564-1642) mathematically described the motion of falling objects.[3] The English mathematician and physicist Isaac Newton (1642-1727) explained all motion in terms of three laws of motion and the law of universal gravitation.[4] These early scholars saw God in their work. Kepler believed that he had discovered the harmonies of God in the dimensions of the planetary orbits. Newton felt that his equations revealed that the solar system was unstable and God had to intervene to keep the solar system functioning.

---

[1] The word *scientist* was not coined until 1833 by William Whewell.
[2] Kepler discovered three laws of planetary motion. He published two of these laws in 1609 in *New Astronomy* and the third in 1619 in *Harmonies of the World*.
[3] Galileo published his findings in his final work, *Two New Sciences*, in 1638.
[4] Although Newton had been working on these ideas since 1665, he did not publish his findings until 1687 in *The Mathematical Principles of Natural Philosophy*.

Others, following application of Newton's ideas, were intoxicated by the fact that only position and momentum (mass and velocity) data were needed to calculate the position and speed of planets thousands of years into the future. To them the solar system was a machine (a clock). According to tradition Napoleon asked the French mathematician and astronomer Pierre-Simon, Marquis de Laplace (1749-1827) how he could write a series of books on the universe and never mention God.[5] Laplace is quoted as saying, "I have no need for that hypothesis."[6] Laplace believed that he could explain everything in terms of forces acting between particles; he believed that his calculations showed that the solar system was stable without the interference of God.[7]

The success with explaining the action of the solar system led those following Newton to believe that everything, even people, could be described as machines. As the French philosopher Voltaire (1694-1778) said,

> There is nothing without a cause. An effect without a cause are words without meaning. . . . It would be very singular that all nature, all the planets, should obey eternal laws, and there should be a little animal, five feet high, who in contempt of these laws, could act as he pleased, solely according to his caprice.[8]

This intoxication with the laws of Newton led to the philosophy of determinism, which states that all actions, including human ones, are entirely predicted by preceding actions. Thus humans would not have free will, and nature would be totally predictable. A totally deterministic universe also would leave no room for the action of God. Up until the beginning of the twentieth century the deterministic view was the dominant scientific model of the universe. Discoveries in the areas of quantum mechanics and chaos would challenge that deterministic view.

---

[5]Laplace published his findings in the five volume *Celestial Mechanics* (1799-1825).

[6]Pierre-Simon, Marquis de Laplace, quoted in Augustus De Morgan and Sophia Elizabeth De Morgan, eds., *A Budget of Paradoxes* (London: Longmans, Green, 1915).

[7]Today astronomers believe that Laplace's calculations were not accurate enough to prove that the solar systems was stable (see A. Celletti and E. Perozzi, *Celestial Mechanics: The Waltz of the Planets* [Berlin: Springer, 2007], pp. 91-93).

[8]Voltaire, *The Ignorant Philosopher*, published in William F. Fleming, trans., *The Works of Voltaire: A Contemporary Version with Notes* (Akron, Ohio: St. Hubert Guild, 1901), p. 231.

QUANTUM MECHANICS

Although a quantum understanding of matter arose in describing very small objects and properties, quantum mechanics has had a major impact on our daily lives through the introduction of inventions such as the laser in compact disc players, semiconductors in computer chips and MRI machines in medicine. Quantum mechanics inventions have had at least a 30 percent impact on the United States gross natural product.[9] The quantum era began with the paper published in 1900 by the German physicist Max Planck (1858-1947), who explained blackbody radiation output by stating that light is radiated in discrete bundles (particles), which Planck called *quanta*.[10] In the following discussion we will highlight some of the findings of quantum mechanics as they relate to the questions addressed in this chapter.

Wave-particle duality. In the classical world that we inhabit, waves and particles are mutually exclusive. Waves are continuous, spread out phenomena characterized by wavelength and frequency, such as sound and water waves. In contrast, particles are discrete phenomena characterized by mass and velocity, such as bullets and balls. Depending on the type of measurement, quantum phenomena show both wave and particle properties. For example, light appears as a particle in blackbody and photoelectric experiments, and as a wave in interference and diffraction experiments. If light's behavior was not bad enough to the classical mind, matter also shows wave-particle duality. First, duality was seen with electrons,[11] and then it was seen for protons, neutrons, hydrogen atoms, helium atoms, hydrogen molecules and the fullerene molecule, which contains sixty carbon atoms.[12] Unlike in the classical world, the behavior one observes at the quantum level depends on what one chooses to observe.

Measurement—collapse of the wave function—unpredictability. In

---

[9]Max Tegmark and John Archibald Wheeler, "100 Years of Quantum Mysteries," *Scientific American* 284, no. 2 (February 2001): 68-75.

[10]Max Planck won the 1918 Nobel Prize in physics for this work.

[11]American physicist Clinton Davisson (1881-1958) and British physicist George Paget Thomson (1892-1975) shared the 1937 Nobel Prize in physics for demonstrating that electrons are "waves." Ironically, Thomson's father, J. J. Thomson (1856-1940) won the 1906 Nobel Prize in physics for demonstrating that electrons are "particles."

[12]Markus Arndt, et al., "Wave-Particle Duality of C_{60} Molecules," *Nature* 401 (1999): 680-82.

1913 the Danish physicist Niels Bohr (1885-1962) proposed a quantum solution for the structure of the atom: the electron orbits around the nucleus were quantized, which means that the electrons will only be found at certain restricted distances from the nucleus. Bohr also postulated that electromagnetic radiation is emitted from an atom only when an electron moves from a higher energy orbit (farther from the nucleus) to a lower energy orbit (closer to the nucleus).[13] These movements of electrons (called quantum jumps) are easy to ob-

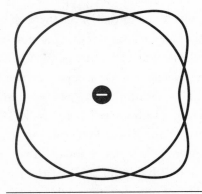

Figure 6.1. De Broglie matter-wave

serve; the brilliant colors of fireworks are the result of these electron jumps. In 1924 the French physicist Louis de Broglie (1892-1987) explained the location of the Bohr orbits by proposing that electrons can only orbit the nucleus at distances in which they will have a whole number of wavelengths (see fig. 6.1). De Broglie called these phenomena "matter-waves," which is another example of the wave-particle duality.[14]

The Austrian-English physicist Erwin Schrödinger (1887-1961) developed differential equations to describe this wave-particle duality. These quantum wave equations were similar in form to the classical physics equations used in music to describe the standing waves in a violin string. The wave function, usually represented by the Greek letter psi, Ψ, is a mathematical expression describing the physical system, for example, the atom with its nucleus and electrons. The selection of the appropriate operator and wave function will allow one to calculate the observed properties of the atom.[15]

An important question in classical physics is the location of an object: Where is the planet? Where has it been? And where is it going?

---

[13]Niels Bohr won the 1922 Nobel Prize in physics for this work.
[14]Louis de Broglie won the 1929 Nobel Prize in physics for this work.
[15]Erwin Schrödinger won the 1933 Nobel Prize in physics for this work.

From the discussion of the Schrödinger equation, one might assume that the location of the electron could also be specified with similar precision. In quantum mechanics, however, we do not obtain certainty of where the object (say an electron) is but rather obtain a probability of where the electron is. The German-English physicist Max Born (1882-1970) showed that squaring the wave function (Ψ^2) results in the probability of where the electron will be in relation to the nucleus (fig. 6.2).[16]

Rather than a sharp line for the trajectory of the electron, the quantum mechanical treatment yields a probabilistic prediction of the electron's position. As can be seen on the left side of figure 6.2, for this particular electron the maximum probability is at a value of 3, but

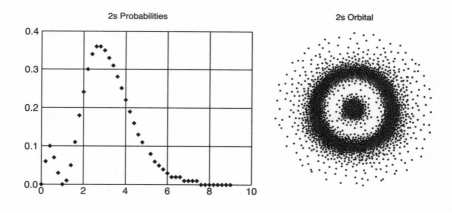

Figure 6.2. Probability density for electron position

there are also probabilities of finding the electron at 1, 2, 4, 5 and so forth. On the right side of figure 6.2 is another representation of the probability of finding the electron.[17] This type of plot models the position of the electron as an electron cloud centered on the nucleus with the intensity of the shading proportional to the probability of finding the electron. Quantum mechanics is not saying that the electron itself

---

[16]Max Born won the 1954 Nobel Prize in physics for this work.
[17]The "2s" description informs us that the orbital will be in the second level while the letter "s" informs the chemist that the shape of the orbital will be spherical.

is smeared into a cloud but rather that the electron can be in a state that is a mixture of all these states; this idea makes no sense at the classical level. Quantum physics allows the mixing of mutually exclusive states (superposition principle), which would be forbidden by classical physics.

Calculations, using the Schrödinger equation, reveal that the system involving this electron will evolve in a continuous and determined fashion with the electron in its superposition states. When a measurement is made on the quantum system, one of the possibilities suddenly surfaces as the position of the electron. Before the measurement the calculations show the position with the largest probability. When the measurement is done, it is impossible to predict with certainty which position will surface as the solution. It is probable, but not certain, that this surfaced position will be near the position of largest probability. And one does not necessarily get the same answer on each occasion that the measurement is made. This process is called collapse of the wave function since the Schrödinger equation does not predict how this solution is reached. (As John Polkinghorne states, "the general definition of measurement is the irreversible macroscopic registration of the signal of a microscopic state of affairs. This happening may involve an observer, but in general it need not.")[18]

Fundamental uncertainty: Heisenberg uncertainty principle. Before quantum mechanics it was assumed that with enough effort one could remove all uncertainty from measurements. The German physicist Werner Heisenberg (1901-1976) realized that for a quantum object it was impossible to know exactly both the position and momentum at the same time. The more certain one quantity is measured, the less certain the other can be determined. The product of both uncertainties will never be less than Planck's constant (6.63 X 10^{-34} joule-seconds). For macroscopic, everyday objects, this limitation is very small compared to ordinary experimental error. But for quantum objects, such as the electron, this uncertainty restriction is very significant. The Heisenberg uncertainty principle raises uncertainty to a universal principle. Even if

---

[18]John Polkinghorne, *Quantum Theory* (Oxford: Oxford University Press, 2002), p. 91.

we could eliminate all errors from a measurement, it would still be impossible to obtain a precise value for both the momentum and position at the same time.[19]

Entanglement. In 1935 Albert Einstein along with Boris Podolsky (1896-1966) and Nathan Rosen (1909-1995), two younger colleagues at the Princeton Institute for Advanced Study, published the paper "Can Quantum-Mechanical Description of Physical Reality Be Considered Complete?"[20] Einstein believed that their thought experiment would reveal that quantum mechanics was incomplete and that there were yet undiscovered hidden variables that are needed to explain the subatomic world; to Einstein these hidden variables would remove the uncertainty of quantum mechanics.

The thought experiment proposed by Einstein, Podolsky and Rosen is called the EPR Paradox, EPR Experiment or EPR Effect. The thought experiment involves a quantum mechanical phenomenon, called quantum entanglement, which states that measurements performed on spatially separated quantum objects have instantaneous influences on one another. Einstein was one of the first to recognize that quantum theory involved entanglement. He did not like quantum entanglement because it looked to him like "spooky action at a distance."[21] If quantum entanglement occurred in the classical world, it would be something like the following: A baseball machine simultaneously ejects two baseballs, one toward right field and one toward left field. If they are quantum entangled, then catching the right-field ball will impact what happens to the left-field ball; say it must always be dropped. Of course this makes no sense in our macroworld. In reality the two baseballs would behave independently. Catching the right-field ball would have no impact on the fate of the left-field ball, which could be caught, dropped, fly over the wall or whatever. Quantum entanglement is not an easy concept. As Polkinghorne stated, "After all, if it did not occur to Bohr, Heisenberg and Schrödinger in

---

[19]Werner Heisenberg won the 1932 Nobel Prize in physics for this work.

[20]Albert Einstein, Boris Podolsky and Nathan Rosen, "Can Quantum-Mechanical Description of Physical Reality Be Considered Complete?" *Physical Review* 47 (1935): 777-80.

[21]Walter Isaacson, *Einstein: His Life and Universe* (New York: Simon & Schuster, 2007), p. 450.

the twenties it cannot be trivially self-evident."[22]

Experiments performed in 1972 and 1982 to test whether Einstein's hidden variables or quantum mechanics would fit the data better revealed that the results of these experiments followed the predictions of quantum mechanics.[23] There is a degree of irreducible nonlocality in the universe. We cannot reduce everything to smaller and smaller non-interacting particles. As Polkinghorne stated, "Even the subatomic world cannot be treated purely atomistically."[24] Rather than viewing two electrons as two separate particles, we should view them as a whole, as a single system. The quantum wave function is not two separate wave functions of two individual electrons but a single wave function including both particles. British physicist Paul Davies (1946-) said, "The system of interest cannot be regarded as a collection of things, but as an indivisible, unified whole."[25] The matter-waves are providing "information" about the whole. As the British biologist and theologian Arthur Peacocke stated, "in a very real sense every fundamental particle, or structure constituted of them (which is *everything*), is interacting to some extent with everything else in the universe."[26] A very strange and amazing world indeed.

Does the epistemology reflect the ontology? The quantum world is so different from the world that we experience every day that the question arises as to whether the electron clouds, quantum jumps and matter-waves really reflect the reality of nature. Or are the techniques of Schrödinger, Heisenberg and Born just mathematical methods that work—that make predictions that accurately reflect the results of our measuring instruments?[27] Both of these questions arise out of phi-

---

[22]John C. Polkinghorne, *The Quantum World* (Princeton, N.J.: Princeton University Press, 1985), p. 70.

[23]Stuart J. Freedman and John F. Clauser, "Experimental Test of Local Hidden-Variable Theories." *Physical Review Letters* 28 (1972): 938-41, and Alain Aspect, Jean Dalibard and Gérard Roger, "Experimental Test of Bell's Inequalities Using Time-Varying Analyzers." *Physical Review Letters* 49 (1982): 1804-7.

[24]Polkinghorne, *Quantum Theory*, p. 80.

[25]Paul Davies, *Other Worlds* (London: Abacus, 1982), p. 125.

[26]Arthur Peacocke, *Theology for a Scientific Age*, enlarged ed. (London: SCM Press, 1993), p. 42.

[27]Cardinal Bellarmine used a version of the latter argument with Galileo when he stated that the Copernican system was just a calculating system that saved the appearances; that the Co-

losophy, where the former question reflects realism and the latter question reflects positivism. John Polkinghorne states,

> How we relate what we know to what is actually the case is a central problem in philosophy, and perhaps *the* problem in the philosophy of science. There are a variety of options, but the one chosen, consciously or unconsciously, by the vast majority of scientists is the strategy of realism. This seeks the closest possible alignment between the epistemology and ontology, what we know and what is the case. After all, if we did not believe what we know about the physical world is telling us what it is like, why should we bother to do pure science at all? I have coined the slogan "Epistemology models ontology" to encapsulate this metaphysical stance.[28]

One person who could never accept that the epistemology of quantum mechanics reflects the ontology of the subatomic world was Einstein. He could never accept the indeterminacy of quantum mechanics—the Heisenberg uncertainty principle, the electron clouds, entanglement and so forth. One of his most famous quotes is "God does not play with dice."[29]

Although the quantum world is strange, its concepts have led to the development of the laser, electron microscope and transistor. Our modern electronic world is based on quantum mechanical understandings. This may be great, but those of you from Missouri want to be shown the quantum world. In 1995 a quantum phenomenon called the Bose-Einstein condensate, which could be seen by the naked eye, was formed in the laboratory. At this point the wavy quantum world became visible. In 1924 the Indian physicist Satyendra Nath Bose (1894-1974) and Albert Einstein proposed that at very low temperatures atoms in a noninteracting dilute gas would enter the same quantum state and lose all their individual identities, essentially becoming one superatom. In 1995 a research group at the Joint Institute for Labo-

---

pernican system told us nothing about the actual structure of the solar system.

[28]John Polkinghorne, 'Science and Theology in the Twenty-First Century," *Zygon* 35 (2000): 941-953.

[29]Albert Einstein, letter to Max Born, December 4, 1926, in *The Born-Einstein Letters*, ed. Max Born (New York: Walker, 1971), p. 90.

ratory Astrophysics (now called JILA and a joint project of the National Institute of Standards and Technology and the University of Colorado) headed by Eric A. Cornell (1961-) and Carl E. Wieman (1951-) successfully cooled two thousand rubidium atoms to a temperature less than 100 billionths of a degree above absolute zero. At this temperature the wave equations of all the individual atoms merged into a single macroscopic wave function, which merged the physical characteristics of the atoms, such as their position and velocity. A model of this phenomenon is that the individual atoms have merged into a superatom that behaves as a single entity. Cornell and Wieman maintained their Bose-Einstein condensate for ten seconds and were able to take pictures of it.[30] A quantum phenomenon had become visible. The shape of the condensate was controlled by the Heisenberg uncertainty principle. As Cornell and Wieman wrote, "The Bose-Einstein condensate therefore is a rare example of the uncertainty principle in action in the macroscopic world."[31]

Dozens of laboratories worldwide have replicated the Bose-Einstein condensate discovery; for example, Wolfgang Ketterle (1957-) of MIT has succeeded in creating a condensate of fifty million sodium atoms.[32] Because of the successful experimental observations of quantum entanglement with larger and larger systems, some physicists are beginning to consider that the classical world is just an approximation of the quantum world, which they would state applies to all sizes of things: atoms, molecules, salt crystals, birds and plants.[33] If this realization is true, why do we see a world that looks classical? The quantum world is bathed in an "almost ubiquitous presence of radiation."[34] A single photon interacting with the quantum world causes the collapse of the wave function resulting in the dissipation of

---

[30]For pictures of the Bose-Einstein condensate, see "What Does a Bose-Einstein Condensate Look Like?" *Atomic Lab*, www.colorado.edu/physics/2000/bec/what_it_looks_like.html.

[31]Christopher Foot, "Triple first for Bose condensates," *PhysicsWorld.com*, May 1, 2001, http://physicsworld.com/cws/article/print/163;jsessionid=A54723AF86536E05CD76E0F267506649.

[32]Eric A. Cornell, Carl E. Wieman and Wolfgang Ketterle shared the 2001 Nobel Prize in physics for their work with Bose-Einstein condensates.

[33]Vlatko Vedral, "Living in a Quantum World," *Scientific American* 304 (2011): 38-43.

[34]Polkinghorne, *Quantum Theory*, p. 43.

the quantum superpositions. This leakage of information results in the classical view. The whole process is known as decoherence.

CHAOS THEORY

Chaos theory or deterministic chaos refers to any system that is nonlinear, dynamical and ultimately unpredictable due to its extreme sensitivity to initial conditions. Let's examine some of the terms in this definition: *deterministic, nonlinear, dynamical* and *initial conditions*. *Deterministic* refers to the fact that a mathematical equation can be written to describe the system's behavior. The equation predicts or determines the future behavior of the system. In a *nonlinear* system the output is not proportional to the input. For example, doubling the force may cause a golf ball to go four times as far, while tripling the force may cause the golf ball to go nine times as far. Plotting this behavior results in a curve rather than a straight line. Most of nature is nonlinear. But most of the examples in elementary science courses are linear because linear systems are much easier to understand and model. In a linear system the output is proportional to the input; doubling the force may cause a golf ball to go twice as far, while tripling the force may cause the golf ball to go three times as far. *Dynamic* systems have constantly changing conditions in contrast to static systems. The *initial conditions* are the variables that are measured to determine how a system will behave in the future. In studying gases the initial conditions may be temperature, pressure and volume. Because chaotic systems are nonlinear, some errors in measuring the initial conditions can result in loss of the ability to predict how the system will behave. For example an error of one part in one thousand (0.706 vs. 0.707) allows us to predict the sequence of events for a chaotic system for only twenty-four steps. Even reducing the error to one part in one million (0.7061234 vs. 0.7061235) allows us to predict the sequence of events for a chaotic system for only forty-eight steps. For nonchaotic systems, errors of one part in one thousand are very common, and with this level of error the nonchaotic systems are predictable.

Modern chaos theory began with the work of Edward Lorenz (1917-

2008), who in 1960 at the Massachusetts Institute of Technology was working on creating computer models that would ultimately lead to accurate weather forecasting. He analyzed the output of his program by graphing the data. The resulting graph looks like wings of a butterfly and is one of the most famous icons of chaos (fig. 6.3). Lorenz observed that the path within the overall pattern was very sensitive to initial conditions; for example, a one-part-in-a-thousand change in input would quickly result in a different path. Lorenz also observed that as the path weaves

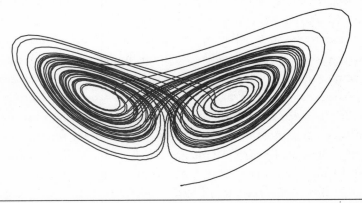

Figure 6.3. Lorenz data plot

back and forth between the "wings," the path never repeats itself. The behavior signaled disorder since no path ever repeated. At the same time, the behavior signaled order since all the paths were confined within the overall pattern called a *strange attractor*.[35] As John Polkinghorne states, "All such possibilities (i.e. different paths traversing the strange attractor) correspond to the same energy; they differ only in the patterns of behavior that they represent."[36] Lorenz had discovered deterministic chaos as well as three of its characteristics:

- sensitive dependence on initial conditions

- the trajectory never repeats

- strange attractor (ordered limits)

[35]An attractor is a set of points that a dynamic system approaches. The attractor pattern may be a point, a curve, a torus (doughnut) or complex. Chaotic systems have complex patterns called *strange attractors*.

[36]John Polkinghorne, *Scientists as Theologians* (London: SPCK, 1996), p. 36.

Finally, Lorenz's work gave us one of the most quoted terms in regard to chaos: *butterfly effect*. The butterfly effect is the idea that because weather is very sensitive to initial conditions, then the flapping of a butterfly's wings in Brazil is enough to change the weather in unexpected ways in the United States.[37]

Further insights into the behavior of chaotic systems came from the field of ecology through the work of the Australian physicist and biologist Robert May (1938-).[38] May studied the relationship between stability and complexity in animal populations using the nonlinear equation $x_{next} = rx(1-x)$, where x represents this year's population, x_{next} represents next year's population, r represents the rate of population growth, and 1-x represents the number of offspring who survive.

As we input values into the equation and graph x_{next} versus r, the predications of the model followed the observations of field biologists (fig. 6.4). Below the r-value of one, there is extinction, while above the r-value of one there is a nonlinear steady increase in the population.

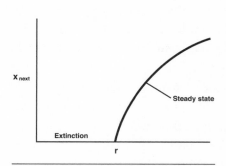

Figure 6.4. Population changes

When the rate of population increase reaches an r-value near 3, an interesting phenomenon occurs. As can be seen in figure 6.5, near an r-value of 3 the population value has two possibilities. This splitting is labeled a bifurcation, either of which may occur in nature with no way of predicting which one will occur. As time passes the population begins to oscillate between these two values. The bifurcating paths are not discriminated by energy differences. A simple model of bifurcation is a bead at the top of vertical, smooth, inverted U-shape wire. The

---

[37]The term *butterfly effect* seems to be derived from a presentation by Edward Lorenz: "Predictability: Does the Flap of a Butterfly's Wings in Brazil Set Off a Tornado in Texas?" Annual Meeting of the American Association for the Advancement of Science, Washington, D.C., 1979.

[38]In 2001 in the United Kingdom, Robert May was elevated to a life peer, and he chose his title to be Baron May of Oxford.

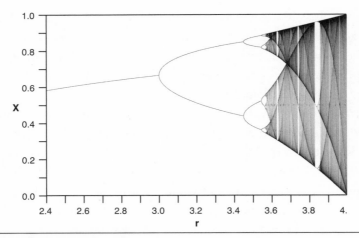

Figure 6.5. Bifurcations to chaos

bead can fall either way with no energy barrier to cause preference for one side or the other.[39]

As an r-value is increased, the population continues to bifurcate with oscillations between four values, then eight, then sixteen and then thirty-two values. Around the r-value of 3.57, chaos begins with slight variations in initial populations resulting in vastly different population values. Looking closely at the graph, we notice that "islands of order" appear within the chaos at r-values around 3.83. Here the period doubling following the pattern of 3, 6, 12, and the shape of the middle part of this region resembles the whole diagram. Geometric shapes whose small-scale and large-scale structures resemble each other are called *fractals*. Figure 6.6 shows a Koch snowflake, which is a fractal formed in just four steps by adding small triangles to the sides of larger triangles. The behavior of this system is truly unpredictable since we can never have sufficient accurate knowledge of the parameters during these fluctuations to predict which way the system will go. This work revealed three other characteristics of chaos:

- the transition to chaos is preceded by period doubling (bifurcation)

[39]John C. Polkinghorne, *Science and Providence* (Philadelphia: Templeton Foundation Press, 2005), chap. 2.

- chaotic systems exhibit fractional dimensionality (fractals)
- order can emerge within the chaotic regions

As scientists developed chaos theory, they realized that some systems that they had previously thought were random were in fact chaotic. Now scientists had a mathematical model for analyzing these systems. Examples appear in fields as far ranging as astronomy, medicine and social sciences. In the asteroid belt between the planets of Mars and Jupiter, there are regions almost free of asteroids, which are

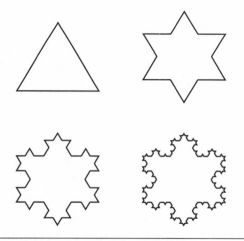

Figure 6.6. Example of a fractal, the Koch snowflake

called Kirkwood gaps in honor of their discoverer. Analysis reveals that interaction between the motions and gravitational fields of the asteroids and Jupiter results in chaotic regions that expel asteroids from certain regions of the belt sending the asteroids on a path toward the inner planets.[40] Chaos theory was used to analyze the historical data for the childhood diseases measles and chicken pox.[41] Epidemics of chicken pox were observed to vary periodically with a period of one year. In contrast, epidemics of measles were observed to occur in a

---

[40]Jack Wisdom, "Chaotic Behavior and the Origin of the 3/1 Kirkwood Gap," *Icarus* 56 (1983): 51-74.

[41]George Sugihara and Robert M. May, "Nonlinear Forecasting as a Way of Distinguishing Chaos from Measurement Error in Time Series," *Nature* 344 (19 April 1990): 734-41.

chaotic pattern; this means that it is much more difficult to predict the direction that measles epidemics will proceed. Attempts have been made to apply chaos theory to social science areas such as economics, advertising, the stock market and strategic decision making. Although applying chaotic processes to social science data has proven problematic, the chaotic model has allowed insights that linear models have not provided. Researchers and policymakers are beginning to realize that the extreme sensitivity to initial conditions imply that small, low-cost policy changes can have large impacts. Because the future tracks of chaotic systems quickly become unpredictable, it is very difficult to know when and where to apply a particular policy. Finally, the concept of chaos has entered the public consensus through movies such as the *Jurassic Park* series. In conclusion, as John Polkinghorne says, "there are at least as many disorderly clouds in the world as there are orderly clocks."[42]

OPEN UNIVERSE

As presented in chapter five, the narrative describing the events from the big bang to today seems like Aristotle's great "chain of being" linking particles and events in such a way that seems very deterministic. What can be easily missed in this narrative is how different the universe was during its first billion years. Today, the universe that we experience on earth is a universe of macro-objects whose interactions involve the four fundamental forces and all the laws of nature. For the first billion years after the big bang the universe was a very different place in terms of size and content:

- from big bang until 10^{-35} seconds: size of universe was less than that of an atom
- from 10^{-10} seconds until 0.001 seconds: just elementary particles
- from 0.001 seconds until 3 minutes: just subatomic particles
- from 3 seconds until 400,000 years: plasma of hydrogen nuclei, helium nuclei and electrons

---

[42]John Polkinghorne, *Exploring Reality* (New Haven, Conn.: Yale University Press, 2005), p. 21.

- from 400,000 years until 1 billion years: atoms form; their gas clouds condense into stars

- about 10 billion years: first-generation stars die producing all the elements beyond hydrogen and helium that form gas and dust clouds which condense into second-generation stars and planets

During this time, quantum mechanical and chaos processes would be much more involved with the actions of the universe's constituents than what we see today. At first the universe is smaller than an atom and would be a total quantum system. Later all the objects (elementary particles, subatomic particles, nuclei, electrons) were quantum objects. In addition, their multibody interactions would be very chaotic. Later, in the gas and dust-cloud remains of first-generation stars, chaotic process created regions of stability and instability allowing for condensation into second-generation stars and planets.

Because of the nature of quantum and chaotic process, the "formative" years of the universe were very open. This openness contrasts with the common and familiar machine model of the universe: the great clockwork universe. Looking at the majestic movement of the heavenly bodies, the clockwork model can easily lead us to overlook the quantum process at the heart of all matter and the chaotic processes that relate the interactions between the bodies of matter. In addition, relying on the clockwork model for today completely obscures the quantum and chaotic early life of the universe. Thus, we belong to an open universe that provides the venue for the Creator to act.

WHERE IS GOD?

This book has been discussing one of the most interesting debates between science and theology: the nature of God's action in the world. First, we will examine two broad types of causality. Then, we will examine arguments against God intervening in the world. Finally, we will examine where the "causal joint" between God and his creation may lie.

Types of causality. Causality takes the form of "bottom-up" and "top-down" causality in our universe.[43] Bottom-up causality involves energy inputs and is described in terms of the behavior of the parts of a system. An example of bottom-up causality is the way that a gas sample's temperature (top) is the average of the kinetic energy of the individual gas molecules (bottom). Top-down causality involves information inputs (pattern formation); here the emphasis is on the overall behavior of the system. For top-down causality to be invoked, there must be ontological gaps in the bottom-up explanation. These gaps must be more than ignorance; they must really be there. In the following discussions it must be remembered that knowledge of causal relationships is still incomplete, and one needs to be humble and modest in any proposals for causal relationships.[44]

Objections to God's action in the world. Before considering how God may be interacting with the world in light of modern science, let us briefly consider some historical objections to divine "intervention" in the world.[45] To some an intervening God is one who is outside his creation and has to come back into his creation to achieve his purpose. Others cannot reconcile the God who, as an expression of his will, sustains the laws of nature (providence) with the God who has to suspend these same laws to achieve his purpose (a change of mind). Some people, including David Hume, believe that the historical record shows no evidence of the laws of nature being intervened. Finally, some people ask why God does not intervene in human affairs to prevent disasters (e.g., Great Lisbon earthquake, Holocaust and cancer) if God can intervene in the natural world. Because of these concerns many theologians and scientists speak of God's interaction with the world rather than his intervention with the world.

How might God interact: An "ontological gap" at the "causal joint." The English theologian and philosopher Austin Farrer coined the

---

[43]Peacocke, *Theology for a Scientific Age*, chap. 3; Donald T. Campbell, "Downward Causation in Hierarchically Organised Systems," in *Studies in the Philosophy of Biology: Reduction and Related Problems*, ed. F. J. Ayala and T. Dobzhansky (London: Macmillan, 1974), pp. 179-86; and Roger W. Sperry, *Science and Moral Priority* (Oxford: Blackwell, 1986), chap. 6.
[44]Polkinghorne, *Exploring Reality*, chap. 2.
[45]Peacocke, *Theology for a Scientific Age*, chap. 9.

phrase *causal joint* to account for how God interacts with his creation.[46] Farrer never explained how this causal joint worked. To the modern theologian-philosopher of science, the regularity of the natural processes reflects the divine faithfulness to the created order. Thus, to them the causal joint of God's actions must be in the ontological gaps in complex systems whose future development is unpredictable. As we saw in the early part of this chapter, both quantum and chaotic systems have this ontological unpredictability. The ontological unpredictability distinguishes this gap from the old "God of the gaps" that merely involved a gap in scientific knowledge.[47]

If these ontological gaps are an area for the causal joint, how should they be viewed? As Peacocke states, "'Does God know the outcome of these situations that are unpredictable to us?' and . . . 'Does God act within the flexibility of these situations to effect his will?'"[48] If we answer in the affirmative to both questions, then Peacocke continues,

> If this were so, God would both have to be able to predict the outcome of God's actions within the "flexible process" and also actually to make some micro-event, subsequently amplified, to be other than it would have been if left to itself to follow its own natural course, without the involvement of divine action. . . . Such a conception of God's action in these, to us, unpredictable situations would then be no different in principle from the idea of God intervening in a deterministic, rigidly law-controlled, mechanistic order of nature of the kind thought to be the consequence of Newtonian dynamics. The only difference, on this view, would seem to be that, given our irreducible incapacity to predict the histories of many natural systems, God's intervention (for that is what it would properly have to be called) would always be hidden from us, whereas previously, God's intervention in a mechanistic, rigidly law-controlled world would always have been regarded as open to verification by us provided we could ascertain the natural laws usually operative.[49]

Because of the nature of the universe (regularity through natural

---

[46] Austin Farrer, *Faith and Speculation* (London: A&C Black, 1967), p. 66.
[47] The second part of this heading is from Peacocke, *Theology for a Scientific Age*, p. 148.
[48] Ibid., p. 153.
[49] Ibid., pp. 154-55. We also wish to thank one of our readers for pointing this out to us.

laws and openness through the unpredictability of complex dynamical systems), some have proposed that God has self-limited his omniscience and omnipotence.[50] This self-limitation allows God to bestow some autonomy not only on humans (free will) but also on all aspects of the creation. This openness in the natural order allowed the development of conscious organisms. As the British statistician David John Bartholomew (1931-) states, "God chose to make a world of chance because it would have the properties necessary for producing beings fit for fellowship with himself."[51]

This line of thought betrays a lingering attachment to the old classical deterministic system, but couched in anthropomorphic terms. When Peacocke speaks of a system taking a route "other than it would have been if left to itself to follow its own natural course, without the involvement of divine action," he suggests that some specific outcome would have occurred had God not acted. The point of chaotic systems is that the system is open and without a predetermined outcome. God's action would not "change" the outcome because no law of cause and effect has determined a specific outcome. As for the system being denied its choice of what course to take, these chaotic systems have no brain or self-consciousness. They really don't care. They have no plans.

Where does this line of thought leave us; are we any closer to the causal joint? Yes, current thought places the causal joint in the indeterminacies but in a way more subtle than the previous discussion of direct intervention. Current thinking focuses on analogy to the only personal agent that we know—ourselves. In the following discussion we have to be aware of the challenges of the analogy relating human and divine action. Humans have physical bodies that operate within the confines of thermodynamic relationships (e.g., conservation of energy), with human knowledge (information) being constrained by these factors. God is not embodied; he is a spirit. As such his knowledge is not constrained by the conservation of energy.

[50]For example the work of theologians such as Peacocke and Polkinghorne and the British statistician David John Bartholomew.

[51]David John Bartholomew, *God of Chance* (London: SCM Press, 1984), p. 138.

Consideration of how we might today conceive of God's continuing interaction with the world has led, not surprisingly, to the perennial model of God as a personal agent interacting with and acting on the world. This model, modified and enriched by recent insights into the unity of the mental and physical in the human-brain-in-the-human-body, is based on the only personal agent we know, ourselves. This model further gives us insight into top-down causation. Although a complete solution to the mind-body problem still eludes us, it appears that how we act in our bodies is a top-down process. As Arthur Peacocke states, "Now the meaning of an action by a human agent is not to be found by scientific analysis of the physiological, chemical, and mechanical processes going on in the agent's body, but by discovering the person's reasons and intentions, that is, the mental events which are involved in the action in question."[52]

Just as we input information, which affects our bodies (worry affects heart rates for example), God in a top-down manner inputs information into the unpredictable processes that has an impact on the unrolling of history, as we shall see in chapter eight. Within the creation the most complete way that God has made himself heard is by furnishing his creation with beings—us—that can discern his meanings. Since the universe, as God's creation, expresses God's purpose, God has created humans with the ability to understand God's self-communication through creation. God is sending signals to humans through the events of the universe's history, the history of humans and our own personal history; God is sending these signals through top-down input of information into the universe. As we discussed in the introduction, the universe has many levels of complexity, ranging from atoms to neural processes. Each level, in its own way, expresses the design and purpose of God. Since human beings mirror God's nature, the fullest expression will be at the human level; certain meanings and purposes can only be expressed at this personal level.

We have discussed two unpredictable processes: quantum events and chaotic events. Before a measurement is made in a quantum system, there

---

[52]Peacocke, *Theology for a Scientific Age*, p. 178.

are certain probabilities of where the quantum particle will be. When a measurement is made of a quantum system, the macroscopic system causes the quantum system to collapse into one of the possible states. This measurement is an example of top-down causality as information flows from the large to the small. As we have discussed, the early universe was very different from the current universe, with the early universe being a quantum system. During this period, divine action would be hidden in the cloudy nature of quantum events. Critical events during this period were the emergence of the four forces. As we have discussed, there is a fine-tuning in the values of the strengths of these forces and in the relative strengths between them. These values depend on "infinitesimal (information-like) triggers" that resulted in these processes to occur in one way rather than another.[53] These values and ratios have anthropic significance, since their narrow range of values appears to be needed for our appearance in the history of the universe. Thus, we can conceive of God inputting information that brought about the values of these forces that fall within the narrow fine-tuning ranges.

In chaotic systems the hierarchical level of these complex dynamical phenomena is the same level as events we deal with in everyday life— turbulent flow in liquids, predator-prey patterns, yearly variation in insect populations and the weather. The bottom-up causality of physical processes provides the envelope of possibilities (strange attractor) within which the future will develop. Within this envelope of possibilities the path actually taken will depend on their extreme sensitivity to initial conditions (any external disturbance). All the paths through the strange attractor in chaotic systems correspond to the same energy. One of the old objections to God's action in the universe involved the idea that God's action would mean an intervention from the outside and thus a change in energy. The open universe of quantum mechanics and chaos, however, provides a model consistent with the biblical idea of a God fully present in the universe as Holy Spirit, while at the same time remaining utterly transcendent. Thus, we would not expect a change in energy due to the activity of God, because God has never been absent.

---

[53]John Polkinghorne, *Science & Christian Belief* (London: SPCK, 1994), p. 79.

Something brings about the future; if bottom-up causality is not sufficient, then information input through top-down causality is necessary to resolve what the future will hold. In the U-shaped wire example discussed previously, the input in chaotic systems is information (this way or that way), which correlates well with the nature of God. The universe is multilevel, with surprising emergences as one goes from one level to another. As John Polkinghorne states

> One example, too familiar to surprise us but remarkable nevertheless, is the way in which the slow increase of temperature suddenly produces a discontinuous change from liquid to gas at boiling point. The detailed physics of such phase change (as they are called) are notoriously difficult to figure out, but certainly the underlying laws of nature do not change at 100° centigrade. That example of the discontinuous change of behavior with changing physical regime, coupled with the unbroken regularity of physical law, may be of some small analogical help in thinking how God might be capable of acting in miraculous, radically unexpected, ways, while remaining the Christian God of steadfast faithfulness.[54]

This "causal joint" for God would be a top-down causality that inputs information into chaotic systems. Through this top-down interaction with the universe (whether in the stellar nursery gas clouds, rain in due season or the amazing survival of a loved one), God is sending signals to humanity. How we view these events (as just a natural event, general providence, special providence or miracle)[55] will depend not only on the characteristics of the event but also on our faith.[56] In the Old Testament story the wind that came up to part the Red Sea could either be seen as God's effect on the chaotic weather systems or just an

---

[54]Polkinghorne, *Science and Providence*, p. 60.

[55]*General providence* refers to God's continuous upholding the universe through his natural laws, and *special providence* or *miracle* refers to God's extraordinary intervention in the life of people.

[56]C. S. Lewis reflected on why it is difficult for some to detect miracles. He wrote, "The moment it [miracle] enters her realm [nature] it obeys all her laws. Miraculous wine will intoxicate, miraculous conception will lead to pregnancy, miraculous bread will be digested. The divine act of miracle is not an act of suspending the pattern to which the events conform but of feeding new events into that pattern. . . . A miracle is emphatically not an event without cause or without results. Its cause is the activity of God: its results follow according to Natural law" (*Miracles* [New York: Collier, 1960], p. 60).

amazing wind that "came out of nowhere."[57] The writer of Hebrews states, "By faith we understand that the universe was created by God's command, so that what is seen has been made from things that are not visible" (Heb 11:3 HCSB). Note that the writer uses *God's command*, which is top-down information causality. In addition, if it takes faith to understand that the universe is a creation, then it is not surprising that individual information patterns that God has put into the history of the universe can be unrecognizable without faith.

This analysis is limited by our ideas about the structure and patterns of the universe, and it assumes a degree of flexibility and openness within the framework of the laws of nature as understood by modern physics. Further this analysis assumes that the purpose of God is reflected in the nature of the universe, and God's interactions with the universe would respect this openness and order. Although limited, we observed that the structure of the universe is open to God's activity through top-down causality (information inputs). Scientists and theologians like Polkinghorne and Peacocke have assumed that God has self-limited his omniscience and omnipotence in order not to violate the laws of nature, but the openness of the universe does not require such a self-limitation. One may say that God does not always choose to micromanage the universe, but such freedom of choice on the part of God does not logically imply a surrender of the power and freedom to act. Just as natural theology could never lead to the Christian God, our analysis only gives a glimpse of how God may interact with his creation. To find the personal God of Christianity, however, we must look at the other book of God, the special revelation of the Bible.[58]

CONCLUSION

The brave new world of quantum mechanics and chaos has profound implications for how we conceive of God's action in the world. The old model of deterministic cause and effect presented what appeared to be

---

[57]Exodus 14 contains an account of the crossing of the Red Sea by the children of Israel.

[58]The English philosopher and pioneer in the scientific revolution Francis Bacon urged studying the two books of God—nature and the Bible; see Francis Bacon, *Advancement of Learning* (Cassell, 1893), chap. 1, www.gutenberg.org/dirs/etext04/adlr10.txt.

an impenetrable philosophical barrier, which God could not cross without damaging or destroying the laws of nature. Quantum and chaos understandings have destroyed the old barrier, and it appears that the universe lays itself bare.

An uncertain universe. At the end of the nineteenth century and the beginning of the twentieth century, Max Planck, Niels Bohr, Louis de Broglie, Erwin Schrödinger, Max Born and Werner Heisenberg made a number of important discoveries about the nature of atoms and sub-atomic particles. These discoveries led to what we now call *quantum mechanics,* because of Planck's view that atoms radiate energy in discreet bundles called *quanta.*

Aristotle taught us that something cannot be *A* and *not A* at the same time. This law of noncontradiction represents a fundamental aspect of Western logic and scientific thinking. It is this logical law that rebels against the notion that Jesus of Nazareth could be fully human and fully divine at the same time. Humanity and deity are mutually exclusive concepts. The philosophers of the Enlightenment inhabited such a universe, but that universe disappeared a hundred years ago.

In spite of the plastic model of atoms that school children grew up seeing, atoms are not actually like billiard balls stuck together with sticks like Tinkertoys. Atoms involve relationships of energy in the form of electrons, protons and neutrons, which are all composed of relationships of energy in the form of subatomic particles, which are relationships of energy. In 1913 Niels Bohr proposed that electrons may orbit the nucleus of an atom at a lower energy orbit close to the nucleus or a higher energy orbit farther from the nucleus. When an electron moves from one orbit distance to another, electromagnetic radiation is emitted when the electron makes its "quantum leap" in orbit. Instead of the steady, perfect circles that Aristotle led scientists to expect, the orbits of electrons oscillate. Twirling a weight tied to the end of a string will create the perfect orbits of Aristotle. Twirling a sparkler at night creates the effect of an oscillating circular orbit like the one Bohr proposed.

J. J. Thomson won the Nobel Prize in 1906 for proving that the electron is a particle, and in 1937 his son George Paget Thomson along with Clinton Davisson won the Nobel Prize for proving that the electron is a wave. A particle occupies a discrete point, while a wave has an extended continuous existence. In 1924 Louis de Broglie had argued that in its orbit around the nucleus, an electron's leap from an inner orbit to an outer orbit constitutes a wave and that it must be able to complete whole wavelengths in each orbit. The conclusion of this mysterious world of quantum physics is that electrons behave as both discrete particles and continuous waves. Electrons are both *A* and *not A* at the same time.

The advances in quantum understanding collapsed the old certainty of physics. Werner Heisenberg observed in his famous Heisenberg uncertainty principle that a physicist could observe the location of an electron but not its velocity, or he or she could observe the velocity of an electron but not its location. The more we can know about one property, the less we can know about the other property. Physics moved from a science of certainty to one of probabilities. The quantum world is an open world to future contingencies. The old determinism of the Enlightenment was dead, but the mindset has continued in the popular imagination. Einstein had great difficulty giving up the certainty of Aristotle's universe, even after he had overthrown Aristotle's concept of absolute time.

One of the strangest aspects of quantum mechanics involves the idea of action at a distance. At the quantum level of the universe, the problem of quantum entanglement occurs whereby measurements performed on one quantum object will have an instantaneous effect on another quantum object spatially at distance from it. In spite of the individual components of an atom, they function as a unity. Moreover, they are open to action at a distance.

A chaotic universe. Within the laboratory where experiments can be controlled in such a way that only one cause and one effect may be observed, the deterministic universe of Laplace makes sense. The closed universe of Laplace, however, only exists within the laboratory, where a barrier may be placed around the laws of nature. Within the closed confines of the laboratory, accurate predictions may be made because no other causes are allowed to interfere with an effect.

The universe is a much messier place than a scientific laboratory.

Whereas the laboratory provides an uncontaminated environment for isolating properties and phenomena, it gives a false picture of how the universe actually works once the dike has been removed. In the universe, everything acts on everything else in a grand game of rock-paper-scissors. One law of nature trumps another law of nature. We can take measurements and in retrospect describe how the laws of nature operated to slam Hurricane Katrina into New Orleans, but the chaotic interaction of the vast complexity of the universe makes it difficult to predict the effect that the laws of nature will cause. The universe of Laplace, with its deterministic predictability, does not exist. This intricate interaction of the complexity of the universe is called "chaos theory." The chaos does not mean that the laws of nature have ceased to operate, but that the complex interaction of the whole creates an indeterminate future.

Edward Lorenz did the most important early research on chaos. Perhaps the most well known popular version of chaos theory comes from a comment by Lorenz that the flapping of a butterfly's wings in Brazil would change the weather in unexpected ways in the United States. The idea of the "butterfly effect" captures the enormous tentativeness of the present to the future in the vast interrelatedness that marks a chaotic system. It also demonstrates the indeterminate and open nature of the universe at the macro level as well as at the quantum level.

At the fundamental building-block level of the universe, we find an openness to manipulation and action by intelligent beings, if we call ourselves intelligent beings. We have learned so much about the atomic and subatomic nature of the universe precisely because the universe is open to interaction, interference, manipulation, alteration and investigation. The universe is an open book to us, and we betray a certain naiveté if we think it is more open to us than to God.

7

GOD AND LIFE

✦✧✦

WHAT DISTINGUISHES A BEAKER FULL OF chemicals from a living cell, which is a membrane full of chemicals? There is no precise definition of life, but in general, living things share the following characteristics:

- Organization: living organisms consist of one or more cells (complex chemical structures enclosed in membranes). Multicellular organisms have cellular corporation in the form of tissues, organs and organ systems.
- Importation: living organisms take food and energy from their environment.
- Homeostasis: living organisms maintain relatively constant internal conditions.
- Sensitivity: living organisms respond to internal and external stimuli.
- Growth: living organisms change during their life span.
- Reproduction: living organisms produce copies of themselves.
- Adaptation: structures, physiology and behaviors of individual organisms as well as the population are suited for survival in a particular environment.

The emergence of life resulted in the emergence of a fourth earth system, the biosphere, which joined the lithosphere, hydrosphere and atmosphere. Living things are found from the upper reaches of the atmosphere to the lowest depths of the ocean. Each of the four systems interact with each other. The biosphere has the ability to alter the relationships between the other earth systems.

Biology is the science that studies all aspects of life: its origin, structure, function, growth, distribution and so forth. In biology the term *species* is the basic category of biological classification and gives an indication of how many different kinds of living organisms there are on the earth. Scientists estimate that the number of species ranges from 5 to 100 million with about 2 million having been identified.[1] Living organisms range from microscopic bacteria (*Mycoplasma genitalium* at 0.2 to 0.3 μm) to blue whales that reach 30 meters (98 ft) in length.[2]

The habitats of living organisms range from the cold Antarctic to boiling deep-ocean trenches to tropical jungles to temperate prairies. Humans, through the use of technology, are able to live in almost any habitat. In contrast some organisms are very specialized. An amazing niche is inhabited by the larvae of the petroleum fly (*Helaeomyia petrolei*), which develop in the petroleum pools of California. This is the only known insect able to live in oil.

Although there is much diversity in the size and habitats of species, there are also many similarities between species. All species are made of cells, which in multicellular organisms are organized into tissue, organs and organ systems. At the chemical level all living organisms are made of six basic building blocks (elements): carbon, hydrogen, nitrogen, oxygen, phosphorus and sulfur.[3] At the molecular level all living organisms have a similar set of molecules of life: polysaccharides, polypeptides and polynucleotides. Living organisms use *polysaccharides* or *carbohydrates* for energy storage and generation, structural materials

---

[1] Andrea Thompson, "How Many Species Exist on Earth?" MSNBC.com, August 3, 2007, www.msnbc.msn.com/id/20109284; and Liz Osborn, "Number of Species Identified on Earth," *Current Results*, www.currentresults.com/Environment-Facts/Plants-Animals/number-species.php.

[2] A μm is one millionth of a meter (or one thousandth of a millimeter). The diameter of a human red blood cell is 8 μm with the average human cell being 25 μm.

[3] Recently NASA scientists discovered a microorganism that can thrive in a normally toxic arsenic environment and apparently can substitute arsenic for phosphorus in its cellular components: "NASA-Funded Research Discovers Life Built with Toxic Chemical," NASA, www.nasa.gov/topics/universe/features/astrobiology_toxic_chemical.html.

and antigenic determinants (antibody binding sites). *Polypeptides* or *proteins* are used by living organisms for the transport and storage of small molecules, structural framework of cells and tissues, antibodies, blood clotting agents and enzymes. Living organisms use *polynucleotides* or *nucleic acids* "as the repositories and transmitters of genetic information for every cell, tissue, and organism."[4] Nucleic acids are also involved in protein synthesis. Not only do living organisms contain similar polynucleotides, they contain the same code for translating the information encoded in the genetic material into proteins. Finally, all living organisms employ similar metabolic pathways. For example, all eukaryotes and the majority of prokaryotes employ the same ten enzymes in the same order in glycolysis, which is the initial pathway in the catabolism of carbohydrates.[5]

Fossils are the preserved remains or evidence of prehistoric organisms found in the succession of rock layers in the earth's crust. In general, in order to be classified as a fossil, the remains have to be older than ten thousand years, the date of the last glacial event.[6] Many of the fossilized remains resemble plants or animals alive today. The insects preserved in amber are examples. Other fossilized remains are very different from today's living organisms. An example would be the dinosaurs. The fossils of simple organisms are found at the bottom of the geological column while the first appearances of the fossils of more complex organisms are in top layers. The distribution of fossils in the geological record reveals that species appear and disappear, and are followed by new species.

THE HISTORY OF LIFE

Figure 7.1 is a symbolic representation of the sedimentary rocks that

---

[4]Christopher K. Mathews and K. E. van Holde, *Biochemistry*, 2nd ed. (Menlo Park, Calif.: Benjamin/Cummings, 1996), p. 86.

[5]Catabolism is the set of metabolic pathways that break large biochemical molecules, such as polysaccharides, lipids, nucleic acids and proteins into smaller biochemical molecules such as monosaccharides, fatty acids, nucleotides and amino acids. Anabolism is the set of metabolic pathways that construct large biochemical molecules from small molecules. Metabolism is the sum of the catabolic and anabolic reactions that living organisms use to maintain life.

[6]Tom Deméré, "Frequently Asked Questions About Paleontology," *San Diego Natural History Museum*, www.sdnhm.org/research/paleontology/paleofaq.html .

make up the earth's crust. The layers of rocks are grouped into categories of eons, eras and periods, where the different categories usually represent a major geological or paleontological event, such as mass extinctions. Eons represent the largest category and cover hundreds of millions of years. Eras are subdivisions of eons and are characterized by distinct life forms, for example, the Cenozoic is the age of mammals. Eras are divided into periods, which usually have a single type of rock system. The dates given to each category come from radiometric dating methods.[7] An important feature of the rocks of the Phanerozoic eon are plant and animal fossils.

The fossil record symbolized in figure 7.1 provides a history of life on earth. Current thought on the history of life begins with the formation of the earth about 4.5 billion years ago.[8] Rocks about 3.5 billion years old contain microfossils of prokaryote organisms similar to bacteria and blue-green algae. The first eukaryote cells (cells with nucleus) appeared about 2 billion years ago, and the first multicelluar organisms (algae) appeared about 1.8 billion years ago.

After about 1.5 billion years of very little change, "suddenly" almost all of the major types (phyla and classes) of different body plans appeared. This period, which occurred about 540 million years ago, is termed the "Cambrian explosion" and generated over one hundred major animal groups, of which about thirty have survived until today. Although many new families would later appear in life's history, these new families would only involve variations on body plans seen in the Cambrian explosion.

---

[7]For Christian overviews of scientific dating techniques, see the following publications: Roger C. Wiens, "Radiometric Dating: A Christian Perspective," American Scientific Affiliation, 2002, www.asa3.org/ASA/resources/wiens.html, accessed December 19, 2008; Davis A. Young, "How Old Is It? How Do We Know? A Review of Dating Methods—Part One: Relative Dating, Absolute Dating, and Non-radiometric Dating Methods," *Perspectives on Science and Christian Faith* 58 (2006): 259-265; Davis A. Young, "How Old Is It? How Do We Know? A Review of Dating Methods—Part Two: Radiometric Dating, Mineral, Isochron and Concordia Methods" *Perspectives on Science and Christian Faith* 59 (2007): 28-36; and Davis A. Young, "How Old Is It? How Do We Know? A Review of Dating Methods—Part Three: Thermochronometry, Cosmogenic Isotopes, and Theological Implications" *Perspectives on Science and Christian Faith* 59 (2007): 136-142.

[8]For a more detailed account of the history of the earth and life on the earth, please see James F. Luhr, ed., *Smithsonian Earth: The Definitive Visual Guide to Our Planet.* (New York: DK Publishing, 2005).

Eon	Era	Period	Age millions of years	First Fossil Evidence
Phanerozoic	Cenozoic	Quaternary	2-present	Humans
		Tertiary	65-2	Mammals (camels, bears, cats, monkeys, rodents, dogs); grasses
	Mesozoic	Cretaceous	142-65	Flowering plants; extinction event (50% of all life forms including dinosaurs)
		Jurassic	200-142	Birds; giant dinosaurs develop
		Triassic	252-200	Dinosaurs; mammals; extinction event (35% of all animal families)
	Paleozoic	Permian	290-252	Reptiles; pine-like trees; largest ever extinction event (60% of genera, both marine and terrestrial, including trilobites)
		Carboniferous	354-290	Reptiles; seed-bearing plants
		Devonian	418-354	Insects; sharks; amphibians; extinction event (30% of animal families)
		Silurian	443-418	First true plants, first air breathers
		Ordovician	490-443	Armored jawless fish; terrestrial moss; extinction event (50% marine genera extinct)
		Cambrian	543-490	Cambrian explosion
Precambrian	Proterozoic		2500-543	Soft-bodied marine animals; marine plants; increasing oxygen levels
	Archean		3800-2500	Chemical fossils; prokaryotes
	Hadean		4560-3800	Origin of Earth

Note: The vertical timeline is not drawn to scale.

Figure 7.1. The history of life reflected in the geological column and timeline

In the oceans, arthropods (trilobites, crustaceans), echinoderms (sea urchins, starfish), mollusks (snails, clams) and chordates (animals with backbones) flourish. By 485 million years ago the first vertebrates with true bones appear (jawless fish). By 434 million years ago, the first plants appear on land. At least two events had to precede the appearance of land plants: enough oxygen had to accumulate to form an ozone layer and the production of soil from oxidation and weathering of rocks. Around 363 million years ago, the earth became more recognizable; insects roamed the land, sharks swam in the ocean and vegetation covered the land. By 300 million years ago, flying insects and reptiles had appeared. The earliest dinosaurs appeared about 215 million years ago with the first mammals about 200 million years ago. At this time gymnosperm (conifer) forests dominated the land. Flowering plants appear about 130 million years ago. Bees appear about 100 million years ago. The age of dinosaurs ended 65 million years ago. After this time, mammals are the dominant species. About 55 million years ago, the modern bird groups diversified into song birds, parrots, swifts and woodpeckers. At this time the first rodents and whales appear. Horses appear by about 50 million years ago. By 40 million years ago the modern-type moths and butterflies appear. Grasses appear about 35 million years ago. Dogs, cats and pigs appear between 35 and 30 million years ago. Hominids appear about 6 million years ago. True humans appear in Africa about 200,000 years ago.

The current scientific explanation for the diversity and similarity of life and for the fossil record is known as biological evolution. The current understanding of evolution developed out of two streams of research: the field biology observations of Charles Darwin (1809-1882) and Alfred Russel Wallace (1823-1913) combined with the genetic work of Gregor Mendel (1822-1884).

BIOLOGICAL EVOLUTION

When Darwin wrote *On the Origin of the Species*, he had two objectives: to present evidence in support of biological evolution and to present a mechanism responsible for evolution. To Darwin evolution was a fact and natural selection was the mechanism responsible. In many discussions evolution and natural selection are intertwined to the point that some feel that discrediting natural selection discredits evolution. What is forgotten is that the concept of biological evolution can be supported even if natural selection is not its mechanism. Thus, in the following discussion we will consider support for evolution separate from any mechanism responsible.[9]

---

[9]This approach follows the pattern of how scientists understand how phenomena develop. First, observations and experiments are collected into an organizing concept. For example, in order to understand the behavior of gases, scientists collected observations and experiments of gases

Biological evolution asserts that species are not immutable (they change through time) and that all living organisms are descendants of a common ancestor. Or as Darwin stated, "species have changed, and are still slowly changing. . . . [P]robably all the organic beings which have ever lived on this earth have descended from some one primordial form, into which life was first breathed."[10] During the preceding six hundred years, Aristotle's concept of the eternal, unchanging form had dominated the Catholic and Protestant interpretation of Scripture. By the time of Darwin and into the twenty-first century, many Christians accepted Aristotle's view as the only valid understanding of God's creation of life.

In his essay "Nothing in Biology Makes Sense Except in the Light of Evolution," the Russian-American biologist Theodosius Dobzhansky (1900-1975) stated, "Seen in the light of evolution, biology is, perhaps, intellectually the most satisfying and inspiring science. Without that light it becomes a pile of sundry facts—some of them interesting or curious but making no meaningful picture as a whole."[11] Why do scientists such as Dobzhansky think that evolution is as valued a concept as gravity, the sun-centered planetary system or atoms? An examination of the two main tenets of biological evolution—common ancestor and mutable species—will demonstrate how well they agree with the data and how fruitful are their predictions.

Agreement with data and fruitfulness. At the beginning of this chapter we discussed the similarity and diversity of living organisms and the fossil record as challenges to any unifying understanding of biology. How well do the ideas of a common ancestor and mutable species agree with the findings of biology, and how fruitful are the

---

at different temperatures, pressures and volumes. Relationships were formulated relating these three variables without knowing the mechanism for these relationships. Later the kinetic-molecular model was proposed as the mechanism (causal connection) for the observed behavior: gases were modeled as billiard balls in constant motion, which gave rise to the observed relationships. Likewise in regard to biological evolution, we will first present the observations/experiments that led to the concept of evolution, followed by proposed mechanisms for biological evolution.

[10]Charles Darwin, *The Origin of Species*, (New York: Gramercy Books, 1979), pp. 452, 455.

[11]Theodosius Dobzhansky, "Nothing in Biology Makes Sense Except in the Light of Evolution," *The American Biology Teacher* 35 (1973): 125-29.

predictions that result from the concept of evolution?

Similarity and diversity of living organisms. All living organisms share the following characteristics—cellular structure, energy utilization, growth and reproduction. The common-ancestor tenet of evolution predicts that all living organisms should have inherited molecular structures that perform all these functions—that there should be a common set of molecules throughout all living organisms. That is indeed what is observed. Within the two cell structures (prokaryota and eukaryota) there exists the same energy storage molecule; the same metabolic pathway; the same mechanism for synthesis of protein cata-lysts; the same polysaccharides, polypeptides and polynucleotides; and the same genetic code. In fact the scientists who solved the genetic code in the 1950s and 1960s assumed a universal code based on evolutionary reasoning; the assumption of a universal genetic code was instrumental in solving the code because this assumption allowed them to avoid certain lines of research.[12]

Having similar structures is an example of molecular homology. *Homology* is defined as the resemblance between organisms in molecular or anatomical structures. It could be advantageous if each species (say, humans and chimpanzees) had different genetic codes; this way a disease virus could not jump from one species to another and humans would be spared transspecies diseases such as HIV. If an uncommon genetic code is advantageous, why do we see a common genetic code? The concept of evolution would postulate that the shared genetic code was inherited from a common ancestor. An advantage of molecular ho-mology is that biomedical research can test potential drugs on or-ganisms (mice) with molecules homologous to humans.

Anatomical homology was observed by early comparative anatomists, such as the French naturalist Baron Georges Cuvier (1769-1832) and the British biologist Richard Owen (1804-1892), who noticed struc-tural similarities between species despite differences in function. In *The Origin of the Species* Darwin referred to the following examples (fig 7.2): "What can be more curious than that the hand of a man, formed

[12]Horace Freeland Judson, *The Eighth Day of Creation: The Makers of the Revolution in Biology* (New York: Touchstone, 1980), part 2.

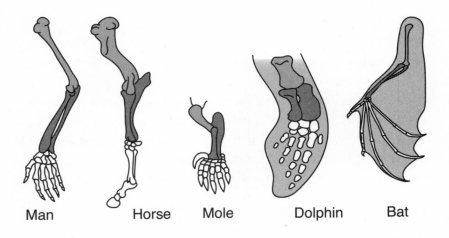

Man   Horse   Mole   Dolphin   Bat

Figure 7.2. Homologous structures mentioned by Darwin

for grasping, that of a mole for digging, the leg of the horse, the paddle of the porpoise, and the wing of the bat, should all be constructed on the same pattern, and should include the same bones, in the same relative positions?"[13] To Darwin this homology supports evolution by attributing the similarities to descent from a common ancestor.

The common-ancestor tenet of evolution predicts both functions and structures of organisms will be gained and lost during the evolutionary development of an organism. Further, evolutionary thinking predicts that organisms will retain vestigial structures as evidence of this evolutionary development. *Vestigial structures* are rudimentary structures homologous to fully functional structures in closely related species. Ostriches have flightless wings that are used for balance when running and for threat and courtship displays. The ostrich wings are vestigial structures because they are rudimentary wings that are useless for flight. The cave-dwelling adult grotto salamander is blind, yet it has eyes with retinas and lenses overgrown by its eyelids.

Atavism is different from vestigial structures in that atavism is the

---

[13]Darwin, *Origin of Species*, p. 415.

reappearance of lost structures that were observed in remote ancestors. Two examples of atavism are the appearance of extra toes in horses, similar to what was seen in the fossils of horse ancestors, and hind limbs in whales, similar to what is seen in the fossils of whale ancestors. One of the most famous horses with atavism was the war horse of Julius Caesar. Suetonius in the *Lives of the Caesars* wrote, "Indeed, [Caesar's] horse was an extraordinary creature, whose feet were almost human, for its hooves were divided so that they looked like toes. When this horse was born on his estate, seers interpreted it as an omen that Caesar would become lord of all the world."[14] Although whalers had occasionally reported hind-limb-like protrusions on whales, the first scientific examination of such protrusions took place at the American Museum of Natural History in 1921. The limb was about four feet in length, consisted of femur, tibia, tarsus and metatarsus, and was attached to the vestigial pelvic bones found in whales. Incidents of these limbs occur in approximately one out of every five thousand adult sperm and humpback whales.[15]

The concept of evolution postulates that the observed diversity of living organisms results in response to the diversity of environments on the earth. As Dobzhansky stated, "the environment presents challenges to living species, to which the later may respond by adaptive genetic changes."[16] Populations that are small and occupy a small area are more likely to encounter peculiar local conditions and in response undergo the most rapid genetic change, which may result in a new species. Or the species may not be able to adapt and become extinct. Are there any observations of one species changing into another? Evolutionary change is a slow process compared to human life spans, but there are some snapshots of species distributions that support the evolutionary arguments.

Cichlid fish (family of *Cichlidae* and order of *Perciformes*) represent

---

[14]Suetonius, *Lives of the Caesars*, trans. Catharine Edward (Oxford: Oxford University Press, 2000), p. 29.

[15]Lars Bejder and Brian K. Hall, "Limbs in Whales and Limblessness in Other Vertebrates: Mechanisms of Evolutionary and Developmental Transformation and Loss," *Evolution & Development* 4 (2002): 445-58.

[16]Dobzhansky, "Nothing in Biology Makes Sense," pp. 125-29.

one of the largest vertebrate families. The cichlids are distributed within the freshwater lakes of Africa and South America. The great lakes of Africa are estimated to contain the following distributions of cichlid species: Lake Tanganyika (300 species), Lake Malawi (500 species) and Lake Victoria (400 species).[17] With few exceptions the cichlid species found in each lake are found nowhere else. Lake Victoria is estimated to be 12,400 years old, which implies that its 400 species "have emerged to fill virtually all possible ecological niches, and in the incredibly brief span of about 12,400 years."[18] An even shorter time period involves the cichlid fish in a small lake that is separated from Lake Victoria by a sandbar. The cichlid fish in the small lake are unique to the lake and different from cichlid fish in Lake Victoria. Charcoal in the sandbar has been radiocarbon dated to about four thousand years old. It is thought that formation of the sandbar isolated a small group of cichlid fish, which evolved into a new species in this short time period.[19]

In the Hawaiian Islands there are moths found nowhere else. One species feeds on a Hawaiian palm. The other five species feed only on bananas. About a thousand years ago Polynesians brought banana plants to Hawaii. Since the moths do not occur in Polynesia, they seem to have evolved in the Hawaiian Islands during the last thousand years.[20]

Another distribution that supports species evolution is the phenomena of ring species. Ring species occur when "a chain of intergrading populations encircles a barrier and the terminal forms coexist without interbreeding."[21] In the phenomena of ring species, variation in space is used to infer variation in time. An example of a ring species is the Tibetan greenish warbler (*Phylloscopus trochiloides*) whose six sub-

[17]George W. Barlow. *The Cichlid Fishes: Nature's Grand Experiment in Evolution* (Cambridge, Mass.: Perseus, 2000), p. 221.
[18]Ibid., p. 226.
[19]G. Fryer and T. D. Iles, *The Cichlid Fishes of the Great Lakes of Africa* (Neptune City, N.J.: T.F.H. Publications, 1972).
[20]E. C. Zimmerman, "Possible Evidence of Rapid Evolution in Hawaiian Moths," *Evolution* 14 (1960): 137-38.
[21]Darren E. Irwin, Staffan Bensch and Trevor D. Price, "Speciation in a Ring," *Nature* 409 (2001): 333-37.

species encircles the Tibetan Plateau (fig. 7.3). Although the songs of the greenish warbler subspecies increase in complexity as one moves from south to north, all subspecies interbreed except where *P.t. viridanus* and *P.t. plumbeitarsus* meet north of the Tibetan Plateau. Biologists interpret these observations to mean that space and time have gradually divided one species into two.

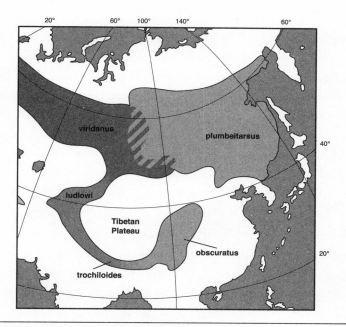

Figure 7.3. Range of the Tibetan greenish warbler

Plants provide examples of a different type of isolation—sterility barrier—that can result in a new species. When two closely related species of plants interbreed, the resulting hybrid can have twice as many chromosomes as either parent. While the hybrid will breed true, the offspring of the cross between the hybrid and either parent species will be sterile, such as mints of the genus *Galeopsis*. Another example is the codgrass of the English salt marshes. During the nineteenth century, people brought American codgrass in contact with European codgrass; the hybrid of this union is a new species of codgrass.

Fossil record. Darwin viewed the fossil record of his day as a challenge to his proposal of evolution:

> Why then is not every geological formation and every stratum full of
> such intermediate links? Geology assuredly does not reveal any such
> fine graduated organic chain; and this, perhaps, is the most obvious
> and gravest objection which can be urged against my theory. The ex-
> planation lies, I believe, in the extreme imperfection of the geological
> record.[22]

One hundred and fifty years of exploration since the publication of
Darwin's *On the Origin of Species* has filled in many of the gaps in the
fossil record and addressed many of Darwin's concerns. Even with this
new information, does the fossil record provide enough information to
understand the history of life? A recent study of the literature compared
the order of fossils in the rocks (stratigraphy) to the order of the evolutionary trees (phylogeny). The researchers found "no evidence of dimi-
nution of quality backwards in time."[23]

If all the living organisms that we see today arose from a common
ancestor through descent with modification, the following predictions
about the fossil record can be made.

- *Prediction:* The oldest rocks would have the simplest life forms.

  Finding: The earliest fossils are found in the Apex Chert of Australia
  and are dated to be 3.55 billion years old. Observations include
  microfossils of prokaryotic cyanobacterium-like organisms that are
  chains of single cells.[24]

- *Prediction:* The youngest rocks would have life forms that are most
  similar to living organisms.

  Finding: In the Tertiary Period (1.8 to 65 million years ago) fossils of
  modern plants and animals have appeared.

- *Prediction:* Lineages should undergo gradual change.

  Finding: To show gradual change in a lineage, one needs a good suc-

---

[22]Darwin, *Origin of Species*, p. 292.
[23]M. J. Benton, M. A. Willis and R. Hitchin, "Quality of the Fossil Record Through Time,"
Nature 403 (2000): 534-37.
[24]J. William Schopf, "Microfossils of the Early Archean Apex Chert: New Evidence of the
Antiquity of Life," *Science* 260 (1992): 640-46.

cession of sediments without missing layers. Trilobites are one of the better known groups of fossils. Trilobites belong to the phylum *Arthropoda,* as do insects and spiders. Trilobites first appear in the fossil record about 540 million years ago and finally disappear from the record in the mass extinction at the end of the Permian period about 250 million years ago. A study of the eight lineages of trilobite fossils in a three-million-year sample of shale revealed that all lineages showed a net gradual increase in segments on the rear section of the trilobite.[25] Similar observations have been made for the fossils of other marine organisms, such as plankton and radiolarian.

- *Prediction 1:* Transitional forms should exist between different types of organisms.

- *Prediction 2:* Transitional forms should be found in rocks located between the two types of organisms.

- *Prediction 3:* Changes in organisms will always involve the remodeling of old structures into new structures.

Finding: These three points are interrelated and will be considered together. Although many transition forms are now documented in the fossil record, such as reptiles to birds or land animals to whales, we will focus on the transition between fish and amphibians.[26] About 390 million years ago there were lobe-finned fish but no terrestrial vertebrates in the fossil record. About 30 million years later the fossil record contains amphibians that are *terapods*, four-footed vertebrates that walked on land. If a transitional form were to be found, scientists reasoned that it should be found in rocks between these two dates (around 375 million years ago) and in freshwater sediment, because both late lobe-finned fish and early terapods lived in fresh water. Sedimentary rock in the Canadian Arctic at Ellesmere Island fit these criteria. After a five-year search, fossils of a new species,

---

[25]Peter Sheldon, "Parallel Gradualistic Evolution of Ordovician Trilobites," *Nature* 330 (1987): 561-63.

[26]Scott Freeman and Jon C. Herron, *Evolutionary Analysis*, 4th ed. (San Francisco: Person Benjamin Cummings, 2007), pp. 46-49.

Tiktaalik roseae, were discovered.[27] *Tiktaalik* had a mixture of both fish and terapod characteristics. Like a fish, *Tiktaalik* had both gills and scales. The characteristics of its limb bones and ears were what have been labeled "fishapod," intermediate between fish and terapod. Like a terapod, *Tiktaalik* had lungs with sturdy ribs that allowed it to breathe air, a mobile neck and a flattened head with eyes and nostrils on top rather than on the side of the head. *Tiktaalik* "fins" had wrist bones and rudimentary finger bones that appear to be modifications of the bone structures of the lobe-finned fish.

In conclusion, these and similar arguments lead most scientists to conclude that evolution is the unifying concept of living organisms, and that the statements of evolution correspond to the data that have been collected.

THE MECHANISMS FOR EVOLUTION

In the previous section we discussed why scientists think that evolution is the unifying principle of biology. This discussion presented no mechanism to explain how evolution could have occurred. Darwin in 1859 stated that just supporting evolution "would be unsatisfactory, until it could be shown how the innumerable species inhabiting this world have been modified, so as to acquire that perfection of structure and co-adaptation which most justly excites our admiration."[28] In this section we will address the proposed mechanisms for evolution: natural selection, mutation, migration, genetic drift and sexual selection.[29] Natural selection involves change in the genetic makeup of an organism's population by adaptation to its environment. The others involve change in the genetic makeup of an organism's population but through processes other than adaptation.

---

[27]Edward B. Daeschler, Neil H. Shubin and Farish A. Jenkins Jr., "A Devonian Terapod-like Fish and the Evolution of the Terapod Body Plan," *Nature* 440 (2006): 757-63; Neil H. Shubin, Edward B. Daeschler and Farish A. Jenkins Jr., "The Pectoral Fin of Tiktaalik Roseae and the Origin of the Terapod Limb," *Nature* 440 (2006): 764-71.

[28]Darwin, *Origin of Species*, p. 66.

[29]Freeman and Herron, *Evolutionary Analysis*, p. 141; Margaret B. Ptacek and Shala J. Hankison, "The Pattern and Process of Speciation," *Evolution: The First Four Billion Years*, ed. Michael Ruse and Joseph Travis (Cambridge, Mass.: Belknap, 2009), p. 177.

Before examining each mechanism in detail, let us review the relationship between the different mechanisms using a hypothetical population of brown butterflies. A *mutation* is a change in the sequence of DNA bases. Enough mutations could occur to cause the allele for a swallow tail to appear in a population that has been mostly brown and tailless.[30] As a result, the population would have some brown butterflies with swallow tails. *Migration* is the movement of alleles between populations or from one gene pool to another. The geneticist's use of the term *migration* is different from the more familiar use of the term to refer to the seasonal migration of animals. Wind could blow some of the swallow-tail butterflies to an island in a lake, increasing the proportion of alleles for the swallow-tail variety in what was originally a brown, tailless population on the island. *Genetic drift* is the random change in allele frequency from generation to generation. One day on the lake as the butterflies flutter around, a rogue wave crashes ashore just as most of the brown, tailless population is near the shore. As the wave comes ashore, it kills 90 percent of the brown, tailless butterflies, which drastically increases the frequency of the allele for the swallow-tail variety. *Natural selection* involves the changes in heritable characteristics (alleles) that allow some members of a population to survive and reproduce better than other members of the population. Because of the butterfly's swallow tail, the birds on the island eat more of the swallow-tail butterflies, making the brown tailless butterflies more likely to survive and reproduce. Over time, natural selection would increase the number of tailless butterflies in the population. Notice in this example, genetic drift and natural selection have not operated in concert; in other cases they could act in concert. *Sexual selection* refers to differences in success at mating due to differences in phenotype (observable characteristics or traits). Female butterflies prefer to mate with the swallow-tail butterflies, which would increase the frequency of the swallow-tail allele. Here natural selection and sexual selection operate against each other. All

---

[30]An allele is an alternative form of a gene that is located at a specific position on a specific chromosome. Organisms have two alleles for each trait located at the same locus in the chromosome pair. One allele is inherited from each parent.

these mechanisms can cause changes in the frequency of the alleles in the population, and thus all these mechanisms have the potential for causing evolutionary change.

Natural selection. Darwin's original title for his 1859 work included his proposed mechanism for evolution: *On the Origin of the Species by Means of Natural Selection.* His proposal for evolution through natural selection can be stated in terms of four postulates:

1. Individuals within populations are variable.

2. The variations among individuals are, at least in part, passed from parents to offspring.

3. In every generation some individuals are more successful at surviving and reproducing than others.

4. Survival and reproduction of individuals are not random; instead they are tied to the variation among individuals. The individuals with the most favorable variations, those who are better at surviving and reproducing, are naturally selected.[31]

As discussed previously, the idea of natural selection was independently and simultaneously conceived by Charles Darwin and Alfred Russel Wallace. During the decades of the 1930s and 1940s, scientists succeeded in showing that Mendelian genetics was consistent with the idea of natural selection. The combination of these two streams of biology is called the "modern synthesis." In this synthesis the variations of natural selection are stated in terms of alleles. Those organisms that survive and reproduce possess the most favorable alleles. Natural selection ultimately produces organisms with the alleles that are well adapted to their environment. If the change in genetic material is great enough, then a new species could result from natural selection.

From the perspective of testing a scientific theory, an important point is that each natural selection postulate can be tested independently. An example of an experimental test of Darwin's four postulates is the recent work of Kristina Niovi Jones and Jennifer Reithel, which investigated how the pollination pattern of bumblebees would affect

---

[31]Freeman and Herron, *Evolutionary Analysis*, p. 76.

the floral traits of snapdragons.[32] They set up the experiment to ensure that postulates 1 and 2 (individuals with heritable variations) were satisfied by selecting a population of snapdragons in which 75 percent had white flowers with yellow spots on the tips and the rest had pure yellow flowers. They confirmed that the color was due to two alleles and was inheritable. They observed which flowers free-roaming bumblebees pollinated and how many seeds were produced per flower. Postulates 3 and 4 (individuals vary in reproductive success and reproduction was nonrandom) were confirmed. Bumblebees visited the white flowers twice as often as the yellow flowers. The white flowers also produced slightly more seed than the yellow flowers. Nature in the form of the bumblebee was selecting snapdragons with white flowers over yellow flowers. The next generation of snapdragons had 77 percent white flowers over the starting generation of 75 percent. At this rate it would not take many years for the white flowers to take over the population. In this experiment the four postulates of natural selection were confirmed and the populations were evolving.

In addition to human-controlled experiments, the following are cited as three examples of natural selection in the wild: insects acquiring resistance to DDT, disease-causing bacteria acquiring resistance to antibodies, and Darwin finches changing body and beak sizes in response to drought. After World War II, DDT became widely available as an insecticide and initially was effective in nearly eliminating many diseases, such as malaria and typhus. Less than thirty years after DDT's introduction, however, over two hundred species of insects have developed resistance to DDT.[33] Biologists explain the emergence of the DDT-resistant insect by natural selection.

After World War II, penicillin was introduced as a miracle drug that would "eliminate" most bacterial infections. A major bacterial pathogen is *Staphylococcus aureus*, commonly referred to as a *staph infection*. *S. aureus* can cause a range of illnesses, from minor skin infections to life-

---

[32]Kristina Niovi Jones and Jennifer Reithel, "Pollinator-Mediated Selection on a Flower Color Polymorphism in Experimental Populations of *Antirrhinum* (Scrophulariaceae)," *American Journal of Botany* 88 (2001): 447-54.

[33]Douglas J. Futuyma, *Science on Trial: The Case for Evolution* (Sunderland, Mass.: Sinauer Associates, 1995), pp. 118-19.

threatening diseases to postsurgical wound infections. Within four years of the use of penicillin on staph infections, *S. aureus* became the first bacteria with penicillin resistance. The antibiotic methicillin was introduced as a replacement for penicillin to treat staph infection. By 1961 MRSA (methicillin-resistant *Staphylococcus aureus*) had appeared. Vancomycin became the next antibiotic of choice. In 2002 the first VRSA (vancomycin-resistant *Staphylococcus aureus*) appeared in the United States. The next antibiotic used was linezolid, with LRSA (linezolid-resistant *Staphylococcus aureus*) appearing in 2003. MRSA is now the most antimicrobial drug-resistant pathogen in American hospitals. In the past ten years MRSA-caused infections have moved out of the hospital to the community.

Some of the most famous birds in science are Darwin's finches, which comprise thirteen species in the Galápagos Archipelago. Although similar in size and coloration, the finches vary in beak size and shape. Since 1973, Peter and Rosemary Grant (both 1936-) have been observing one species, the medium ground finch, on Isla Daphne Major. This population is ideal to study as few birds migrate on and off the island, and the total population is small (about 1,200 individuals). The Grants found that beak size is correlated with the size of seeds eaten; for example, smaller-beak birds eat smaller seeds and large-beak birds eat large seeds. It was also shown that the beak size of parents and offspring are similar; this suggests that variation in beak size is related to variation in alleles. When the Grants started studying the finches, they had a medium-size beak and their favorite food was small, soft seeds. In 1977 a severe drought struck the island, causing plants to produce few flowers and seeds. As the drought continued for twenty months, only larger, hard seeds were available and over 84 percent of the finches died. At the end of the drought the surviving population had larger beaks than the population that existed before the drought. Natural selection had changed the characteristic of the finch population.[34]

If the adaptation of an organism to its environment is a result of

[34]Freeman and Herron, *Evolutionary Analysis*, pp. 88-89.

natural selection, then the following predictions can be made about how natural selection should be manifested.

- If adaption is the result of natural selection, then we should expect to see less than optimal engineering design. (Why less than optimal engineering design? Because natural selection is postulated to operate on existing body parts and thereby modify them for a new function rather than making a new body part just for a particular need.) Pandas are fascinating animals that amaze us with all the bamboo that they eat. They manipulate the bamboo stalks by holding the stalks with an "opposable thumb." But the panda has five claws like a bear and the "thumb is an extension of the radial sesamoid bone. (A sesamoid bone is embedded within a tendon.) The panda's thumb is not an optimal design, but is apparently an existing anatomical structure that was modified by natural selection for its current function.[35]

- If adaption is the result of natural selection, then we should expect to see many different genetic solutions to environmental challenges. We have discussed the response of insects to the insecticide DDT. Different populations of the same species of fly have adapted to DDT differently by using either a single dormant gene, a single dominant gene or a combination of genes. The physiological response varies from synthesizing a new enzyme that breaks down DDT to changing cell membrane permeability, which slows down the penetration of DDT into nerve cells.[36]

Sexual selection. Darwin coined the phrase *sexual selection* to refer to the difference in success in obtaining mates due to differences in phenotype (observable characteristics or traits). Sexual selection comes in two forms. One form is direct competition between males for access to females, where the selection involves stronger weapons (antlers or tusks) or larger body size. The other form is female choosiness among possible mates, where the selection involves ornaments, bright colors or mating displays. In the greenish warbler ring species, the males use song both

[35]Stephen J. Gould, *The Panda's Thumb* (New York: W. W. Norton, 1980).
[36]R. D. O'Brien, *Insecticides: Action and Metabolism* (New York: Academic Press, 1967).

to attract females and to defend their territories. Sexual selection has apparently gradually separated the greenish warbler into two species. What about natural selection in regard to the greenish warbler? As the investigators state, "As illustrated here for body size, natural selection may often lead to parallel or convergent evolution, resulting in little difference between incipient species when they meet."[37]

Mutation. One way to classify mutations is by the effect on the structure of the DNA molecule. Small-scale mutations affect either one or a few nucleotides or a gene. Large-scale mutations affect many genes and chromosomes. Among small-scale mutations are:

- *Point mutations* involve base pair substitutions in a DNA sequence that occurs from copying errors or during repair of damaged DNA. Because of the redundancy of the genetic code, many point mutations have no effect on the amino acid expression. When point mutations result in a change in a gene, then a new allele is formed. Normal and sickle cell hemoglobin differ by one amino acid, with glutamic acid being replaced by valine. Only one base change is needed for this mutation to occur; glutamic acid or Glu has the genetic code of GAG while valine or Val has the genetic code of GUG.

- *Insertions* add one or more extra nucleotides into the DNA strand. This mutation is also called a frameshift mutation since it changes the gene's reading frame. Groups of three nucleotides code for one amino acid. The addition of the extra nucleotide changes the code for the amino acid, usually resulting in a nonfunctional protein.

- *Deletions* remove one or more nucleotides from the DNA strand. Again a frameshift may result affecting the function of the protein.

The following are among large-scale mutations:

- *Gene duplication* involves duplication of a stretch of DNA, creating an extra copy of this stretch. It is thought that the α-chain gene and β-chain gene of hemoglobin resulted from gene duplication.

- *Deletions of large chromosomal regions* lead to the loss of genes. Gene duplication and deletions are also called *copy-number variation muta-*

---

[37]Irwin, Bensch and Price, "Speciation in a Ring," p. 337.

tions. The Human Genome Project revealed that these types of mutations occur in about 12 percent of human genomic DNA, which is a higher rate than small-scale mutations.

- *Chromosomal translocations* involve the movement of a series of genes from one chromosome to another, which decreases the number of genes in the first chromosome and increases the number of genes in the second chromosome. Some human cancers are caused by translocations.

- *Chromosome inversion* involves radiation breaking a chromosome segment in two places, with a segment flipping before the chromosome is repaired. This inversion of a chromosome segment results in a change in the order of the genes. The alleles within the inverted segment tend to be transmitted as a unit (a single supergene). The American Paint Horse has two spotting patterns: Overo (white color is scattered and splashy, and usually does not cross the back; at least one leg is dark; and the tail is usually one color) and Tobiano (white crosses the back with spots regular and distinct; all four legs are white; and tail is often two colors). Brooks and colleagues provided evidence that the Tobiano color pattern is due to a chromosome inversion on chromosome 3.[38]

- *Genome duplication* results in the doubling of the number of chromosomes in the cell. This duplication can occur from either error in meiosis (formation of gametes and spores) or mitosis (cell division, especially in plants). Previously, we discussed mints and codgrass, which are examples of genome duplication.

Migration. In population genetics *migration* is the movement of alleles from one population to another. This gene flow can involve the dispersal of juvenile animals over a large area or the dispersal of seeds, pollen or spores by wind, water or animals. Migration tends to homogenize the allele frequency between populations and thus prevents the evolutionary divergence of populations. An example is the water snakes

---

[38]S. A. Brooks, T. L. Lear, D. L. Adelson and E. Bailey, "A Chromosome Inversion Near the KIT Gene and the Tobiano Spotting Pattern in Horses," *Cytogenetic Genome Research* 119 (2007): 225-30.

that live on the mainland and islands in and around Lake Erie. Migration of individuals from the mainland to the islands could be preventing the divergence of the island and mainland snake populations.

Genetic drift. Of the nonadaptive mechanism, genetic drift is the only one that is totally random. In each generation, some individuals of a population, by chance, may have a few more descendents than other individuals. In the next generation there will be more genes of the first group of individuals, not because they were healthier or more adapted but because they were lucky. Since genetic drift is not driven by adaptive pressure, as natural selection is, genetic drift may be beneficial, neutral or detrimental to reproductive success. Genetic drift has a greater effect in small populations than in large populations. An example of genetic drift is Ellis-van Creveld syndrome, where an individual has extra fingers or toes. This syndrome is more common among the Old Order Amish of Pennsylvania, which is a small population that marries within their own community. The Ellis-van Creveld syndrome can be traced to one couple, Mr. and Mrs. Samuel King, who came to Pennsylvania in 1744.

In summary, mutations provide the genetic variety that is seen in populations. Migration tends to increase the similarity of the gene pool of the individuals remaining after the migration event. Thus migration can decrease the genetic variety in a population. Genetic drift is most pronounced in small populations and may be a big problem in endangered species, which have small populations. Since an organism is always subject to changing environmental conditions, natural selection is considered the most important influence on the evolution of a population. During an environmental stress, the fittest survive and pass their genes to their offspring.

EPIGENETICS

Epidemiological studies showed relations between parents' experiences early in their lives and the health of their children, their grandchildren and beyond. During World War II, western Netherlands was affected by a severe famine from October 1944 to May 1945. As expected, children of the women who were pregnant during the famine were smaller. Surprisingly, the famine seemed to affect the second generation, as the grandchildren of these women were also born smaller.[39] Another set of studies examined the effect of food availability on the parents, children and grandchildren of Överkalix, northernmost Sweden.[40] Researchers discovered that overeating during a child's slow-growth period before their prepubertal peak in growth causes a drop in the life span of their children and grandchildren, with cardiovascular and diabetes mortality being greater in this population.

The challenge with these types of epidemiological studies is that we really do not know what food was available to a particular ancestor. In a "proof of concept" experiment, Randy Jirtle and Robert Waterland of Duke University fed methyl-rich diets to agouti mice, so-called because they contain the agouti gene, which makes them fat, yellow and susceptible to cancer and diabetes.[41] Pregnant agouti mice that were fed methyl-rich supplements (folic acid, vitamin B_{12}, choline and betaine) produced offspring that were slender, brown and lived longer than traditional agouti mice.[42] The researchers concluded that methylation of cytosine (C) shut off the expression of the agouti gene. Epigenetic control was affecting the phenotype. Another study examined the effect of environmental toxins on the male descendants of gestating female rats. Increased male infertility was observed through four generations. Analysis of the male rats revealed altered DNA methylation of the male germ line.[43] Even more

---

[39]L. H. Lumey, "Decreased Birthweights in Infants After Maternal *In Utero* Exposure to the Dutch Famine of 1944-1945," *Paediatric and Perinatal Epidemiology* 6 (1992): 240-53.

[40]Lars Olov Bygren, Gunnar Kaati, and Sören Edvinsson, "Longevity Determined by Paternal Ancestor' Nutrition During Their Slow Growth Period," *Acta Biotheoretica* 49 (2001): 53-59; Gunnar Kaati, Lars Olov Bygren, Marcus Pembrey and Michael Sjöström, "Transgenerational Response to Nutrition, Early Life Circumstances and Longevity," *European Journal of Human Genetics* 15 (2007): 784-90.

[41]Robert A. Waterland and Randy L. Jirtle, "Transposable Elements: Targets for Early Nutritional Effects on Epigenetic Gene Regulation," *Molecular and Cellular Biology* (2003): 5293-5300.

[42]Since folic acid and multiple vitamins are routinely prescribed to pregnant women to reduce the incidence of birth defects, one has to wonder if unintended epigenetic consequences may also be occurring.

[43]Mathew D. Anway, Andrea S. Cup, Mehmet Uzumcu and Michael K. Skinner, "Epigenetic Transgenerational Actions of Endocrine Disruptors and Male Fertility," *Science* 308 (2005): 1466-69.

amazing is evidence that parental care can alter the epigenome of their offspring. The newborns of mother rats that licked and groomed them grew up to be braver and calmer than newborns whose mothers did not lick or groom them. The calmer offspring passed this behavior on to their offspring. This appears to be an epigenetic effect as the groomed rats have more DNA methylation in their hippocampus cells.[44]

How permanent is the epigenetic change? One of the longest observed epigenetic changes involves the common toadflax, *Linaria vulgaris*, whose flowers have bilateral symmetry. In the 1740s, Linnaeus was presented with a variety of the toadflax whose flowers have radial symmetry.[45] Linnaeus called this variety "peloria," Greek for "monster." It was a monster to Linnaeus because it implied to him that species were not stable, that they can change. This variety, *Linaria peloria*, has one gene shut off, which results in its flowers having the deviant form, which results from epigenetic methylation.[46] This epigenetic change has been around for over 250 years.

What is the relationship of epigenetics to evolution? Epigenetic insight says that not only do some organisms respond better to environmental stress because of their genetic makeup but that the organism can respond to the stress by reprogramming how the genetic makeup is expressed. Since changes to the epigenome are partially reversible, the resulting phenotypes are possibly more variable and the changes to the phenotype less final than phenotype changes due to modification of the genome sequence. This could give the organism more flexibility in responding to an environmental stress in contrast to that due to genome sequence change. The grooming rat studies also imply that epigenome changes give the organism one last chance to mold their progeny to suit the current environment.

---

[44]Frances A. Champagne et al., "Maternal Care Associated with Methylation of the Estrogen Receptor-α1b Promoter and Estrogen Receptor-α Expression in the Medial Preoptic Area of Female Offspring," *Endocrinology* (2006) 147: 2909-15.

[45]Å. Gustafsson, "Linnaeus' Peloria: A History of a Monster," *Theoretical and Applied Genetics* 54 (1979): 241-48.

[46]Pilar Cubbas, Coral Vincent and Enrico Coen, "An Epigenetic Mutation Responsible for Natural Variation in Floral Symmetry," *Nature* 401 (1999): 157-61.

WHERE IS GOD?

Almost as soon as *On the Origin of the Species* was published, Darwin and his contemporaries began debating God's relationship to evolution and especially evolution by means of natural selection. Two philosophical currents affected Darwin. One current was natural theology; the other was Darwin's evangelical background that included the William Perkins dichotomy, which was discussed in chapter two. Darwin studied William Paley's (1743-1805) book *Natural Theology, or Evidences of the Existence and Attributes of the Deity Collected from the Appearances of Nature* while he was a student at the University of Cambridge. As the subtitle of his book states, Paley presents the idea that the design in nature leads to a belief in God. When Paley looked at nature, he saw design; he saw the great "watches" of nature reflecting the perfection of the watchmaker. When Darwin looked at nature, he saw nature "red in tooth and claw"; he saw parasites consuming their still-living hosts.[47] Darwin was repelled by the vision of God this view of nature presented: "There seems to me too much misery in the world. I cannot persuade myself that a beneficent & omnipotent God would have designedly created the Ichneumonidae with the express intention of their feeding with the living bodies of caterpillars, or that a cat should play with mice."[48] Adopting the dichotomy of Perkins, Darwin saw the either-or proposition of either God has done everything or God has done nothing beyond setting the laws of nature in motion:

> It has always seemed to me that for an Omnipotent & Omniscient Creator to foresee is the same as to preordain. . . .
>
> I am inclined to look at everything as resulting from designed laws, with the details, whether good or bad, left to the working out of what we may call chance. . . .
>
> I cannot believe that there is a bit more interference by the Creator in the construction of each species, than in the course of the planets. It is

---

[47]Alfred Lord Tennyson, *In Memoriam A. H. H.*, 1850, canto 56. Although published before *The Origin of the Species* in 1859, the phrase "red in tooth and claw" was adopted to evoke the process of evolution by natural selection by both those in favor of and opposed to the concept.

[48]Charles Darwin, *The Correspondence of Charles Darwin* 8 (1860; reprint, Cambridge: Cambridge University Press, 1993), p. 224.

only owing to Paley & Co, as I believe, that this special interference is thought necessary with living bodies.[49]

A contemporary supporter of evolution was the American Asa Gray (1810-1888). Harvard University professor Gray was the leading botanist of his day. Gray was the only American to whom Darwin revealed his ideas before the publication of *On the Origin of the Species*. When Gray considered nature and Darwin's proposal, Gray saw design and the action of God. Some of Gray's statements include "we think that a theistic view of Nature is implied in his book. . . . [G]radatory, orderly, and adapted forms in Nature argue design. . . . [V]ariation has been led along certain beneficial lines."[50]

How could Gray see design and direction to the origin of species while at the same time Darwin could not? Gray did not begin with Paley, as Darwin had done, and Gray did not restrict everything to the either-or thinking of Perkins's dichotomy. Gray described himself as "one who is scientifically, and in his own fashion, a Darwinian, philosophically a convinced theist, and religiously an acceptor of the 'creed commonly called the Nicene,' as the exponent of the Christian faith."[51] Gray knew the attributes of God from Scripture and could see them reflected in nature, even with its waste and suffering, just as he could see God in the joys and suffering of humans. In addition, Darwin held the duality that either everything was designed or nothing was design; this belief could not reconcile random events with any overall plan.[52] As he said about humans, "But, surely, all human doings are not 'products of design'; many are contingent or accidental."[53] Gray took a more global approach to all of nature by seeing design in an overall plan

---

[49]Ibid., pp. 106, 224, 258.

[50]Asa Gray, "Natural Selection Not Inconsistent with Natural Theology," in *Darwiniana: Essays and Reviews Pertaining to Darwinism* (New York: D. Appleton, 1889), pp. 87-178. The article was originally printed in the July, August and October 1860 *Atlantic Monthly*.

[51]Asa Gray, preface to *Darwiniana*, p. vi.

[52]In an 1860 letter to Gray, Darwin talks about a man killed by lightning and a gnat killed by a bird and asked if these deaths were designed or accidents. Darwin then states, "If the death of neither man or gnat are designed, I see no good reason to believe that their first birth or production should be necessarily designed," Charles Darwin, *The Correspondence of Charles Darwin* 8, (1860; reprint, Cambridge: Cambridge University Press, 1993), p. 275.

[53]Asa Gray, "Evolutionary Teleology," in *Darwiniana*, pp. 356-90.

with some specific details the result of contingence or accidents. From his Congregational background, Gray knew it was a fallen world; a world in which God may work either by modifying species through the elimination of unfavorable traits or refining the elect through suffering. The Darwin-Gray discussions show the importance of the philosophical framework that one uses in approaching the study of nature.

OPEN UNIVERSE

Was Gray giving a God-of-the-gap argument? As he admitted, "the physical cause of variation [was] utterly unknown and mysterious."[54] Once this cause became known would another God-of-the-gaps door close along with Gray's vision of design? As we shall see, once the cause was discovered, a very deterministic paradigm developed which seemed to exclude any room for the action of God.

A lot of science has been carried out since Darwin and Gray discussed whether the theory of evolution by natural selection removed design from nature.

As discussed previously, the "physical cause of variation" is now known to be due to genetic variations. Modern science favors a reductionist mode of thought that tries to break complex phenomena into their simplest parts and then use these simple parts to explain the behavior of the complex phenomena. The success of the reductionist method for some disciplines, such as physics, encourages its application to all disciplines. Thus the reductionist mode of thought was applied to heredity with, as discussed previously, scientists looking for the smallest unit that carried the hereditary information. Mendel's genetic laws seemed to support this way of thinking, as he found one gene was related to one characteristic of his peas. When the structure of DNA was finally solved and the gene was now related to a series of nucleotide base pairs, the tendency was to relate complex properties of organisms back to their genes.

This view is called *genetic reductionism* and can be expressed at three levels: cellular, organism and society. The *cellular level* is expressed in

---

[54]Ibid.

Francis Crick's proposed "central dogma" of molecular biology: DNA makes RNA makes proteins. In this view information flows unidirectionally from nucleic acids to protein and never vice versa. At the *organism level* one adds a further step to the central dogma: DNA makes RNA makes proteins makes a body. In this view everything about the body (its size, health, life span) is determined by the genes. This view underpins the drive in medicine to find genetic markers for all diseases. The genetic reductionist view at the *society level* moves from pure biology into the areas of psychology and sociology, and adds one more stage to the central dogma: DNA makes RNA makes proteins makes a body makes all the behaviors. As the April 1998 cover of *Life* stated: "Were You Born That Way? Personality, temperament, even life choices. New studies show it's mostly in your genes." So the ultimate machine model had been created. The gene cog turned to cause the RNA cog to turn which caused the protein cog to turn which built a body and its personality. This is genetic determinism, with everything being set by the genetic code. The American biologist and Nobel Prize winner Walter Gilbert (1932-) reflects this view when he stated that once your DNA has been sequenced, "one will be able to pull a CD out of one's pocket and say, 'Here is a human being: it's me!'"[55] If this view is true, then Gray was making a God-of-the-gaps argument, and there is little openness in the universe.

The "death" of this genetic reductionist-deterministic view came with the triumph of one of the greatest achievements in the science of genetics: the completion of the Human Genome Project. In 1990 the Human Genome Project began as a joint project of the U.S. Department of Energy and the National Institutes of Health, with support from the United Kingdom, Japan, France, Germany and China. The thirteen-year mission of the Human Genome Project was to sequence all the base-pairs in human DNA as well as determine the number and location of all the genes in the forty-six human chromosomes. When the project began, it was assumed that the human genome contained over 100,000 genes, with the number 142,634

---

[55]Walter Gilbert, "A Vision of the Grail," in *The Code of Codes: Scientific and Social Issues in the Human Genome Project*, ed. Daniel J. Devles and Leroy Hood (Cambridge, Mass.: Harvard University Press, 1992), p. 96.

widely advertised.[56] Why 142,634 genes? This is the number of genes that is needed for the central dogma to work: that is, one gene making one protein, and so forth.

On February 12, 2001, the anniversary of Darwin's birthday, the initial working draft of the human genome sequence was published and stated that the number of genes in the human genome is about 35,000. (In 2004, the number was revised downward to between 20,000 and 25,000 genes.)[57] This latter number is only 1.3 times the number of genes (19,000) that the lowly roundworm, *C. elegans*, with only 959 cells, has. This was the death of the central dogma. As the American evolutionary biologist Stephen Jay Gould (1941-2002) remarked,

> Human complexity cannot be generated by 30,000 genes under the old view of life embodied in what geneticists literally called . . . their "Central Dogma": DNA makes RNA makes protein—in other words, one direction of causal flow from code to message to assembly of substance, with one item of code (a gene) ultimately making one item of substance (a protein), and the congeries of proteins making a body. Those 142,000 messages no doubt exist, as they must to build our bodies' complexity, with our previous error now exposed as the assumption that each message came from a distinct gene.[58]

The American biologist and cosequencer of the human genome J. Craig Venter (1946-) agreed with Gould, stating, "We simply do not have enough genes for this idea of biological determinism to be right. The wonderful diversity of the human species is not hard-wired in our genetic code. Our environments are critical."

Gould and Venter are calling for biology to go beyond genetics and consider epigenetic processes to understand complex living organisms. How a gene is expressed is influenced by a vast array of signals within the cellular environment (hormones, nutrient supply and signals from other cells). In addition, all of these signals are influenced by the ex-

---

[56]Stephen Jay Gould, "Humbled by the Genome's Mysteries," *New York Times*, February 19, 2001.
[57]"Major Events in the U.S. Human Genome Project and Related Projects," *Genomics.Energy .gov*, www.ornl.gov/sci/techresources/Human_Genome/project/timeline.shtml.
[58]Gould, "Humbled by the Genome's Mysteries."

ternal environment. Although new individuals can have the same gene sequence, their epigenetic environment will determine how this gene sequence is expressed or even if it is. Who we are is not determined by our genes but by the totality of our experiences and even the experiences of our ancestors.

Epigenetics is not a God-of-the-gaps type of argument. This is not a case of missing knowledge but rather the ontological structure of the universe. As the International Theological Commission of the Roman Catholic Church stated,

> The appeal to divine causality to account for genuinely *causal* as distinct from merely *explanatory* gaps does not insert divine agency to fill in the "gaps" in human scientific understanding (thus giving rise to the so-called "God-of-the-gaps"). The structures of the world can be seen as open to non-disruptive divine action in directly causing events in the world.[59]

The latest biological research has revealed that the universe of life is not closed to outside input. Life has arisen in an open universe, providing many opportunities for the activities of God.

PURPOSEFUL UNIVERSE?

Even if the universe of life is open to the actions of God, what good is an open universe if it is a universe without purpose? Isn't that one of the hallmarks of the modern view of evolution—that the story of life has no purpose or direction? As the following quotes indicate, Darwin's rejection of purpose or direction to evolution has become the dominant, popularized view:

> Man is the result of a purposeless and materialistic process that did not have him in mind. He was not planned. He is a state of matter, a form of life, a sort of animal, and a species of the Order Primates, akin nearly or remotely to all of life and indeed to all that is material—American paleontologist George Gayland Simpson.[60]

---

[59]International Theological Commission, "Communion and Stewardship," *The Vatican*, www .vatican.va/roman_curia/congregations/cfaith/cti_documents/rc_con_cfaith_doc_20040723_ communion-stewardship_en.html.

[60]George Gayland Simpson, *The Meaning of Evolution: A Study of the History of Life and of Its Significance for Man* (New Haven, Conn.: Yale University Press, 1949), p. 344.

The entire phrase and not merely the words Natural Selection is important, for the denial of purpose is Darwin's distinctive contention. In this way the notion of a Deity or Providence or Life Force having a tendency of its own, or even of a single individual having a purpose other than survival or reproduction, was ruled out.—French-American cultural historian Jacques Barzun[61]

History includes too much chaos, or extremely sensitive dependence on minute and unmeasurable differences in initial conditions, leading to massively divergent outcomes based on tiny and unknowable disparities in starting points. And history includes too much contingency, or shaping of present results by long chains of unpredictable antecedent states, rather than immediate determination by timeless laws of nature. Homo sapiens did not appear on the earth, just a geologic second ago, because evolutionary theory predicts such an outcome based on themes of progress and increasing neural complexity. Humans arose, rather, as a fortuitous and contingent outcome of thousands of linked events, any one of which could have occurred differently and sent history on an alternative pathway that would not have led to consciousness.—American paleontologist Stephen Jay Gould[62]

The universe we observe has precisely the properties we should expect if there is, at bottom, no design, no purpose, no evil and no good, nothing but blind, pitiless indifference. As that unhappy poet A. E. Housman put it: "For Nature, heartless, witless Nature Will neither care nor know." DNA neither cares nor knows. DNA just is. And we dance to its music." —British evolutionary biologist Richard Dawkins[63]

Darwin's idea—bearing an unmistakable likeness to universal acid: it eats through just about every traditional concept, and leaves in its wake a revolutionized world-view, with most of the old landmarks still recognizable, but transformed in fundamental ways.—American philosopher Daniel Dennett[64]

---

[61]Jacques Barzun, *Darwin, Marx, Wagner: Critique of a Heritage* (New York: Doubleday Anchor, 1958), p. 11.
[62]Stephen Jay Gould, "The Evolution of Life on Earth," *Scientific American* (October 1994): 85-86.
[63]Richard Dawkins, *River Out of Eden: A Darwinian View of Life* (New York: Basic Books, 1996), p. 133.
[64]Daniel Dennett, *Darwin's Dangerous Idea: Evolution and the Meaning of Life* (New York: Simon & Schuster, 1996), p. 63.

Paleontologist Stephen Jay Gould was one of the most widely read popularizers of modern science through his *Natural History* articles and books. In *Wonderful Life* (1989) he used Cambrian Burgess Shale fossils to popularize the idea that evolution had no purpose because of contingency. The Burgess Shale contains fossil remains of what is called the "Cambrian explosion" or "Cambrian radiation," the relatively rapid appearance (over many million years) of most major phyla around 540 million years ago. The American paleontologist Charles Walcott (1850-1927), while secretary of the Smithsonian Institution, collected over 60,000 fossils between 1909 and his death; he interpreted his findings in terms of then-currently known categories. After years of neglect, British geologist Harry B. Whittington (1916-2010), along with graduate students Derek Briggs and Simon Conway Morris, began reexamining Walcott's work, as well as collecting new specimens. They concluded that the fauna represented were much more unusual and diverse than proposed by Walcott and that most of these lineages were evolutionary experiments that went extinct. Gould relied on and acknowledged Conway Morris's reinterpretation of Walcott. Gould's theme is "if we could perform the great undoable thought experiment of 'rewinding the tape of life' back to the Cambrian and 'distributing the lottery tickets' at random a second time, the history of animals would follow an entirely different but equally 'sensible' course that would almost surely not generate a humanoid creature with self-conscious intelligence."[65]

As the British paleontologist Simon Conway Morris (1951-) continued to study the Burgess Shale fossils as well as similar fossils found in Greenland and China, his interpretation of the implications of these fossils in regard to purpose/direction in evolution changed, which he expressed in his book *The Crucible of Creation: The Burgess Shale and the Rise of Animals* (1998). This work was followed by *Life's Solution: Inevitable Humans in a Lonely Universe* (2003) and *The Deep Structure of Biology: Is Convergence Sufficiently Ubiquitous to Give a Directional Signal?* (2008). In all these works, he has challenged Gould's idea that contingency played such an important role in evolution.

---

[65]Simon Conway Morris and Stephen Jay Gould, "Showdown on the Burgess Shale," *Natural History* 107, no. 10 (1998): 48-55.

Convergence is the biological concept that Conway Morris proposes as evidence of a constraint on the unfolding of evolution—"replaying the tape" would result in similar lineages and properties evolving again. Convergence in evolution refers to an organism acquiring similar biological traits (wings, consciousness) in unrelated lineages. Convergent traits are called analogous structures in contrast to homologous structures, which have a common origin. Bat, bird and pterosaur wings are considered analogous structures (convergence) while, as discussed previously, the wing of the bat, the leg of the horse and the hand of man are considered homologous structures. As Conway Morris states,

> Similar environmental selection pressures, acting on differing anatomies, can create convergent or parallel adaptations. . . .
>
> Given certain environmental forces, life will shape itself to adapt. History is constrained, and not all things are possible. . . .
>
> [P]erhaps there is a course and a direction to evolution that would be achieved despite diverse anatomical starting points.[66]

Other scientists are exploring whether there are laws or tendencies in evolution that give it a predictive power. In 2010 the NASA Astrobiology Institute hosted the workshop "Molecular Paleontology and Resurrection: Rewinding the Tape of Life," which addressed this question. The American evolutionary biologist Lynn J. Rothschild (1957-) of NASA Ames Research Center and Stanford University proposed that there are likely universal biological patterns based on

- the likelihood of life being based on organic carbon because of the prevalence of organic carbon in comets, meteorites and interstellar medium
- the likelihood of water as a solvent because of widespread occurrence and chemical properties of water
- the universality of the laws of chemistry and physics
- the universality of the principle of natural selection
- the selective tyranny of the environment

---

[66]Ibid.

- the likelihood of the availability of solar radiation as a source of energy
- the observations of convergence at both molecular and organism level[67]

Using these principles, Rothschild demonstrated why she thinks that photosynthesis is a predictive property in the history of life. In another presentation the evolutionary biologist Stephen J. Freeland of the NASA Astrobiology Institute at University of Hawaii presented evidence that the twenty amino acids found in living systems are the result of chemical and physical constraints rather than random chance.[68]

The overall theme of the workshop was, as Rothschild concludes, "This amalgam creates a surprising amount of predictive power in the broad outline. . . . [T]here are certain tendencies, if not 'laws,' that provide the predictive power."[69] Does everyone agree that evolution is predictable based on physical, chemical and biological principles rather than being contingent or a product of the quirks of history? As Rothschild stated in her presentation, "Some yes, some no."

The fine tuning (anthropic principles) discussed in chapter five have provided a potential common ground between science (cosmology) and religion. It has been much harder to find a common ground between biology and religion because of the evolutionary emphasis on contingency and necessity (selection), which seems to remove all purpose from the story of life. Simon Conway Morris proposes that the addition of convergence to the story of life returns "purpose" to the story of life. The use of convergence adds these insights:

1. *The story of life is constrained where not all possibilities are possible.* Probability calculations imply that an almost "infinite" number of pos-

---

[67]Lynn J. Rothschild, "Replaying the Tape of Life: The Potential of Evolution as a Predictive Science," *Molecular Paleontology and Resurrection: Rewinding the Tape of Life*, NAI Workshop Without Walls, November 8-10, 2010, conference presentation.

[68]Stephen Freeland, "Making Sense of Life's Amino Acid Alphabet," *Molecular Paleontology and Resurrection: Rewinding the Tape of Life*, NAI Workshop Without Walls, November 8-10, 2010, conference presentation. The twenty amino acids found in living organisms are from a possible pool of fifty found in the Murchison meteorite and twenty-six that are seen as intermediaries in biosynthetic pathways. The twenty found in living organisms are the most robust in terms of hydrophobicity, charge and size.

[69]Rothschild, "Replaying the Tape of Life."

sibilities are available.[70] However, as we discussed earlier, the work of Rothschild and Freeland, among others, has shown the physics and chemistry of organic carbon greatly restrict the possibilities. As Conway Morris stated,

> This ubiquity of convergence and the likelihood that the great majority of the examples are almost certainly the result of selective processes operating in the context of adaptation has the obvious corollary that common evolutionary destinations presuppose specific, and restricted trajectories. . . . Yet, trends imply directionality, and perhaps progress."[71]

Another way of visualizing this is as "something analogous to 'attractors,' by which evolutionary trajectories are channeled towards stable nodes of functionality."[72] He further states, "One such node is, of course, that of the humanoid, and from the present evolutionary perspective, we are undeniably unique."[73]

2. *Movement toward complexity.* The biological world of today is built on the worlds of the past. Although simple organisms are still with us, in general, through deep time, we see the emergence of more complex worlds. As the English evolutionary biologist Julian Huxley (1887-1975) stated,

> [Over] the whole range of evolutionary time we see general advance—improvement in all the main properties of life, including its general organization. "Advance" is thus a useful term for long-term improvement in some general property of life. [But] improvement is not universal. Lower forms manage to survive alongside higher.[74]

3. *Movement toward sentience.* As Conway Morris states, "within the animals we see the emergence of larger and more complex brains, sophisticated vocalizations, echolocation, electrical perception, advance social systems including eusociality, viviparity, warm-blood-

---

[70]Temple Smith and Harold Morowitz, "Between Physics and History," *Journal of Molecular Evolution* 18 (1982): 265-82
[71]Simon Conway Morris, *Life's Solution: Inevitable Humans in a Lonely Universe* (Cambridge: Cambridge University Press, 2003), p. 304.
[72]Ibid., p. 309.
[73]Ibid., p. 310.
[74]Julian Huxley, *Evolution in Action: Based on the Patten Lectures Delivered at Indiana University in 1951* (London: Chatto & Windus, 1953), pp. 152-53.

edness, and agriculture—all of which are convergent."[75]

Has Conway Morris and convergence returned purpose to biology? The American theologian John F. Haught states, "I proposed that any process that is bringing into actuality what is undeniably valuable is purposeful."[76] By this definition we could argue that Conway Morris has indeed returned purpose to biology. So the latest biological research has revealed a universe that is not only open for interference but displays a purposeful direction.

CONCLUSION

An important distinction lies between the idea of gradual change in a life form over many generations and the idea of increasing complexity of a life form over many generations. The increasing complexity does not mean simply a reordering of the sequence of the genome but the addition to the genome of new information. It involves not simply the altering of existing information but the creation of new information to add to the genetic code.[77] The light-sensitive patch of skin does not simply get bigger from one generation to the next. The genome itself must instruct it to get bigger and more complex through its code. We describe the progress of biological life in terms of changes that give the organism an advantage in the competition for survival. This explanation for biological evolution, however, does not work for the physical evolution of the rest of the universe. The appearance of particles does not give energy a greater advantage to survive. The appearance of hydrogen atoms does not give particles a greater advantage to survive, nor the collection of atoms into clouds, nor their combustion into stars, nor their explosion into many elements. The fact of the advantage of life in biological evolution is not explanatory but descriptive. It happens. It does not cause; it is a result.

---

[75]Conway Morris, *Life's Solution*, p. 307.

[76]John F. Haught, "Purpose in Nature: On the Possibilities of a Theology of Evolution," in *The Deep Structure of Biology: Is Convergence Sufficiently Ubiquitous to Give a Directional Signal?* ed. Simon Conway Morris (West Conshohocken, Penn.: Templeton Foundation Press, 2008), p. 227.

[77]Mutations change the DNA sequence. The new sequence can be information that alters the organism in a positive way, but the new sequence can be meaningless "information" that may have no impact on the organism or even prove to be fatal.

The openness of DNA. Perhaps the strangest example of how Enlightenment thinking is out of step with modern science rests with the case of DNA and the advances in genetics. Richard Dawkins represents a way of talking about DNA and the whole genetic field that betrays a commitment to an Enlightenment philosophical system as the matrix for interpreting reality.

Without a mechanism for change, Darwin's theory had an embarrassing hole that Darwin acknowledged until Mendel's experiments with peas led to an understanding of how heredity works in living organisms. Darwin provided a theoretical basis for thinking of evolution, but Mendel provided the biology. DNA proved to be the mechanism by which heredity passed on traits from one generation to the next. Mixed with the philosophy of the Enlightenment, however, DNA and the genetic code becomes a deterministic mechanical conception that flies in the face of its organic nature.

If the hereditary process were closed and deterministic, then no evolution would occur because the offspring's DNA would be identical with the parents' DNA. Instead of a closed, deterministic system, the hereditary process from parent to child is open to alteration, which is called *mutation*. Mutations occur as a result of changes in the base sequence of the DNA molecule. DNA molecules do not cause the mutation in an effort to improve the offspring. Mutation happens to the DNA molecules. With 3,000 base pairs in the average human gene, and the largest gene having 2.4 million base pairs, DNA has an enormous number of base pairs exposed to the possibility of mutation. Any number of things within the chaos system that makes up the human environment can cause mutation, such as cell division copying errors, ionizing radiation, chemical mutagens and infectious diseases.

In addition to the hardware of the DNA is the software of the *epigenome.* The epigenome refers to the collective instructions that tell the cells what to do as the body develops from a simple two-cell organism into something much more complex. Environmental factors like hunger and plenty affect the instructions of the epigenome. Rather than a dictator that determines the biological future of an organism's descendents,

DNA is a servant at the disposal of other influences. The genetic structure is an open system to outside influence.

The direction of life. Following his God-of-the-gaps mindset, Darwin thought that evolution had no place for the involvement of God because he had described a situation in which nature selects which organisms will survive and which will go extinct. In Darwin's proposal, the gradual, small mutations that occur from one generation to the next over vast periods of time give some organisms an advantage over the other members of their species under the onslaught of nature. With a change in weather patterns, from lush wetlands to dry desert, from semitropical jungle to frozen tundra, some organisms are advantaged and others disadvantaged in the competition for survival. Volcanoes, continental drift, hurricanes, forest fires and the occasional asteroid and ice age all create situations in which some animals win and others lose in the journey from simplicity to complexity. Since Darwin assumed that any activity by God must follow the scheme described by Aristotle and supported by the model of God as King, he saw no gap where God was needed or where God had anything to do.

Besides bringing an enormous number of philosophical assumptions to the table that do not come from biblical faith, Darwin made the enormous assumption that God is not involved in the rest of nature. Darwin reasoned that God had nothing to do with the evolution of the species because nature performed the function of selecting which mutations would survive. With his fundamentalist orientation, however, Darwin did not recognize that God can be active throughout all of nature. The problem of pain and suffering was a powerful emotional and intellectual issue for Darwin as he struggled with the role of God in the universe. Volcanoes, earthquakes, drought, hurricanes and asteroids cause death. Darwin's own daughter died. One may protect God from the criminal charge of murder by claiming that God is not involved in nature at all. This assertion makes it possible to say that God has no role in the mutation of animals through the genetic code or in the selection of animals through the processes of nature. But this existential declaration has nothing to do with science. It is based solely on the fact that people do not want to die.

As John Donne advised four hundred years ago:

Send not to know for whom the bell tolls;
It tolls for thee.

So often the discussions of the existence of God or the activity of God have very little to do with science and everything to do with our emotional disposition. Our emotional disposition toward death then sets us a-wondering. The question of how a good God can allow suffering and death, or, worse yet, *cause* suffering and death is a perfectly valid theological or philosophical question. It has nothing to do with science, but it is a perfectly valid question.

Without death, the universe has no direction. The early universe "died." The great plasma soup was swept away by the fundamental forces as they interacted to create atoms, and from atoms they formed stars. That first universe of stars has passed away, and a new universe of over a hundred elements has replaced it. The old universe without life died a violent, dramatic death, but without pain and suffering, in order for a new universe to take its place which is fitted for life. Death is another indicator of the kind of universe we live in. Our universe is not one in which we continue in a never-ending circle. We have passages that lead to death, which signals the direction of the universe. The problem of death for people is quite different from the problem of death for the rest of the cosmos: we know we are going to die. Eating of the tree of knowledge gives us profound understanding, but it also comes at the price of knowing that our time is limited.

Deism had placed God's involvement in establishing the laws of nature with an original act of creation which then continued without further divine involvement. Darwin's observations actually argue for a continuous involvement in selecting organisms from one generation to the next, but Darwin did not know what mechanism transmitted the information for heredity from one generation to the next. We now know that DNA carries the information that allows cells to grow with slight modifications from one generation to the next. The DNA chain is an open data program that allows for modification, the way a computer program is updated or revised from an older version to a newer version. DNA does not shift its own code around. Mutation shifts the DNA code around, which creates new information to the code that may be useful or meaningless, just like the Internet.

Chaos theory does not mean the absence of order, but it does mean that chaotic interactions are so complex that predictability becomes very difficult. The greater the complexity of the science, the lower its capacity for long-range predictability. Biology cannot predict what will happen next in evolution, except that whatever happens, it will be good for some organisms and others will go extinct. For the subject at hand, however, we can say that the lower the capacity for science to predict the future, the greater is the openness of the universe at that point for the activity of God.

8

GOD AND HISTORY

✦✦✦

Any DISCUSSION OF THE RELATIONSHIP OF GOD to the physical world must take account not only of physics, chemistry and biology, but also of human history. The question of God's involvement in nature cannot be separated from God's involvement in history. History forms the extended study of humans in social relationship. As products of star dust and biological creatures, humans are part of nature. Historians do not have the comfort about their subject that physicists and chemists enjoy. Physicists and chemists may not know with certainty the outcome of their observations, but they know that they are dealing with matter and energy. They know that four fundamental forces are at work. They know what they are studying. In the twentieth century, historians lost confidence in the idea of "world history." Historians have lost a consensus about what they are studying. They know they are studying humans over time, but they are not sure what it is about humans that they are studying. The idea that human history may be moving toward a goal or objective has metaphysical undertones that seem ominously unscientific. Perhaps it would be more helpful to point out that these undertones do not seem very naturalistic or materialistic. Confusing science with philosophies like naturalism and materialism commits the same fallacy as confusing science with a religion. Historians who commit this fallacy and confuse philosophy with history have severely limited their field of investigation as we shall see.

THEORIES OF HISTORY

History as a discipline emerged from the telling of stories. Homer's

Iliad and *Odyssey* tell stories of great heroes of the Trojan War that are designed to instill in the listener (for these stories originally were recited) the values of the culture that made them regard the heroes as great. A thousand years later Virgil (70-19 B.C.) wrote the *Aeneid*, another epic tale of the Trojan War from the perspective of the Trojans. Virgil does something quite different from Homer. His story draws a relationship between two points of time, the Trojan past and his Roman present, to show how the past creates the present and prepares for the future. Virgil wrote to explain the greatness of Rome in terms of Rome's historical antecedents, the Trojans. Augustine (354-430) stood in the cultural tradition of Virgil three hundred years later when he explained the decline of Rome as the result of actions and behaviors in the past. But Augustine also stood in the tradition of the historians of Israel.

The first five books of the Bible, known as the Pentateuch, form the heart of the law of Israel. In Hebrew tradition this section of the Bible is also known as the Torah, which is usually translated into English as "law," but which has a more nuanced meaning as "teaching," "instruction" or "tradition." The Torah involves more than the rules and commandments. It also involves the story of what God did over time in the lives of individuals as he created the nation of Israel from a single family descended from Abraham and Sarah. The giving of the commandments to Moses over five hundred years after Abraham comes relatively late in the story of God's involvement with people.

In many ways the Bible seems to be the same sort of story as the *Iliad* or the *Aeneid*. It relates the feats of great heroes with the help of the God of Abraham. It tells about how the God of Abraham created a nation from wandering nomads. These similarities can lull one into the false perception that the Bible is no different than the stories of Greece and Rome. In his discussion of epic poetry, C. S. Lewis explained that the first thing a person must do before interpreting a text is to understand what kind of text it is and what it was intended to do.[1] A huge

---

[1] C. S. Lewis, *A Preface to Paradise Lost* (New York: Oxford University Press, 1961), p. 1. Lewis spends the first sixty pages of this book explaining what an epic poem is, how it works and what it does, as he distinguishes between primary and secondary epics.

difference exists between *primary epics*, like the *Iliad* and *Bhagavad-Gita*, which tell of individual heroes and teach virtues, and *secondary epics*, like the *Aeneid*, which speaks of collective human destiny based on past exploits. The Bible does something quite different from either of these even though it has elements of both.

Several features distinguish the Torah from the great epics. First, the form of the Torah is not poetry, as was common in most Mediterranean and Near Eastern cultures. It is highly poetic and contains brief moments of striking poetry, but for the most part, it comes as prose narrative. Second, the narrative focuses on the initiatives of the God of Abraham rather than on the human actors. Third, the narrative involves promises and their fulfillment in time. Its very style and form gave to it an authority which the *Iliad* and the *Aeneid* never enjoyed within their cultures. Because God made extravagant, impossible promises that he kept over a period of generations, all of what God said and expected became sacred and binding upon the Hebrew people. Their story was their law. We shall return later to the issue of the fulfillment of promises.

Because Augustine accepted the Hebrew tradition, he accepted the idea that God works in history both to create and to destroy. Augustine's *City of God* represents the blending of the Roman and Hebrew understandings of history. During Augustine's day as the barbarian invasion resulted in Aleric's sacking of Rome in 411, many pagan writers argued that Rome's calamity resulted from the abandonment of the old gods. In *The City of God*, Augustine responded with his own historical analysis of Roman corruption and decay that led to Rome's decline.

Augustine's theory of history finds its roots in the fifth book of the Pentateuch, Deuteronomy. *Deuteronomy* is a word that means "the second law." The book represents a recapitulation of God's promises to Israel and his expectation of the nation. It includes an extensive narration of blessings that would accompany obedience to God and curses that would accompany disobedience. Augustine applied the Deuteronomic concept of history to Rome and argued that Rome's troubles came as a result of generations of immoral behavior. He also dealt with why Christians would also suffer with their pagan neighbors. Augustine argued that

God is no talisman of protection from harm to be used superstitiously by a people. Likewise, he argued that the suffering of Christians during the invasion was no sign that God had abandoned them or that he was powerless to protect them. Contrary to modern cultural Christianity, Augustine taught that Christians were called to suffer and die to demonstrate their faith in Christ, who rose from the dead.

Benedetto Croce (1866-1952), the Italian philosopher of history, drew a distinction between chronicle and history. A chronicle provides a record of an event or events. The boredom of history for many people lies in their experience of having been exposed to chronicle rather than history during their education. Many people associate history with rote memorization of a chronological table of information about events that took place. Croce contrasted chronicle with history, which explains the *meaning* of events over time. Chronicles recite the deeds of mighty men of yore, but history explains how and why those deeds shaped the world. To a certain extent, Homer's story of the *Iliad* was chronicle, but Virgil's story of the *Aeneid* was history. In the present day, however, we also ask whether the events ever actually took place. Modern people have a greater concern for factual information than for meaning. The Germans have two different words for this, story (*Geschichte*) and history (*Historie*), but French maintains the ancient relationship between story and history with a single word (*histoire*).

For centuries in the West those who studied history sought to explain the meaning of events against the backdrop of the passage of time. History provides the luxury of stepping back and contemplating the long view apart from the heat of the moment. The study of history has also assumed that the past has lessons to teach the present, by which people can avoid past mistakes. The idea of learning from the past involves the important idea that people play a role in determining their future. The Deuteronomic history of the Bible lays out options that people may choose. This view of past and future contrasts dramatically with the common view of many cultures of antiquity that humans were bound to a fate laid out for them. In most cultures of the Near East and Europe, the gods themselves are bound to their fate. The Deuteronomic history of the Bible involves a teaching that people have freedom to act in determining their future, but God has freedom to act as well.

In the Gospel record, Jesus called people to follow him. Some responded while others did not. In creation God called for things to respond, such as when he called for the waters and for the earth to bring forth life (Gen. 1:11, 20, 24). Somehow the relationship of God to the world involves a call or beckoning from God that invites a response. In terms of matter, this beckoning involves the establishment of a physical law for nature, but for people this beckoning involves the establishment of a direction of human development that has been called a moral law.

The biblical understanding of history introduces the idea of freedom in human action, but it also introduces the idea that history has a direction from beginning to end. This linear view of history contrasts dramatically with the cyclical or circular view of history present in the pagan societies of nature religion with their emphasis on fertility. The nature religions reflected the cycles of nature seen in crops, from birth to maturity to death to rebirth. The culture of ancient Egypt, dependent as it was on the seasonal flooding of the Nile to replenish the soil by laying down fresh layers of silt, built massive monuments to the unchanging nature of things. The rigid formality of Egyptian architecture, with its long walls and rows of columns and statues, lays out the path set for all to follow from the lowliest slave to the god pharaoh. The unchanging nature of things was state policy for Japan and China until forced to change by the West in the nineteenth century through military intervention.

A cyclical view of history does not lend itself to the development of scientific methods of inquiry and observation, with the exception of astronomy, which involved plotting the cycles of the heavenly bodies in order to learn what fate had in store. With the adoption of a view of history that progressed from past to future in linear fashion, however, a new understanding of the world came into existence that allowed for observation and repetitive experimentation. In many ways, the experimental sciences are a form of history.

Scientific data is history in its purest form. It involves the chronicle of a series of experiments or observations, but this carefully tabulated raw data of the chronicle requires interpretation. Scientific data is a record of the past rather than the present, regardless of how recently the data was collected. Scientific data is nothing but meaningless information until someone interprets it to discover relationships, coincidence and meaning. Intellect assigns meaning to data. A popular materialistic aphorism states: The universe has no meaning; it just is. This aphorism is almost true. The universe has no meaning until it is *interpreted*. A great number of historians in the late twentieth and early twenty-first centuries began to argue that history has no meaning or purpose because, they suppose, this view sounds more "scientific."

Science, history and religion have had an interesting relationship since the late seventeenth century, when the West began to push God out of the universe. The argument for God's noninvolvement in the universe is rather simple, though problematic from a purely logical point of view. Though *God of the gaps* is a recent term, it is not a new idea. The human race has long tended to say that what it did not understand in the physical world was to be explained by the direct action of God. As soon as people could describe the process of a phenomenon, they concluded that God had nothing to do with it. It was "natural." With the successes of chemistry, astronomy and physics in the seventeenth century, a new religious idea developed that taught that God created the world and established the moral and physical laws of nature, but is no longer involved in the continuum of cause and effect. We call this view *deism*. The logic of this view may be stated as: I can describe what I observe; therefore, God is not involved. The underlying assumption of this logic is that if I can describe something, then God could not have been involved in it.

Deism led to a new approach to history that continued to recognize the linear direction of history and the idea that history has some underlying meaning, but without the God of Abraham. The philosophers wanted a more scientific history that allowed for meaning without God. In *The History of the Decline and Fall of the Roman Empire*, Edward Gibbon (1737-1794) presented just such an approach. Gibbon focused his study on efficient causes. Though he attributes the fall of Rome to "the triumph of barbarism and religion," he discusses religion, or the success of Christianity, exclusively in terms of cultural matters without reference to any activity by God. Gibbon was influenced by Montesquieu, Voltaire, Locke and Hume, but his *Decline and Fall* quickly became a watershed approach to history that continues to be influential despite its many errors of fact and judgment.

Georg Wilhelm Friedrich Hegel (1770-1831) developed a philosophy of history based on Spirit or Mind (*Geist*) manifesting itself in a meaningful way. Over time Mind becomes aware of itself, recognizes its transcendence and realizes that it has the freedom to act as the subject of its activity. History is made up of epochs in which Mind, understood as humans, makes advances, but each epoch is also incomplete and full of error. In history, Mind moves gradually toward a state of completeness or final perfection. This view finds the meaning of history in the goal toward which it moves, but the meaning comes from within the process of Mind expressing itself in dialectic process. Hegel redefined *dialectic*, the old Greek philosophical term for the concept of logic, in terms of his own concept of thesis answered by antithesis resolved in synthesis, which forms the new thesis. Notably, Hegel's approach has rid itself of God, but his system depends on the biblical assumptions of freedom, linear progress and an ultimate goal. Karl Marx (1818-1883) built on Hegel's system for his philosophy of history. Marx did not consider his work philosophical at all but scientific. He interpreted history as the struggle toward a utopian workers' society free of wages, money, classes and government. The system of Marx replaces freedom with determinism, which seemed more scientific before quantum mechanics.

In the midst of the great ideological wars of the first half of the twentieth century that brought the colonial period to an end, several philosophers of history struggled to understand the rise and fall of civilizations. Oswald Spengler (1880-1936), working in Germany, published *The Decline of the West* in 1918. In it he distinguished between science, which looks for causes, and history, which seeks out destiny. Science is systematic and looks for universal laws that operate regardless of time or place. History, on the other hand, must deal with unique cultures that arise and express themselves in a variety of ways without the constant necessary for scientific study. While the scientist relies on systematic method, the historian must have "intuitive vision."[2] Spengler viewed cultures analogically as organisms that pass through four stages of life before dying: childhood, youth, manhood and old age. He added to the poetic metaphor by speaking of the spring, summer, autumn and winter of a culture. He returned to the pre-Christian cyclical view of history that lacks linear direction toward a goal that Hegel and Marx had retained from a biblical view of history, while embracing the determinism of the cyclical view. Each culture lives and dies on its own without an overarching direction for human history.

In contrast to Spengler's view, Arnold Toynbee (1889-1975), working in England, developed a different understanding of the rise and fall of civilizations. In *A Study of History*, published in twelve volumes beginning in 1934 and not completed until 1961, Toynbee recognizes the cyclical patterns of civilizations, but notes that young civilizations borrow from older civilizations as history moves in a forward progression. Civilizations develop and flourish when *mimesis* or imitation is focused on creative personalities who command a following rather than focusing on the past. Civilizations flourish in the delicate balance between challenge for survival and creative response. Toynbee had a greater appreciation for empirical study than Spengler and sought to correct Spengler's disregard for the facts. Toynbee also found fault with "antinomian historians" who denied that history contained any patterns. Toynbee saw patterns and sought to understand them.

Toynbee's conclusions surprised him. He concluded that all existing civilizations in the twentieth century had their backgrounds in a "universal church" that had survived a previous civilization. The earliest civilizations fostered higher religion from which later civilizations developed universal churches that survived the collapse of the civilization. Despite his lack of religious convictions at the beginning of his study, Toynbee argued that the rise and fall of civilizations is a vehicle for carrying forward religion in which the multiplicity and repetitiveness of civilizations is contrasted with the unitary and progressive nature of

---

[2]Oswald Spengler, *The Decline of the West: Form and Actuality*, vol. 1, trans. Charles Francis Atkinson (New York: Alfred A. Knopf, 1950), p. 102. Spengler argues that "poetry and history are kin."

religion. In contrast with the tradition of the Enlightenment, Toynbee felt compelled to conclude that the meaning of history and the future of the human race is found in religion.

SCIENCE AND HISTORY

History sought to become a scientific discipline in the eighteenth century, which meant gradually moving to the view that history has no meaning, because the universe has no meaning. In an odd twist, science had deferred to history for an explanation for meaning, but history abandoned its proper role in order to be a discipline it could never be. History cannot use the method of chemistry and physics because of its subject matter. It may borrow the qualities of objectivity, careful observation and extensive tabulation of data that mark the scientific method, but many historians confuse the scientific method with philosophical views held by some scientists about what can be known and what can exist.

The certainty, determinacy, infinity and eternity of the eighteenth-century universe have now been replaced by a much smaller, younger, open and uncertain universe. Does such a universe have anything to say to history about the possibility of meaning and purpose? Do physics, chemistry, cosmology and biology have something to say about history? Is the eighteenth-century view of history in need of revision in light of the radical revisions to the scientific understanding of the universe since the deists?

The mechanical universe of the eighteenth century was infinite in size and eternal in duration. It had always been. It was a static thing. Yes, it moved, but it moved with an inevitable determinacy without beginning or end in its cycles. It was static. In such a universe Hume imagined an infinite number of possibilities, eon after eon, which would inevitably result in life happening by chance. Charles Darwin was born and lived in Hume's universe. In an eternal universe of infinite possibilities, life did not depend on anything but chance. In such a universe, it was natural to think of evolution and natural selection as the same thing.

In this eternal, infinite universe Edgar Allan Poe (1809-1849) was called a mad man when he proposed that the universe began from a single "primordial particle" from which everything expanded outward. For the first three quarters of the twentieth century, Poe biographers discussed the "misapplications and misapprehensions of the data of science" found in Poe's *Eureka* (1848) and explained it by suggesting that Poe "was very ill, mentally and physically, when he wrote it."[3] Now we live in Poe's universe. It had a very hot beginning, and the latest measurements strongly suggest that it will have a very cold end. The idea of a rhythmic, pulsating universe that expands and contracts seems put to bed for the present. We have the hypothesis of a multiverse, but we have no proposal for how to move the hypothesis to scientific theory by means of experimental observation. For the moment, we live in a universe that has a direction.

History, or the course of humanity on earth, has a direction because every level of organization below the complexity of human life and social organization has a direction. As we have seen, with the movement from simplicity to complexity at every level, the universe expresses a valuing of progress, but with self-conscious life, the meaning of progress and other values takes on new depth and breadth. Some things are good for progress while other things are bad. At the human level, however, the meaning of progress grows in multiple layers.

Unlike the rest of the universe, humans tell their own story and reflect on their own experience of what is good and bad. Progress involves improvement of the experience of life in terms of increasing what seems good and decreasing what seems bad. The experience of good and bad provides an incentive to encourage the human race toward the future. When people learn from bad experience they take steps to prepare against the cold and against drought. The pursuit of something good, whether the food or property of other people, results in what the other person experiences as bad against them. We may experience the same activity as good until someone stronger takes what belongs to us. Pain and suffering teach us something about ourselves and urge the progress of society.

---

[3]Hervey Allen, *Israfel* (New York: Farrar & Rhinehart, 1934), pp. 591-92.

The Bible as a historical resource. Secular history focuses on chronicling the events of the past, the development of technology, conquests of rulers, the growth and collapses of empires and the development of ideas. When considering the place of God in history, the focus falls elsewhere. God cares about the progress in how people treat each other. Kingdoms, artifacts and knowledge come as byproducts of the trajectory God has in mind for human history. Inflicting pain and suffering on someone weaker seems a good way to get ahead and experience an advantage as humans emerged from the collective ooze of life, but violence as a bad thing appears as the earliest lesson God teaches humans across the span of their interaction. From the earliest pages of Genesis through the books of the prophets, God condemns individual, institutional and cultural violence. The punishment for violence is violence. Though we normally think of religion as an institution designed to prop up, reinforce and defend the power structure of a culture, the Bible records an experience of centuries across several cultures in which God speaks counterculturally.

God does not treat people as mere objects in the biblical narrative, even in the earliest periods when we might expect it from the general ethos of Near Eastern culture 3,500 years ago and earlier. God offers alternative choices. God gives warnings. God allows wrong choices. In all of this, God models behavior for people to treat each other as people rather than as mere things.

The Bible is a unique document of human history, whether God exists or not. It is a narrative of a defeated people that spans over a thousand years of written history and even more of oral tradition. At one time in the early development of higher criticism in the nineteenth century, it was popular to regard the Hebrew Bible as a product of the Jewish community in Palestine during the Persian period and later, which was intended to relegate figures like Abraham, Moses and David to historical myth-making by the priestly community. Development in higher critical method, involving advances in cultural and archaeological studies, now indicate the antiquity of the Abrahamic, Mosaic, Davidic and other early accounts. The narratives make frequent reference to customs related to family structure, marriage, village organi-

zation, religious practices and geographical sites that had long since
been forgotten by the time of the Babylonian conquest, which modern
archaeology and anthropology confirm. The Bible is a panorama of a
people of faith who live in a variety of cultures in which they are the
minority over a period of more than fifteen hundred years. The text
reflects oral history from the clash of a hunter-gatherer society with
stable agriculture communities, migrations of the Semitic Akkadian
culture into Mesopotamia, Canaanite culture following the collapse of
the old Babylonian kingdom, Egyptian culture Hebrew tribal culture,
Israelite culture, Babylonian culture, and Persian culture. By the time
the books of the New Testament were written, we must add the experience of Greco-Roman or Hellenistic culture. Such a narrative has no
parallel in any other culture or time period on earth. It is an anthropological gold mine.

In the historical context of ancient Near-Eastern despotic rulers,
God is represented as concerned for barren women, which was considered a mark of divine displeasure. God is concerned for slaves. God
favors younger sons over older sons. God continually goes against the
cultural pattern of the people who worship him.

Though the Bible describes God as manipulating the heavens and
the earth like someone setting up a tent or rearranging the furniture, it
describes God's relationships with people in a different way. The Bible
claims that God moves historical events with the same authority and
power that he moves the direction of the universe, but the mechanism
for the experience of authority is different. By the prophets, God made
dramatic claims that he would hand Israel over to Nebuchadnezzar,
king of Babylon (Jer 27:8). He declared that he would bring judgment
on the nations, leading to ruin, devastation, death, famine and destruction (Jer 25:15-38). He claimed to hand over Zedekiah, king of
Judah, to Nebuchadnezzar and that he would hand over Pharaoh
Hophra of Egypt to his enemies (Jer 44:30). God is credited with
sending King Rezin and King Pekah against Judah (2 Kings 15:37).
God calls Cyrus of Persia "his anointed" even though Cyrus did not
acknowledge him as God (Is 45:1, 4-5).

On the other hand, the instruments of destruction who carry out the judgment of God do not receive a reward for their efforts. They destroyed Israel from their own selfish motives. They did not consider themselves engaged in a holy crusade for God. They did not wreak havoc to please God but to satisfy their own desires. God declared that he would punish Nebuchadnezzar and the Babylonians for their guilt in their violence against Judah (Jer 25:12). Assyria was the instrument of God to punish Israel, but it was not a self-conscious servant. Assyria was useful because of its own sinfulness and received punishment in return (Is 10:5, 7, 12, 15). After warning Judah that it must alter its victimization of the poor or face punishment, God declared,

> But all who devour you will be devoured;
>   all your enemies will go into exile.
> Those who plunder you will be plundered;
>   all who make spoil of you I will despoil. (Jer 30:16)

God "sent" the hostile armies to attack Israel and Judah by ceasing to protect his people. He ceased to constrain the nations and gave free reign to their inclinations for land, wealth, power and fame. When God removes his influence, chaos ensues.

Human spirit. But what is the mechanism by which God influences and constrains people? The prophets frequently spoke of God "stirring up" someone to action (Is 41:2-4; Jer 51:11; Hag 1:14), both to destroy Jerusalem and rebuild Jerusalem. More specifically, God stirs the *spirit* or the *heart* of people. In Hebrew thought, the heart is the metaphor for the human spirit. The heart should not be understood in this poetic sense as the physical organ where the spirit resides. Instead, the heart represents the spirit. In Hebrew poetry, we may say that heart "rhymes" with spirit, as in the psalm of David:

> Create in me a *clean heart*, O God,
>   and renew a *right spirit* within me. (Ps 51:10, italics added)

In this passage, "clean heart" and "right spirit" mean the same thing.

In Hebrew thought expressed throughout the Bible, the human spirit is not a ghost that inhabits a body. The body and spirit form a psychosomatic unity. The body affects the spirit and the spirit affects the body, because they are no more separable in a person than flesh and blood. Translations of the Bible usually refer to this unity as "soul," but in modern language it might be more appropriately translated as "person." In English, the word *person* and the word *soul* are interchangeable. The Greek philosophical tradition, with its pagan background, has an entirely different understanding of soul and spirit that influenced several important theologians, like Augustine and Thomas Aquinas, but this study focuses on the biblical faith rather than the philosophical tradition of the West.

In Hebrew thought people experience many things through their bodies, but they experience other things through their spirits or hearts. In the Bible the human spirit is the domain of intellect, character, emotion, will, imagination and vitality. These qualities of human spirit are not separate functions that can be isolated from each other. Rather, they exist in a dynamic relationship with each other. A modern analogy would be water, which technically speaking is a compound of oxygen and hydrogen. As water, however, the oxygen and hydrogen become a third thing dynamically different from its parts.

God acts in history by interaction with human spirit. Process theologians tend to speak only of the mind, that intellectual dimension of humans, but the biblical narrative indicates that God has a much greater understanding of what it means to be human. At the conclusion of the Chronicles, we are told that God "moved the heart of Cyrus" (2 Chron 36:22) to allow the rebuilding of the temple in Jerusalem. The impulse toward morality and generosity, justice and mercy, kindness and compassion does not simply "emerge" naturally of itself from base and selfish brute animal impulses. In the biblical narrative, God draws these qualities forth over time through involvement with people (Zech 7:8-14).

Do we have any evidence that divine encounter with people actually has occurred such that it can be distinguished from the "natural" flow of history? Other than the biblical claim that God has guided history, is there anything about the biblical texts, in the context of the cultures in which they were written over time, that suggests that the flow of history corresponds to the claims about God? As it happens we do find such a subtext within the grand sweep of the biblical narrative that fits well with a modern Western value system, but which stands oddly out of place in its original context stretching back more than fifteen hundred years before the rise of imperial Rome.

THE DIRECTION OF MORALITY

One of the disturbing aspects of God's dealing with Israel in the first half of the Bible concerns the pervasive violence that punctuates the story. The human story begins with the specter of death hanging over humanity as the ever-present background of life. The enormity of violence in the early chapters of Genesis reflects what we would expect in a world in which the competition for dominance within a species requires winners and losers. Whereas most species move forward by the small variations from generation to generation that give one animal a greater advantage in survival than their neighbors, which often involves skill in getting food and not becoming food, humans tend to kill their human competition.

In his brief discussion of the development of religion in human society in *The Problem of Pain*, C. S. Lewis identifies the experience of the numinous as the first stage. The second stage involves the appearance of morality. Moral judgment is not found in the facts of experience; rather, people bring the sense of morality to the experience. The third stage of religious development occurs when people identify the numinous as the source and foundation for morality.[4] Morality did not come to humanity, however, as a fully developed attribute. The development of morality came in stages that the Bible reflects.

What one would not expect of the Bible is the movement of the story from a God involved in violence and death to a God who enters into space-time for the purpose of experiencing violence and death in order to free people from violence and death. The biblical interpretation of the human story reflects the same linear movement that we find at all levels of organization in the universe. Does this movement represent a changing view of God by a variety of cultures over time, or does this movement represent a change in cultures over time as a result of inter-

---

[4]C. S. Lewis, *The Problem of Pain* (New York: Macmillan, 1948), pp. 4-11.

action with God? Is God merely an artifact of humanity, or is humanity an artifact of God? What makes the Bible a valuable resource in approaching these questions is that it does not have a single author with a single perspective or thesis to argue by marshaling supportive data. It was not written as a theory of how God changed culture. Any pattern that may be present cannot be seen in the details of the text but by stepping back from it. Yet, even in the selection of details by authors who never knew each other, separated by centuries as they were, the narrative normally focuses on the hinge moment when a person goes through a change, transformation or conversion from one way of understanding the world, or one way of behaving, to another.

Innocence. In the garden Adam and Eve lived in a state of innocence. Innocence is a neutral state of existence. It implies the absence of negative characteristics such as wickedness, evil and guilt. Innocence involves the absence of malice or wrong intentions. The absence of negative content has tended to give innocence a positive connotation it does not necessarily deserve. Innocence comes from not knowing. To the Athenians, Paul used the term "ignorance" (Acts 17:30). While Adam and Eve could not do anything morally bad in a state of innocence, they could not do anything good either. They knew neither good nor evil. They were totally innocent.

Innocence also had other ramifications for Adam and Eve. They were the center of their universe. Everything existed for them, and they viewed everything quite possessively. They even named all the other creatures. The account of the Fall illustrates the egocentric and impulsive character of innocence. Even God held a secondary position to the urges of the creatures. They explored things around them because it was their world.

For all its simplicity and purity, innocence is not the same as holiness or righteousness. Unlike the neutral character of innocence in which neither good nor evil are possibilities, holiness and righteousness are positive attributes. These attributes are exclusive qualities of God. They are not merely the absence of evil; they are the presence and nature of God. Though people began with innocence, they did not begin with holiness. Holiness would come later as a distinct act of creation by God beyond the natural physical dimension of creation and birth.

God appears never to have intended for the creatures to remain in a state of innocence. On the contrary, his eternal plan calls for depth of knowledge and understanding as the great prayers of Ephesians make plain. The prayer in Ephesians 1:16-19 calls for a spirit of wisdom and of revelation in the knowledge of God. The possibility for these qualities and deep faith only comes with enlightenment. Rather than dwell in perpetual innocence, God intended that people should comprehend the breadth and length and height and depth of the love of Christ which is beyond knowledge (Eph 3:18-19).

Paul looked forward to the endpoint of God's plan when he declared: "Now we see but a poor reflection as in a mirror; then we shall see face to face. Now I know in part; then I shall know fully, even as I am fully known" (1 Cor 13:12).

Knowledge, understanding and wisdom play a part in God's purpose for people. Holiness becomes a possibility for people only when wickedness becomes a possibility. Without knowledge, neither option is a possibility.

Punishment. In the opening chapters of Genesis, humans have no particular sense of moral concern. Self-interest drives the decisions that the narrative discusses. A sense of right and wrong relates exclusively to consequences. Moral judgment is no different from that of other animals. Something is wrong if it involves pain and suffering. Otherwise, behavior has no limits. The human understanding of right and wrong begins when God warns people that punishment will follow certain behaviors. At this level of moral understanding, people do not arrive at a sense of moral values through intellectual reflection but through physical or emotional pain. The prehistorical section of Genesis mentions no other moral understanding than punishment, which is an interesting matter if this material was a creation of the postexilic period when the community of faith had a vastly different basis for moral understanding. By the postexilic period, we find a variety of approaches to moral decision making, which we would expect to be reflected in the text of Genesis if it dated from that late period. As we move through the Bible, we will find people continually regressing to a lower form of morality. By analogy, we find simple forms of life throughout the fossil record, but we do not find higher forms of life in the most ancient strata of the fossil record.[5]

Reward. With the appearance of Abraham, something radically different happens with human moral understanding. With Abraham, God finds a person who begins to understand moral choice on the basis of reward. People had experienced grace prior to Abraham, but we do not find God using reward for behavior before Abraham. While reward still involves selfishness or self-interest, it is a dramatic advance above pain as a motivation. It is the difference between the carrot and the stick. If Abraham will leave his culture and community and travel to another culture where he has no safety and protection from others, God will cause Abraham's very old wife to have a baby. We also see an intriguing effort by people to manipulate God on this same level of moral understanding. Jacob attempts to barter with God by offering God a "reward" if he will only do something for him. Jacob offers to give God a 10 percent cut if God will make Jacob rich (Gen 28:20-22).

Reward has another important ingredient. Reward points toward the future. Reliance on reward means believing a promise and deferred gratification. The relational dimension of this level of morality involves trusting the promises of someone who keeps promises. Thus, the understanding of morality provides a foundation for beginning to see the world in a linear way that moves to the future.

Group expectation. With the sons of Jacob and the tribes that develop from their offspring, the expectations of the group grow more powerful than fear of suffering or desire for reward. The community may risk disaster and forgo advantage for the sake of what the group wants to do. Peer pressure cuts both ways. It may restrain behavior and cause one to reflect on "what would the neighbors think?" On the other hand, the group provides the kind of anonymity that allows people to go to excesses they would never have pursued on their own. The group may become the mob.

---

[5]This study assumes an early date for the books of the Pentateuch, which is based largely on the presence in the text of place names and customs that had long since disappeared by the post-exilic period. Much of this cultural history of the ancient world had been lost until archaeological and anthropological developments in the twentieth century.

When the brothers of Joseph decide to kill him, Judah does not want to do it, but he has no choice. He cannot go against the group. When the Hebrew people decide to return to the worship of the gods of Egypt while Moses is away on the mountain speaking with God, Aaron fashions a golden calf for them. From his perspective Aaron has to do it because he cannot go against the group. After the giving of the law, however, we begin to see isolated cases of people who are willing to stand up to the group, as is the case with Joshua and Caleb when they dissented from the majority report of the spies who investigated the Promised Land (Num 13:26–14:9).

Law. The law of Moses contains a proportionate understanding of punishment, but it defaults to a punishment basis for enforcement of the moral code. On the other hand, the law is presented to Israel on the basis of reward. If Israel will keep the law, great rewards will follow. God makes promises to Israel as a community and expects the community to enforce the law.[6] With the giving of the law and the establishment of a covenant with Israel, nothing new has actually happened. The Babylonians had the codified law of Hammurabi a thousand years before Moses.

Several centuries later, however, something new happens in relation to law and morality. King David has an entirely different attitude toward the law: a person does not follow the law to avoid punishment or to gain reward. One does not even follow the law because of the group expectation. A person follows the law because the law is good. Throughout the psalms he composed, David sang of the law as a gift from God and a thing to be prized:

> Blessed is the man
>   who does not walk in the counsel of the wicked
> or stand in the way of sinners

---

[6]In terms of the covenants that we find God making with people, it is important to distinguish the covenant with Abraham from the covenant with the nation of Israel. As we see in the Deuteronomic history of Israel, the covenant with Abraham remains in effect even after Israel forfeits its integrity as a political state. The covenant with Israel, which included civil and religious matters, came to an end with the conquest of Israel by Babylon, but God continually promised that he would make a new covenant with the people unlike the one mediated by Moses (Jer 31:31).

or sit in the seat of mockers.
But his delight is in the law of the LORD,
and on his law he meditates day and night. (Ps 1:1)

While this attitude forges the basis for legalism and the rigid view that "the law is the law," it provides a much more stable basis for human society than the lower forms of moral orientation.

At the heart of this attitude toward the law lies David's view of God. David does not regard God as capricious like the other deities of the ancient Near East at that time. God is faithful, steady and consistent. God provides a sure point of reference. Despite David's own moral fluctuations in which he violated most of the Ten Commandments, the Bible calls David "a man after God's own heart." The catalytic change in attitude toward law as good comes about because of a significant experience that David has with God, according to the biblical narrative. The experience might have fallen to Saul who also had powerful spiritual experiences but who enjoyed them as an end in themselves. Saul did not choose God the way God chose Saul, for Saul was not after God but power.

Higher principle. For several centuries the idea of the goodness of the law gained strength, but political turmoil also arose. Civil war resulted in a divided kingdom split between Israel in the north and Judah in the south. The ceremonial law continued as before with its elaborate temple worship and sacrificial system. Under the cover of a fervent religion, however, the moral dimension of the law suffered.

Over a period of centuries a steady stream of prophets who claimed to speak for God brought messages to the political and religious establishment and to the people. Their message may be summarized by a startling pronouncement from Amos to the northern kingdom of Israel during the reign of Jeroboam in the eighth century before Christ:

I hate, I despise your religious feasts;
I cannot stand your assemblies.
Even though you bring me burnt offerings and grain offerings,
I will not accept them.
Though you bring choice fellowship offerings,
I will have no regard for them.

Away with the noise of your songs!
  I will not listen to the music of your harps.
But let justice roll on like a river,
    righteousness like a never-failing stream! (Amos 5:21-24)

Something lies behind the law to which the law points. The law merely represents a means to achieve the higher principle of justice. Higher principles are at stake, which the law only serves to advance. When the law becomes an end in itself, however, it only becomes a burden that may actually prevent the purpose for which it was intended. Of course, the problem with higher principles raises the issue of how the principles may be known. This view may also generate foundationless relativism. Is a higher principle only a personal preference, or is a higher principle rooted in some eternal, objective value? The prophets claimed that the new interpretation of the law and the history of Israel came from God through dreams, visions and voices. Once they had these experiences, however, they were willing to go against the force of community opinion and the power of the political and religious authorities to deliver their message. They had no doubt about the authenticity of their experience. What resulted from the experiences was a radical new way of conceiving of morality and ethics. Before the prophets of Israel, other people like the warriors in Homer's *Iliad* had appealed to their core values such as duty and courage, but these operate at the group expectation level. The appeal to higher principles that stood above the group, the king or the religion was new.

Costly morality. With the coming of Jesus the basis for morality comes full circle with a paradoxical shift. Instead of doing the right thing to avoid suffering, Jesus does the right thing in spite of suffering. With Jesus, enduring the suffering is the cost of loving people. Thus the cross of Christ is not the great tragedy of a failed ministry. The cross is the goal of ministry. Jesus intentionally embraced suffering. Many martyrs from many religious and political traditions have done so as testimony to the depth of their convictions. The death of Jesus, of course, only has meaning if God actually broke into history, time and space completely. By taking on flesh God would have absolutely interfered, violated or intervened in the physical world. The gospel claims that such an intervention took place with Jesus.

By taking on human life, including birth and death, God experienced suffering from the inside. Thus the author of Hebrews declares the good news that God is sympathetic with us because he knows how it feels. And because he knows how it feels, he is able to help us in our own weakness (Heb 1:9-18; 4:14-16).

Observations on moral development. Fundamentalists, legalists and other literalists tend to read the Bible as a flat document, like the income tax code. The Bible tells a different story that involves God relating to different people in different ways, depending on how they respond through resistance or cooperation. In the self-consciousness of the peoples involved in the biblical narrative, the critical change in attitude and moral orientation came as the result of a personal encounter with God. In the encounter they had the option of responding differently. The biblical narrative follows the stream of those who responded to God positively over centuries. God selects those who respond in a way that moves the story along.

We also note that in the biblical narrative intermittent moral failure does not mean rejection by God. Abraham, Moses and David failed from time to time, but all remained committed to the relationship with God. God remains committed to the relationship with them, but we find God relating to people on the moral level at which they have chosen to live. Throughout the biblical narrative we find that people sink to the subhuman level in which they only understand morality as a function of punishment. Thus the theme of divine punishment continues throughout the narrative for those who choose to live at a subhuman level. When someone begins to function at a higher moral level in some area of life, they will continue to retain lower levels of morality in other areas of life:

> Even a man who is pure in heart
>   and says his prayers at night,
> Can exceed the speed limit when the wolfbane blooms,
>   and no patrol cars are in sight.[7]

---

[7]With apologies to *The Wolf Man* (1941), directed by George Waggner.

The good news of the biblical narrative concerns how God finally settles the problem of human immorality by entering into time and space, taking on human flesh, dying in our place, conquering sin and death, and rising from the dead with a transformed body. Just as new forms of life appeared over millions of years from old forms of life, the biblical story proposes that God has begun to change people into a form of life that continues beyond the grave and transcends physical existence. The focus of this transformation involves the spiritual dimension of people, which also provides the elusive locus for interaction with God. The Holy Spirit who transforms us into children of God also interacts with us cognitively.

HUMAN IMAGINATION

With the human imagination we find an opening in the cause-and-effect continuum of the universe through which God may interact with people. Imagination comprises one aspect of human spirit. To a great extent the modern world does not take imagination seriously as a reliable source of knowledge. We have tended to relegate it to the impractical world of painters, composers, novelists, poets and their ilk. We do not think of imagination as having anything to do with reality. Imagination is a means of escaping reality for many people.

Some forms of knowledge have their basis in physical experience, such as seeing, hearing, smelling, touching and tasting. This kind of knowledge, which comes to us through our body, we call empirical knowledge. Dogs experience empirical knowledge and so do clams. The simplest organisms with nerve endings and a rudimentary nervous system use empiricism. One might argue successfully that sunflowers and daylilies that demonstrate light sensitivity experience a form of empiricism. Empiricism is the lowest form of knowledge that humans have, rising slightly above automatic functions like breathing and blinking. One of the most foolish philosophical movements of the last three thousand years was positivism (and its near relation logical positivism). At the beginning of the twentieth century these schools of thought argued that only things that can be known through the senses actually exist. Though the positivist schools of thought were easily discredited, they have had a profound influence on the average person's ideas about what we can know and what can exist.

Our ancestors plodded along through forest and field with scarcely anything to distinguish themselves from other animals for hundreds of thousands of years. They made a tool of primitive design every hundred thousand years or so, and then an explosion of creativity and ingenuity came spurting forth. The trajectory of the human race arched suddenly skyward in the last fifty thousand years. The acquisition of knowledge and the production of artifacts accelerated with the creation of more sophisticated societies. Human culture came into being just as stars had originally gathered in the early universe. Something that had never been before came into being. People began to imagine on a grand scale.

One reason that we have so identified the imagination with fiction and fantasy is because the Romantic poets took such an interest in imagination in contrast to the love of rationality by an earlier generation. In a famous letter William Blake (1757-1827) discussed imagination in relation to his painting:

> To me this world is all one continued vision of fancy or imagination, and I feel flattered when I am told so. What is it sets Homer, Virgil and Milton in so high a rank of art? Why is the Bible more entertaining and instructive than any other book? Is it not because they are addressed to the imagination, which is spiritual sensation, and but mediately to the understanding or reason? Such is true painting, and such alone valued by the Greeks and the best modern artists. Consider what Lord Bacon says: "Sense sends over to Imagination before Reason have judged, and Reason sends over to Imagination before the decree can be acted."[8]

Samuel Taylor Coleridge (1772-1834) and William Wordsworth (1770-1850) joined Blake in extolling the imagination, but they did so as poets who contrasted poetic knowledge with scientific knowledge, and somehow science always came out the loser. In his "Preface to Lyrical Ballads," Wordsworth tended to associate imagination with

---

[8]William Blake, "To the Rev. Dr. Trusler," in *Anthology of Romanticism*, ed. Ernest Bernbaum, 3rd ed. (New York: Ronald Press, 1948), p. 129.

feelings and passion while dismissing science as cold and remote. Wordsworth condescended to remark,

> If the time should ever come when what is now called science, thus familiarized to men, shall be ready to put on, as it were, a form of flesh and blood, the poet will lend his divine spirit to aid the transfiguration, and will welcome the being thus produced as a dear inmate of the household of man.[9]

Discussions of this sort that stood at the center of intellectual conversation in Great Britain at the beginning of the nineteenth century made it easy for the culture at large to think of imagination as the sphere of the arts while rationalism and empiricism belonged to the sciences as the basis for knowledge.

While the Romantic poets saw science and poetry as two entirely different enterprises, Edgar Allan Poe came to see them profoundly alike. He created the mystery story in 1841 as a demonstration of how the exercise of imagination by the detective leads to knowledge. In 1848 Poe published *Eureka*, his extravagant essay on everything in which he first proposed the big bang theory and the basic principles of relativity. Poe called this essay a "prose poem" because he regarded science as a poetic exercise. The introduction to the essay involves a comic science-fiction story set a thousand years in the future in which people in vast flying machines comment on the silliness of the ancients who thought that empiricism and rationalism were superior forms of knowledge to imagination.[10]

What Poe and most great scientists understand is that new scientific knowledge does not come from doing the old science harder. The imagination is the human faculty that sees what has never been seen before when a new scientific breakthrough occurs. Imagination visualizes what has never been. Imagination involves the ability to see what is not, to recognize what is unknown, to understand the unintelligible

---

[9]William Wordsworth, "Preface to Lyrical Ballads," in *Anthology of Romanticism*, ed. Ernest Bernbaum, 3rd ed. (New York: Ronald Press, 1948), p. 306.

[10]For a full discussion on Poe's understanding of science, the big bang and relativity, and how imagination leads us to new knowledge, see Harry Lee Poe, *Evermore: Edgar Allan Poe and the Mystery of the Universe* (Waco, Tex.: Baylor University Press, 2012).

and to name the mysterious. Imagination peers through the mist and sees clearly. Imagination creates the future. Imagination knows what has not been known. Imagination grasps the parts and sees the whole. Imagination does something quite different than mere rationalism or calculation. Induction, deduction and other forms of logical reasoning attempt to tell us what is. Imagination tells us what *could* be. An astronomer can do the math of Ptolemy's universe over and over without ever reaching the Copernican universe by calculation. Calculation can never take us outside the past and what is already known unless it has a guide. Imagination points the way.

The history of the sciences, in fact the history of human progress in all areas of knowledge, is the story of people who suddenly understood something, often by analogy or correspondence, the way that poetry works. Reason and sensory experience play a part in the advance of knowledge, but they are tools at the disposal of imagination.

It is not necessary to be a Copernicus, Newton or Einstein to experience imagination in the same way that they did. Everyone experiences the same remarkable capacity of imagination to see things in a new light. Anyone who has lacked the right tool to do a job in the garage or the kitchen has had the experience of discovering another way to do the job by the same poetic power of analogy that imagination provides. We see that a dime is really like a screw driver. Thomas Edison "saw" a wire glowing with brilliant light as a result of running a charge of electricity through it long before he discovered what kind of wire he would need to use. Imagination visualizes questions and wonderings. Lightning lights up the night sky, and lightning is just electricity. What would it be like to capture lightning in a glass jar the way we capture lightning bugs? Poe was quite right. Science is poetry.

It is not the purpose of this book to prove that God exists. In fact, one of the presuppositions of this book is that God exists. The book merely suggests avenues God has available for interacting with the physical world. Any discussion of imagination, however, requires some treatment of the argument that God is a figment of human imagination. This argument is a polite way of stating the position of the Soviet state that religious people suffer from psychosis. Richard

Dawkins makes reference to the same argument when he speaks of "the God delusion." By this view, belief in God is a form of mental illness like believing that little green men are under the bed.

The mental illness view of imagination is based on the very real phenomenon of paranoiacs who "hear voices" and "see things." As a prison chaplain I knew a man who claimed to have been visited by an angel who asked him to prove his love for God by sacrificing his wife. He obliged. Another man was visited by an angel who warned him that the only way to protect his daughter from the mark of the Beast was to send her on to be with Jesus. Send her on he did. While these kinds of experiences tell us that human minds are susceptible to terrible frailty, they tell us nothing about whether God exists. It is important for reasoning people to recognize this difference lest they fall into another example of mental frailty known as the logical fallacy.

Almost everyone hears voices and sees things every day. We do not normally talk about it because it is such a commonplace occurrence. We visualize where we will eat lunch. We visualize meetings on our schedule. We rehearse in our minds the conversations we will have with people. Our imaginations combine our memories of people, places and events together with our feelings about them to create dramas that unfold before our minds. Normal people see visions and hear voices. The fact that mentally ill people also see visions and hear voices does not disqualify the legitimacy of our experiences of imagination. Like our emotions and our reason, our imagination is prone to error. Human emotion is often regarded as the least reliable aspect of the human spirit. Because of the dynamic relationship between emotion, reason, character, imagination and will, the Enlightenment emphasis on the reliability of human reason may be overstated. Our Western educational system devotes an enormous amount of time to training people how to reason accurately, and then Einstein introduces his cosmological constant, thus demonstrating the frailty of human reason and our default to feelings. The imagination is unreliable in the same way that reason and emotions are unreliable. It is unreliable in the same sense that character and human will are unreliable. Imagination is unreliable in the same way as the rest of the human spirit, but not more so.

Nonetheless, following the Romantic vision of imagination, most people in our culture continue to think of imagination as having no connection with reality. To sort the issue out, it may be helpful to note the variety of ways in which people experience the imagination.[11]

First, the imagination provides the means for people to "have an idea." We have ideas all the time without ever deciding to have an idea or even trying to have an idea. The imagination constantly produces ideas or thoughts about everything "imaginable." The imagination allows us to process the variety of experiences we have in the course of a day and somehow manages to connect today with yesterday and tomorrow.

Second, the imagination provides a helpful and ever-present means of relaxation in the form of the daydream. Everyone spends time in every day leaving their physical location as the imagination carries them away in what could almost be called an out-of-body experience. We travel where we have never been before. We have experiences we have never had before. We spend time with people we have never known before. We have conversations we have never had before. The daydream may also be called a fantasy. It involves wish fulfillment and egocentrism.

Third, the imagination provides the facility for invention. This level of imagination involves the imitation, innovation or adaptation of something to a new use. It may involve the development and advancement of preexisting material, like the development of the Model T Ford to the Model A Ford to the Edsel. This mundane form of invention uses the dime as a screwdriver. Imitation involves small changes from one thing to its next state and most closely resembles Darwin's concept of evolution by natural selection, which cannot operate by big stages.

Fourth, the imagination involves the poetic grasp of reality in a way that elicits wonder. C. S. Lewis observed that this form of imagination corresponds to the experience of the most gifted and groundbreaking physicists and mathematicians who describe their imaginative discoveries, theories and equations in terms similar to those

---

[11]I have borrowed many of the basic ideas in this list from C. S. Lewis, who never wrote an essay on imagination but spent forty years of his life trying to sort out the problem of imagination. See especially his letter to Dorothy L. Sayers of December 14, 1955, in C. S. Lewis, *The Collected Letters of C. S. Lewis*, ed. Walter Hooper (New York: HarperSanFrancisco, 2007), 3:683.

used by poets, with special emphasis on wonder. According to Lewis, this fourth sense of imagination involves an experience that goes beyond ordinary life to "another dimension."[12] Instead of the mere innovation, adaptation and imitation of invention, the wonder of imagination takes us to something that has never been known before. We find this experience occurring in every field of human endeavor, from economics to engineering.

This fourth aspect of imagination is not like Darwin's concept of evolution, for it involves cataclysmic changes at a single stroke. This aspect of imagination is at work in the science of Copernicus and Einstein, who did not simply modify the trajectory of science or draw out yet another conclusion based on the principles and discoveries already known. Copernicus and Einstein took knowledge to an entirely different realm by a complete break with the knowledge that had existed before. Astronomers could do the math of Ptolemy's universe over and over with great accuracy, but it could never lead to the universe of Copernicus by mere reason. Empiricism can observe the stars and reason can calculate their movements, but only imagination creates the universe in which they travel. Empiricism knows the past, but imagination anticipates and creates the future. The imagination allows scientists to know things about the physical world that they have not learned.

Imagination is not the same as intuition. Intuition belongs to the affective domain and provides us with a "feeling" about something. Imagination, on the other hand, belongs to the cognitive domain and provides us with information, often in the form of pictures or sounds. We know something we did not know before. Even the daydream provides us with a script for what we might say and do under the right circumstances. It may be the wrong thing to say and do, but it is information.

Fifth, the imagination produces the hallucinations experienced by mentally ill people.

Sixth, the imagination is the human faculty for perceiving transcendent experience, just as the eyes are the faculty for perceiving physical light and the ears are the faculty for perceiving sound waves.

---

[12]C. S. Lewis, *Surprised by Joy* (New York: Harcourt, Brace, 1956), p. 17.

Imagination allows us to see what does not lie physically before us and to hear what is not physically spoken to us. Like the empirical senses, we process imagination physically in our brains, which brings us back to Descartes' efforts to dislocate mind from body.

Imagination goes beyond the nonrational experience of "the Other," about which some philosophers of religion like Rudolf Otto and Friedrich Schleiermacher have spoken. The universal phenomenon of "religious experience," as they have studied it, focuses more on the affective dimension that Otto calls "numinous" or spiritual experience. For Otto it is encapsulated by the experience of *mysterium, tremendum* and *fascinans*—the encounter with the mysterious "Other" that is frightening and yet draws us to itself, like Moses with the burning bush.[13] Imagination, on the other hand, allows a basis for divine encounter that involves cognitive knowledge.

In the Greek philosophical tradition kept alive in the West by Descartes's mind-body dualism, we must place the imagination either in the mind or the body, either the spirit or the brain. In the Bible no such dualism of human nature exists. A person, or a soul, involves both the physical and the spiritual aspect in dynamic, inseparable unity. The physical affects the spiritual and the spiritual affects the physical. This unity is reflected in the biblical understanding of resurrection, which preserves the knowable aspect of a person together with the aspect that knows. Thus we do not dismiss the imagination as the bridge between the physical and the metaphysical simply because the imagination involves the brain and the central nervous system. More to the point, the imagination involves the entire physical body of a person. At the same time, it interacts seamlessly with those dimensions of consciousness that we call reason, emotion, character and will. The imagination provides the medium by which people may "hear" God.

The human imagination, a faculty we use and take for granted throughout every waking day, provides God with access to every person

---

[13]Otto is too well known to devote more space at this point in the discussion, but those who have not yet read his argument should read Rudolf Otto, *The Idea of the Holy*, trans. John W. Harvey (New York: Oxford University Press, 1979). Originally published as *Das Heilige* in Germany in 1917, Oxford published its English edition in 1923.

on earth. The imagination processes information that it receives from any source. Just as the imagination allows us to know things about the physical world that we have not learned, the imagination allows us to know God. Paul argued that the imagination is why people have so many conceptions of God (Rom 1:21 KJV). People have the facility to receive cognitive information from God, but we also have the facility to create our own image of God. Humans have the freedom to respond as they please, but the existence of the imagination provides God with access to humans without any violation of the laws of nature. This feature of human experience raises the question of how we might know we are hearing from God and not simply from an overactive imagination. It is the question raised by Moses when God said that he would send prophets to Israel. In the answer, God stresses the importance of experience over time and not simply in the static moment. A prophet's word will come to pass (Deut 18:15-22). Thus, part of the validity of the Bible depends on its reception by a community over time. Imagination must be tested, whether in science or religion. At one level, personal experience with God has a subjective, individualistic, private and mental/psychological dimension. In fact, most of religious experience is personal and private. At another level, however, religious experience comes as revelation to the entire community of faith, corporately shared and tested before it is appropriated. Israel rejected the message of the prophets for several centuries before the fall of Jerusalem. The destruction of the city, however, confirmed the message so that those who believed realized that they had to attend to the rest of what the prophets had to say.

That the revelation of God unfolds over time in the Bible lies at the essence of the credibility of the message as revelation from God. Empiricism and rationalism play a part in the evaluation of the imagination's claims to revelation from God. The idea of the fulfillment of prophecy was understood by the early Christians as lying at the heart of their faith alongside the death and resurrection of Jesus (1 Cor 15:3-4). Anyone can announce they have come to start a new religion. Jesus did not announce a new religion but the fulfillment of what God had foretold by the prophets over a period of centuries (Mt 5:17-18).

A major portion of the New Testament deals with how the Holy

Spirit of God relates to people. People have immediate, personal experience with God because of the presence of the Holy Spirit. Because of the frailty of the human imagination, which shares with rationality and emotions the capability of self-deception, the apostles warn that not all spiritual experiences have objective validity. While Paul stresses that the human mind is constantly tempted to accommodate encounters with God to suit personal desire and need (Rom 1), John reminded the early Christians to "test the spirits to see whether they are from God" (1 Jn 4:1). Because the human imagination is open to the influence of God, it is also open to the influence of other personal beings. Among other things, the disciplines of psychology and sociology explore the influence people have on one another for good or ill.

Humans constantly deal with fears, aspirations, insecurities, longings, dreads, joys, sorrows and a plethora of other emotions that interact with our knowledge, logic, memories, understandings, assumptions and prejudices, while our character balances choices based on what we value, what we consider good, true and right. Within ourselves, we engage in a continuing conversation as we create the next moment of our lives, but in this conversation the Holy Spirit has a voice. This conversation strikes at the heart of what the Bible means by prayer and why Paul can speak of prayer "without ceasing" (1 Thess 5:17 KJV). It also strikes at what Paul means when he says that the Holy Spirit prays for us "with groans that words cannot express" (Rom 8:26). Out of this conversation, God stirs our hearts, strengthens us, encourages us and finishes the plot of the human story.

CONCLUSION

The world of imagination is not merely the world of pretend or make-believe. We may retreat to the imagination for relaxation and renewal, but that is only one of the many functions of the imagination. The world of the imagination is a real world, but not a physical world outside our own brains. The world of imagination is the world of progress, invention, innovation and knowledge. All progress and knowledge begins in the world of spirit before it becomes physical and open to experience by others.

All religions involve some aspect of experience with the transcendent or ultimate beyond the physical. Some speak of this experience in terms of enlightenment, but some go further and claim that revelation has occurred by which a personal, sentient ultimate being has communicated cognitively to us. Our experience of imagination tells us that humans have a capacity that can allow for receiving such revelation. Our experience of the importance of imagination for scientific discovery and technological invention tells us that imagination provides cognitive knowledge beyond the affective. Whether in science or religion, we do not know how the imagination works. The fact that it works within the body does not preclude it from having access to God.

Openness and revelation. The very idea of revelation from God and the Bible as a source of authority does not mesh with a closed universe. The old deists understood this problem and rejected the Bible as revelation from God. Any involvement of God within the natural order would represent a violation of the laws of nature, and humans are part of the natural order. The nature of scientific discovery, however, demonstrates that humans have a capacity for knowledge and understanding that transcends the physical world. Just as humans have the capacity for receiving knowledge of the physical world through their senses, humans also have the capacity for receiving knowledge of a metaphysical nature through the imagination. The same capacity that allows people to daydream, fantasize and innovate provides an avenue of access between God and people. A damaged imagination provides the venue for hallucination and schizophrenic episodes, but a healthy imagination provides the basis for spiritual experience and scientific discovery.

There are two kinds of scientists: (1) those who preserve the received tradition, and (2) those who discover new knowledge. Those in the first group are the worker bees who rely on empiricism and rationalism to repeat the received tradition and use it. The second group relies on imagination to see what has never been seen, to hear what has never been heard, to understand what has never been understood. The imagination carries the discovering pioneer across the universe and across time to see the beginning of time and the depths of matter. Rationalism and empiricism cannot take them there. Rationalism will allow them to record, calculate and transmit the empirical observations that imagination made possible, but rationalism and empiricism do not open the door to knowledge.

Calculation could never take Copernicus, Newton, Einstein, Bohr or Hubble from the universe of Aristotle to the universe we now inhabit.

Poor Aristotle. Without defenders like the relics of Enlightenment thought, his influence would have declined by now. With such a poor

Aristotle's Teaching	Scientific Refutation
Perfect circles in the heavens	Kepler's elliptical orbits
Perfect spheres in the heavens	Galileo's craters on the Moon
Nature abhors a vacuum	Pascal's vacuum
Infinite universe	Lemaître's expanding universe
Eternal universe	Lemaître's expanding universe
Fixed forms	Darwin's evolving species

Figure 8.1. Aristotle's influence. Aristotle's explanation of the universe has inhibited both the discovery of new scientific knowledge and the interpretation of the Bible

track record, one wonders at Aristotle's continuing hold on the modern world (fig. 8.1).

Rationalism and empiricism allow the pioneering scientist to mark out the trail that imagination has revealed to them. Not every idea that passes through the imagination has validity, and the tools of rationalism and empiricism provide help in sorting knowledge from fancy. The test for verification of the experience for the prophets in the Bible was empirical. Do their prophecies come to pass? The fulfillment of the prophecies is the feature that distinguishes the Hebrew Scriptures from the holy books of other cultures. The holy books of other religions teach different beliefs about deity, but prophecy distinguishes the Bible from the writings of other religions. The followers of the pioneers see the marks and signposts of scientific formulations, but they do not use their imaginations to do it.

In *Eureka* (1848), the treatise in which Edgar Allan Poe first proposed the big bang theory and the basic ideas of relativity, Poe remarked that science is poetry. All discovery of new knowledge comes from the imagination in analogical models, like poetry.

In a closed universe of cause and effect, God has no access to communicate with people. Revelation has no theoretical basis. In a universe in which imagination is the primary source of all knowledge and understanding, however, the biblical description of how revelation occurs has perfect validity in keeping with the common experience of everyone who has ever "had an idea" or experienced having a thought "come to them." All people have spiritual experience because we are spiritual beings, but not all people have faith.

9

CONCLUSION

✦✧✦

IN PONDERING HOW GOD RELATES to the physical world, this book has taken a path different than the centuries-long tradition of science-and-religion discussion in the West. With the fragmentation of theology since the Reformation into discrete disciplines of biblical studies, philosophy, church history and systematic theology, the science-and-religion discussion has tended to belong to the Christian philosophers. Most of the tradition has focused on how "god" relates to the physical world without much attention to the God of the Bible and more particularly the God who is triune in nature.

This study has sought to place the trinitarian faith of Christianity in perspective with the other major religious streams of the world. God is totally other than the physical world, as Islam and Judaism affirm. God completely identifies with the physical world, as Hinduism and traditional nature religions affirm. God is totally immanent, as Buddhism affirms. God the Father, Son and Spirit does not relate to the physical world in a single way but in a variety of ways and in ways appropriate to each level of organization and complexity of the universe. Rather than reducing God's options for activity to a single model, as most theological systems tend to do, the Bible presents a panorama of models to describe God's way of relating appropriately to different aspects of the universe.

The great conflict between science and religion has little to do with science or religion. For the most part the conflict lies in the philosophical biases that people bring to the table when they think about science and religion. Five hundred years ago Francis Bacon took a page from the Protestant Reformation and concluded that scientific progress had been inhibited for over fifteen hundred years by the philosophical assumptions of the learned community. In the twenty-first century, philosophical assumptions continue to be a serious threat to scientific knowledge and theological understanding.

The Enlightenment's closed universe. The twin philosophies of naturalism and materialism gained their respectability in the eighteenth century largely due to the success of chemistry and physics in describing how the world works. The clockwork universe fit together tightly, like a series of gears and wheels in constant motion. The mechanical model of the universe provided absolute certainty and absolute predictability. One set of laws governed all action. Laplace (1749-1829) argued that if he knew all current conditions, he could calculate or predict all future events. With his confidence in the certainty of scientific knowledge, Laplace could reason that the present state of the universe is "the effect of its anterior state and as the cause of the one which is to follow."[1]

When Christian philosophers in the seventeenth century set out to discover the laws of nature laid down by God, their method involved the examination of nature to determine the natural laws of God. With the development of the mechanical model, however, God as law-giver stood outside the gears and wheels of nature. In keeping with the tradition of the English Calvinists, God determined the laws of nature from the foundations of the earth and his eternal decree sustained them. An uninvolved deistic God made perfect logical sense.

It is only a short step under the influence of the mechanical model to shift from the idea that science is concerned with describing natural causes to the conclusion that only natural causes exist. We refer to this view as naturalism. Materialism is a logical consequence of naturalism. If only natural causes exist, then only physical matter exists. Within the framework of naturalism and materialism, we have only two ways of knowing anything: through our senses (empiricism) and through our reason (rationalism). People who inhabit the eighteenth-

---

[1]Pierre Simon Marquis de Laplace, *A Philosophical Essay on Probabilities*, trans. F. W. Truscott and F. L. Emory, 6th ed. (New York: John Wiley, 1961), p. 4.

century intellectual world might logically be expected to be materialistic naturalists, who only accept knowledge acquired through empiricism and rationalism. The average person on the street continues to
be influenced by the intellectual view of the eighteenth century. A
shocking number of theologians and scientists continue to live and
think in an eighteenth-century intellectual environment.

In this book we have argued that our universe is unusually suited for
God's involvement. Unlike the closed, mechanical universe of the Enlightenment, our universe reveals an openness that invites interaction.

An inflation-prone universe. Another interesting feature of our universe is that at every major level of complexity we have seen a sudden
inflationary stage that then levels off. The early expansion of the universe is referred to as the inflationary period during which the expansion rate accelerated tremendously and caused the universe to increase from the size of an atom to the size of a pumpkin in less than the
twinkling of an eye. The ex-
pansion rate slowed again just
as quickly as it had started, like
someone stomping on the gas
pedal and then stomping on the
brake (fig. 9.1). String theory
and M theory attempt to account for this anomaly mathematically, but as we have seen in
the unfolding of this book, the
anomaly seems to be a recurring
situation that string theory and
M theory do not address.

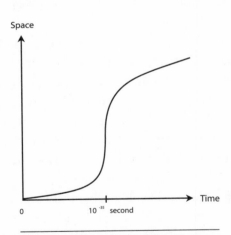

Figure 9.1. Rate of expansion of space

As we have seen, inflation
also occurred with the number of elements in the universe. The universe had gone on for its entire existence when the first three elements
formed, which constituted an enormous inflation in and of itself. The
great inflation of elements occurred, however, eons later in the furnaces
of the first-generation stars that synthesized elements and compounded
the effect when they exploded as supernovas (fig. 9.2). At a critical re-

lational point, dramatic things happen in exponential ways. The inflationary effect involves both the increase in the number of elements as well as the earlier expansion rate of the universe.

From the elements generated by the first-generation stars, the second-generation stars and their satellites were produced. In time this dust of the earth became the stuff out of which life was formed. According to the current consensus of evolutionary biology, the form of life remained simple and consistent for about 1.5 billion years, until what we call the Cambrian explosion occurred. During the Cambrian explosion, another inflationary event occurred, but this time it involved the exponential and dramatic expansion of the number of living "body plans" to over one hundred

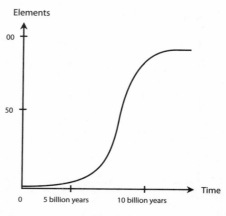

Figure 9.2. Increase in diversity of elements

(fig. 9.3). All current living things are merely subtle variations of these basic body plans that occurred suddenly about 500 million years ago. Since then, the number of body plans has remained stable.

With the growing complexity of life and the appearance of humans, a new feature is introduced into the universe: human culture. For several hundred thousand years, humans made a handful of artifacts, from clothing to

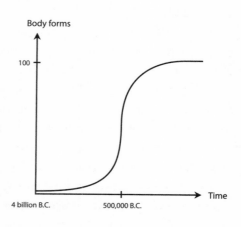

Figure 9.3. Increase in diversity of body forms

shelter to hunting implements. Then human culture exploded with innovation and creativity (fig. 9.4). We live in the midst of the inflationary expansion of knowl-
edge and technology in which
the rate of growth of new
knowledge and invention continues to surge. We cannot
predict how long this inflationary period will last or what
the fate of the human race will
be as a result of it.

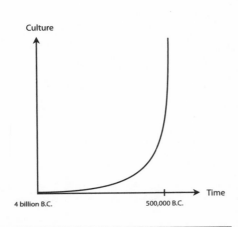

Figure 9.4. Diversity of cultural artifacts

What can we make of the
inflationary aspect of the universe at every level of organization? First, its implications
go beyond what string theory
attempts to explain. It is im-
portant that the periods of inflation begin, but it is equally important
that they end. We should also note that they are all different in terms
of the occasion for their occurrence. We could say that they are merely
odd coincidences, but this approach never leads to new knowledge and
understanding.

We may say that the universe not only moves from simplicity to
complexity at every level of organization, but we may also observe the
intriguing way it does it. In each case the universe makes dramatic
leaps and does things that have never been done before. The universe
is full of one-time occurrences, from the singularity known as the big
bang to the Cambrian explosion. We have the kind of universe that
allows one-time events of an unexpected nature. Repeatability is a
necessary aspect of valid scientific experimentation, but nonrepeatable
events are also a feature of our universe.

Intervention without violation of nature. One of the most remarkable
features of the universe involves its accessibility for observation, measurement, manipulation, alteration, interference, redirection and other
forms of involvement without actually violating the laws of nature. In

fact, the laws of nature seem suited to allow for this wide array of interventions. Whatever humans look for, they somehow discover it right where everyone can see.

The most compelling case for the absence of God from nature is the view that God's involvement in nature would constitute a violation of the laws of nature. The history of science over the last five hundred years, but particularly in the last hundred years, lays this argument to rest as having no validity. The discipline of scientific inquiry and experimentation represents a blatant interference with nature at every level, as those experimenting at the quantum level have called to our attention, yet without violating the laws of nature. Even though humans are part of nature, we have the ability to interfere with nature. Environmentalists complain about this feature of humans. The growth of human civilization from the very simple to the very complex is the story of human interference with nature. We defy the forces of weather with houses and clothes. We defy the caprice of food availability by domesticating plants for crops as we alter their "natural" way of growing. We defy the calamities that affect our bodies by creating artificial limbs, from walking sticks to prosthetic arms to false teeth to hearing aids and glasses. We split the atom and engineer our own genes. We defy the laws of gravity. We breathe underwater. At every turn we discover that though the laws of nature are never suspended, they do not form the barrier that we supposed. Instead, we discover that the laws of nature seem designed for interaction, interference, manipulation, contradiction and employment to our purposes. Part of our problem in understanding how God may be active in the universe comes from the confusion of the scientific model of "law" with the legal model of "law."[2] Scientific laws are models or metaphors for the patterns we discern in nature.

Scientific discovery and technological progress would not be possible except for the openness of the universe to intervention. In half a millennium, humans have only just begun to realize the flexibility of the universe and its openness to interaction. We have only just recognized that the universe is not the closed, deterministic machine with

[2]For a helpful discussion of the difference, see Dorothy L. Sayers, *The Mind of the Maker* (London: Methuen, 1941).

no place for God to relate. Rather than no place for God to be involved, the universe seems designed for involvement. It has ready accessibility at every level of organization. Quantum mechanics has demonstrated that action at a distance is the everyday norm in our universe. If humans are free to intervene in nature, it would seem that God would have at least as much freedom and ability as us. One may protest that human interference and God's interference are not comparable, but that incomparability suggests that God has even greater freedom of involvement.

Bad philosophy. Some critics of divine involvement in the world repeat a concern voiced many times in the past about the way religion inhibits the advance of science and progress. Some forms of religion certainly do, but the Christian faith has not. Instead, the greatest hindrance to the advance of science is the stubborn adherence to a philosophical system that predetermines how the world must work and what can be known. By extension, this same adherence to a philosophical system or cultural view may lead to faulty interpretations of Scripture that inhibit science.

Galileo's Christian faith did not inhibit his discoveries, but the official Aristotelian philosophy of the academy threatened to destroy his work. Since Galileo, some of the most important work in science has been hindered because of the commitment of the scientific community to a philosophical perspective. Einstein could not accept the idea of quantum mechanics because it violated his deeply ingrained assumptions of how the world works as inherited from Aristotle. Einstein went so far as to "fudge" his conclusions by introducing the cosmological constant to make his theory work with the received philosophical tradition. Edgar Allan Poe first proposed the big bang theory in his solution to Olbers' paradox in *Eureka* published in 1848. The scientific community regarded him deranged for denying Aristotle's eternal universe with its infinite size. Because of the refusal to question the philosophical biases that permeated the scientific world, the progress of science suffered a setback of almost a century.

These examples are the most conspicuous of many cases in which science was hindered from pursuing knowledge because of philosophy. It is not difficult to find prominent theologians and scientists that range in perspective from the new atheists to the scientific creationists who have just such a commitment to a philosophical system based on outmoded eighteenth-century science that has long since been discredited.

CONCLUSION

The tradition of the Enlightenment is alive and well. During a time of rapid cultural change of global proportions, many people take comfort in the familiarity of the past. Tradition provides a way of ordering our lives against the onslaught of uncertainty. Conservatives and liberals, believers and unbelievers have found comfort in their idealization of the intellectual respectability of the eighteenth-century Enlightenment. Unfortunately for them the scientific assumptions on which the naturalism and materialism of Enlightenment philosophy stand no longer have any validity within the hard sciences. Physics, chemistry, astronomy and cosmology have said, "Oops! Sorry about that."

Physics is a much humbler discipline after the revolutions of the twentieth century, and is much more tentative about its assertions, while being much more open to new ways of understanding the world. Having had a giant like Newton to lay down the foundational principles of classical physics, by the end of the nineteenth century the discipline tended to think it had nothing more to learn. Then, along came Einstein, Bohr and Hubble.

Biology and the social sciences spawned by the Darwinian revolution are handicapped in their perspective because biology has had its Newton in the form of Darwin, but it has not yet had its Einstein, Bohr and Hubble. Epigenetics is opening a door that will lead to many marvelous discoveries about life, but it will also require a rethinking of fundamental understandings that continue to be based on the Enlightenment framework within which Darwin operated.

The quantum behavior of electrons, the macro behavior of chaotic systems and the instructional behavior of the epigenome do not give us a picture of a tight-fitting mechanical model of cause and effect, but of broad patterns of behavior that interact holistically with enormous openness to personal influence by cognitive beings. The universe is not the tightly sealed machine that Enlightenment thinkers still suppose. It is open to the initiatives of any personal being, including God.

Name and Subject Index

Aaron 267
Abraham 46-47, 49, 51, 69-70, 250, 254, 259, 266, 270
Abu Bakr 52
accretion disk 170
acetic acid 14-15
acids and bases 15
action at a distance 206
Adam and Eve 264
adaptation 208, 276-77
Advishta 39
Aeneid 250-52
aether 84-85, 152
Aga Khan 53
Against Heresies 70
agnostic 15
agouti mice 231
Albert the Great 19, 75
Aleric 251
Alexander, Samuel 103-5
Alexander the Great 48
Alexander of Hales 75
algae 211
Ali 52
Allah 53, 55
allegory 67, 75
alter(s) 29, 134-35, 289
alteration 134, 136, 288
amber 210
Ambrose 73
American Paint Horse 229
Ames, William 83
amino acids 242
Amitabha 44
Amos 268
amphibians 221
anabolism 210
analogies 99-100
analogous structures 241
analogy 136, 142, 146, 262, 265, 274
anatomy 25
Andromeda Galaxy 149
Anselm 23
antacids 15
Antarctic 209
anthropic principles 202, 242
anthropology 25
antibodies 225

antimatter 163
anti-particle 163
Apex Chert 220
aphorism 26
Apostles' Creed 71
Aquinas, Thomas 19, 20, 22, 60, 75-76, 98, 262
Arabs 51
archaeology 25
Arian 87
Arianism 87
Aristarchus 154
Aristotelian 64, 76, 95, 122, 124, 130, 133, 290
Aristotle 21, 24, 28, 34, 60-61, 65-67, 75-79, 81, 83, 88-89, 95, 101, 116, 118, 124, 129, 131, 150-52, 196, 205-6, 214, 246, 282, 290
Arminian 84, 92
Arminianism 120
arthropods 212
Ashkenazi 49
Assassins 53
Assyria 48, 261
asteroid belt 195
asteroids 166, 170
astronomy 21, 25, 195
astrophysics 25
atavism 216-17
atheist 13, 15-16
atmosphere 171, 208
atom(s) 15, 21-22, 25, 28, 161, 165-67, 169, 180-81, 184, 205, 207, 247
Atoms Era 162, 164
attractor 192, 243
Augustine 18, 20, 59, 62, 72-76, 81, 84, 97-98, 108, 250-51, 262
Augustinian 61
authority 60, 62-65, 77, 260, 281
Babylon 48, 70, 260
Babylonian(s) 260-61, 267
Bacon, Francis 16, 20, 34, 64-68, 78, 82, 84, 123-25, 130, 137, 272, 285

Bacon, Roger 19
bacteria 211
baking soda 13-16
Baptists 50
Barbour, Ian 101, 117-19, 126
Barth, Karl 93-94
Bartholomew, David John 200
baryonic matter 167
base pairs 245
beauty 24, 107-8, 118
Becquerel, Antoine Henri 160
behavior 25, 236
ben Zakkai, Johann 49
Bergson, Henri 104-5
Berkeley, George 86
Bessel, Friedrich Wilhelm 159
Beta Israel 49
Bhagavad-Gita 250
bhakti marga 36, 37, 40
Bible 31-34, 55, 57, 59, 60, 62, 65-69, 71-75, 77-78, 88-97, 99, 124, 130, 134, 204, 250-52, 259-65, 268, 270, 272, 278-82, 284
bifurcation 193-94
big bang theory 29, 104, 129, 144, 159, 161, 163, 174-75, 179-80, 273, 283
binomial nomenclature 127
biochemistry 181
biology 22, 25, 170, 209, 214, 248
biosphere 110, 208-9
Birth of Venus, The 88
black holes 149
blackbody radiation 183
Blake, William 272
blueshift 160
bodhisattvas 44-45
body plans 211
Bohr, Neils 146, 184, 188, 205, 282, 291
bonds, covalent 170
bonds, ionic 170
bonds, metallic 170

Born, Max 185, 188
Bose, Satyendra Nath 189
Bose-Einstein condensate 189-90
botany 25
Botticelli 88
bottom-up causality 197-98, 203
Boyle, Robert 16, 21, 68, 82
Boyle's Law 82
Brahe, Tycho 156
Brahman 36, 38, 41
brains 243
Brazun, Jacques 239
Briggs, Derek 240
Brownlee, Donald 173
Brunner, Emil 93
Bruno, Giordano 172
Buddha 42-45
Buddhism 31, 41-45, 56, 59, 72, 142, 284
Buddhist(s) 15, 46, 131, 137
Budhi 39
Bultmann, Rudolf 93-94, 107
Butler, Joseph 86
butterflies 192, 213
butterfly effect 193, 207
Caesar, Julius 217
Caleb 267
caliph 52
Calvin, John 20, 77, 79-83, 86-87, 97
Calvinism 81, 84, 97, 120, 137
Calvinist(s) 79, 82, 87, 137, 285
Cambrian Burgess Shale 240
Cambrian explosion 211, 240, 287-88
carbohydrates 209
carbon 166, 241
carbon dioxide 14
Cardinal Bellarmine 188
caste 36, 47
caste system 36
casuistry 83
catabolism 210
Cathedrali Notre-Dame of Strasbourg France 21

Catholic(s) 35-36, 124
cats 213
causal joint 199-200, 203
cause and effect 79, 81, 85, 94, 127, 254, 271, 283, 291
causes 15, 81
cell 209, 215, 235
cell biology 25
central dogma 236
CERN 161, 163
chain of being 196
Ch'an 43, 45
chaos 22-23, 116, 180-82, 191, 194-95, 197, 201-4, 207, 239, 248
character 262, 275, 278, 280
Charles I 89
Charles II 84
chemicals 208
chemist 21
chemistry 13-15, 25, 170
Chichen-Itza 148
chicken pox 195
chordates 212
Christendom 49, 50, 122
Christian 13, 15-18, 31, 35, 46, 57, 63, 70, 72, 74, 77, 94, 96, 98, 114, 117, 120, 122, 132, 137, 139, 141, 203, 285, 290
Christianity 17-18, 26, 33-35, 45, 56, 71-72, 74, 90, 92-93, 97, 111, 115, 117-18, 254, 284
Christianity Not Mysterious 86
Christians 31-33, 35, 46, 50, 70-71, 93, 128, 132, 138, 251-52, 280
chromosomal translation 229
chromosome 236
chromosome inversion 229
chronicle 252-53
chronological snobbery 118
Cichlid fish 217-18
City of God, The 74, 251
classical world 183
clockwork machine 21
clockwork model 182

clockwork models 179
clockwork universe 22, 181
closed machines 22
clusters of galaxies 149, 166-69
coal 21
Cobb, John B., Jr. 92, 101, 112, 114-15
codgrass 219, 229
cogito ergo sum 125
Coleridge, Samuel Taylor 272
collapse of the wavefunction 183, 186, 201
colonialism 35
comets 166, 170
common ancestor 214-15, 217
common course of nature 18-19
communicative civilizations 173
complexification 109-10
complexity 25-26, 28-29, 57-58, 105, 110, 116, 146, 167, 177, 179, 244, 248, 258, 284, 286, 288
Comte de Buffon 102
Confessions 74
congregational 235
conservation of energy 200
Conservative Judaism 50
Constantine 70-71
Constantinople 74
contingency 239-42
convergence 242-44
Conway Morris, Simon 174, 240-41, 243-44
Copernican 123, 274
Copernicus, Nicolaus 21, 60, 77, 125, 154-58, 274, 277, 282
copy-number variation mutation 228
cosmic microwave background radiation (CMB) 164
cosmological constant 275, 290
cosmology 25, 85
cosmos 21, 28

Coulson, C. A. 126, 128-29
Council of Chalcedon 71
Council of Constance 63
Council of Constantinople 71
Council of Ephesus 71
Council of Nicaea 71
Counter-Reformation 82
Craig, William Lane 138
creatio ex nihilo 114, 116
creation 26, 123, 137, 201, 247
creation science 95
Creator 69-71, 86, 89, 108, 116, 131, 133, 136-38, 143, 178
Crick, Francis 236
Croce, Benedetto 252
Cromwell, Oliver 84
crust, earth 211
Cudworth, Ralph 127
culture(s) 33-35, 45-47, 49, 56-59, 68, 90, 96-97, 99, 129, 131, 250, 252-53, 255-56, 259-60, 262-64, 266, 272-73, 276, 282, 288
Curie, Marie 160
Curie, Pierre 160
cursus communis naturae 18-19, 21, 179
Cuvier, Baron Georges 215
cyanobacteria 220
cycle of rebirth(s) 36, 38-41, 43-46
cyclical view 46, 48, 55-56, 253, 256
Cygnus-Lyra region 173
Cyrus 260, 262
cytology 25
Dalai Lama 45
Dante 13
dark energy 149, 166-67
dark matter 149, 167
Darwin finches 225-26
Darwin, Charles 29, 88-89, 91-92, 101-2, 119, 128, 136, 142, 213-15, 220, 224, 129, 233-35, 237-39, 245-47, 257, 276-77, 282, 291

Darwin, Erasmus 102
David 99, 259, 267-68, 270
Davies, Paul, 188
Davisson, Clinton 205
Dawkins, Richard 239, 245, 274-75
day 148
DDT 225, 227
de Broglie, Louis 184, 206
de Vreis, Paul 15-16
death 247
Decline of the West, The 255
decoherence 190
decree(s) 79-80, 82, 85, 87, 89, 272, 285
deep-ocean trenches 209
deferent 21, 152-53
deism 13, 15, 21, 86-87, 142, 247, 254
deist(s) 116, 137, 157, 281
deistic 90, 285
deity 239
deletions 228
demiurge 141
Democritus 22
Dennett, Daniel 239
density gradient 169
Descartes, René 82-86, 125-26, 129-31, 278
design 234, 239
design argument 101, 127
destiny 255
determinism 22, 29, 120, 126, 182, 191, 200, 204, 206-7, 245
deuteronomic 251-52
Deuteronomy 251
dialectic 102-3, 255
dichotomy 79, 83-86, 91-93, 125-26, 233-34
diffraction 183
dinosaurs 210, 213
direction 28, 56, 247, 253-54, 258, 260
discipline 25
divine 17, 20-21
divine action 200
divine involvement 17
Divine Light Mission 40
DNA 17, 143, 223, 228-29, 231-32, 235-36, 244-48

Dobzhansky, Theodosius 214, 217
dogs 213
Donne, John 247
Doppler Effect 160, 172
Drummond, Lewis A. 92
Druze 53
dualism 73, 102, 112, 130, 278
dust clouds 149
dynamic universe 28-29, 191
earth 149, 181, 239
earth structure 170-71
earth-centered universe 24
East 58
echinoderms 212
ecology 193
economics 25, 195-96
Edison, Thomas 274
effervescence 14-15
efficient cause 91, 254
Einstein, Albert 104, 108, 129, 133, 146, 160-61, 179-80, 187-89, 206, 274-75, 277, 282, 290-91
élan vital 104
electromagnetic force 24, 161, 163
electromagnetic radiation 184
electromagnetic spectrum 148
electron(s) 112, 120, 163-64, 169-70, 176, 183-84, 186, 197, 205-6, 291
electron cloud 185, 188-89
electron microscope 189
Electroweak Era 163
electroweak force 163
elementary particles 25, 165, 167, 169, 196-97
elements 28, 247
elements of life 209
Eliot, T. S. 96
elliptical orbits 181
Ellis-van Creveld syndrome 230
emerge 262
emergence 104, 116, 143, 168, 177, 179, 203, 208

emergent 104
emotion(s) 262, 275, 278, 280
empiricism 24, 29, 124, 271, 273, 277, 279, 281-82, 285
energy 23-24, 26, 28
energy storage 209
Engels, Friedrich 103
engineering design 227
English Reformation 64
Enlightenment 24, 28, 83, 87, 187, 189-90, 205-6, 245, 257, 275, 282, 285-86, 291-92
entropy 116, 165
environment 22
eons 211
epicycles 21, 152-53, 155
epigenetics 22-23, 230-32, 237-38, 291
epigenome 245
epistemology 131, 188-89
EPR Paradox or Experiment 187
equant 21, 152-53, 155
equilibrium state 165
eras 211
Erickson, Millard 139
eschatology 143
Euclidean geometry 179
Eudoxus of Cnidus 21, 150
eukaryote 211, 215
Eureka 29, 258, 273, 282-83, 290
Evangelical Revival 86-87
evaporation 172, 213-15, 217, 232, 244, 246, 248
evil 105, 108, 111-12, 117-18, 264
evolution 91-92, 103, 105, 109, 111, 257
evolutionary philosophy 102, 104-6, 112, 116
evolutionary process 107, 109
evolutionary theology 107, 116
exaltation 138
exodus 47
exoplanet 172-73
exosphere 172
expectations 266-68

experiment 18-19, 25
extinction 211, 246
extrasolar planet 272
extreme sensitivity to initial conditions 181
Fairie Queen, The 67
Farrer, Austin 198-99
fate 47, 252-53
Father 28, 59, 68, 73, 78, 137-43, 284
Fermi Lab 163
feudal system 74
Feuerbach, Ludwig 103
fiat 28-29, 88, 95, 123
filaments 169
final cause 67, 91
fine-tuned for life 174, 176-78, 202, 242
Finney, Charles Grandison 90, 92
fireworks 184
first cause 76, 81, 128
first generation stars 166-67, 175, 181, 197
fish 221-22
fishapod 222
Five Fundamentals 91
foreknowledge 108
fossils 210, 240
four elements of Arisotle 151
Four Noble Truths 41-42
Fourth Lateran Council 61
fractals 195
Francke, August Hermann 90
free 38-39, 41, 47, 76, 88, 114, 120, 137, 263, 290
free will 55, 140, 182
freedom 26, 37, 40-42, 63, 108, 113, 117, 119-20, 135-36, 141, 252-53, 255, 279, 290
Freeland, Stephen 242
Freud, Sigmund 23
fulfillment 251, 279, 282
fullerene 183
fundamental forces 24, 26, 142, 144-45, 161, 180, 196, 202, 247, 249
fundamental particles 180
fundamentalism 25

fundamentalist(s) 36, 91, 95, 270
fundamentalist-modernist controversy 91, 93
future 202
Gabriel 51
galaxies 25, 149, 166-69, 181
Galaxy Era 162, 166
Galileo 13, 16, 21, 65-66, 78, 82, 84, 124-25, 157, 159, 181, 188, 282, 290
Gamma Cephei 172
gamma rays 149, 162
Gandhi, Mohandas "Mahatma" 36
gas 198
gaseous planets 170
Gautama, Siddhartha 41-42
gene(s) 22, 28, 222, 235, 237-38, 245-46, 289
gene drift 230
gene duplication 228
general theory of relativity 160, 162
Genesis 88, 91, 94-95, 127, 139, 141, 259, 263, 265
Genesis Flood, The 94
genetic code 22, 215, 244, 246, 248
genetic determinism 236
genetic drift 222-23
genetic engineering 136
genetic information 210
genetic markers 236
genetic reductionism 235
genetics 22, 180, 237, 245
genome duplication 229
geocentric model 150-51, 153
geoheliocentric model 156
geological column 210
geology 25, 220
Gibbon, Edward 254-55
Gifford Lectures 103
Gilbert, Walter 236
glycolysis 210
goal 249, 255-56
God 13, 15-17, 19-24, 26, 28-30, 178-82, 197-204, 208, 233, 235, 246-48

God, characteristics of 177
God-of-the-gaps 23, 118,
  128-29, 131-32, 199, 235,
  238, 246, 254
God's action 204
Golden Chaine, A 79-82, 84,
  97
goodness 24, 107-8, 139
gospel 59, 71, 73, 103, 269
Gould, Stephen Jay 237,
  239-40
governor 21
grace 108, 117, 266
Grant, Peter 226
Grant, Rosemary 226
gravitational law 181
gravity 24, 28, 143, 161, 163,
  165, 169-70, 175-76, 178
Gray, Asa 16, 234-36
great wall 169
Greeks 21
Grosseteste, Robert 18
growth 208
habitable zone 174
habitats 209
Hadith 54
Hallett, Joseph 87
hallucinations 277
Hammurabi 267
Hanbalite 53-54
Hanifite 53-54
hardware 245
Hartshorne, Charles 92,
  112-14
Haught, John F. 244
Hawaiian Islands 218
heart 261-62, 280
heaven 31, 52, 69-70, 77,
  82, 86, 98, 140
heavens 25, 81
Hebrew(s) 56, 69-70,
  95-96, 130, 139, 141, 251,
  259-62, 267, 282
Hefner, Philip 101
Hegel, Georg Wilhelm
  Friedrich 102-3, 131,
  255-56
Heisenberg uncertainty
  principle 142, 186,
  189-90, 206
Heisenberg, Werner 186,
  188, 206

heliocentric model 154-55
helium 164, 166, 170
helium nuclei 164, 169
hemoglobin 228
Henry VIII 64
heredity 235, 245
hermeneutics 120
Herod 48-49
Herschel, John 16
Herschel, William 159
Hidden Imam 53
hidden variables 187-88
hierarchy 74, 81
higher critical method 259
higher principle 268-69
Hillel 49
Hindu(s) 15, 40-41, 44, 46,
  131, 137
Hinduism 31, 36-41,
  44-45, 56-57, 59, 142,
  284
history 24-25, 45-46, 48,
  56-57, 73, 96, 102-3, 108,
  118, 121, 134, 138, 239,
  241, 249, 251-59, 262,
  269, 274, 289
*History of the Decline and
  Fall of the Roman Empire,
  The* 254-55
Hocking, W. E. 92
holiness 138, 141, 264, 265
holism 105
Holy Spirit 28, 59, 63, 68,
  73, 78, 84, 86, 119,
  137-43, 202, 271, 279-80,
  284
homeostasis 208
Homer 249-50, 252, 269,
  272
hominids 213
Homo sapiens 239
homology 215-16, 241
homology, anatomical 215
homology, molecular 215
hope 117
Hophra 260
horses 213
Hoyle, Fred 177
Hubble Space Telescope
  150
Hubble, Edwin 150, 282,
  291

human action 200-201
Human Genome Project
  229, 236
humans 24, 201, 209
Hume, David 119, 129,
  198, 255, 257
Hurricane Katrina 207
Hus, John 63, 66, 77
Hussain 52
Huxley, Julian 243
Huxley, Thomas H. 16
hybrid 219
hydrogen 164, 166, 170
hydrogen nuclei 164, 169
hydrosphere 171-72, 208
hypothesis 22
igneous rock 172
Iliad 250-52, 269
imagination 262, 271-83
imagine 134, 272
imam 52-54
imitation 276-77
immanence 107-9
imminant 108, 140
imminence 142
imminent 68, 139, 142, 284
immutable 214
importation 208
incarnation 28, 87, 106,
  108, 111, 132, 138-41
indeterminacy 108, 189,
  207
individual(s) 76, 84, 89,
  102, 105, 113, 143, 259
inflation 143, 162-63, 165,
  169, 286
information 28, 203, 244
information input 198, 201,
  204
infrared radiation 149
initial conditions 191-92
innocence 264-65
innovation 276-77, 280
insects 210
insertions 228
*Institutes of the Christian
  Religion* 82
intellect 262
intelligent design 101
interact 29, 93, 135-37, 143,
  146, 271, 274, 278, 280
interaction 134-37, 146,

259, 262-64, 271, 286, 289
interfere(s) 28-29, 86, 93, 135, 269, 289
interference 136-37, 183, 207, 288-90
International Society for Krishna Consciousness 40
interpret(s) 254
interrupt 29, 134
interruption 134
intervene 29, 92-93, 134, 269, 290
intervention 29, 134-36, 198, 270, 288-89
intuition 277
invention 276-77, 280-81
involvement 286
Iqbal, Muzaffar 55
Irenaeus 70
iron 166
irreducible nonlocality 188
Isaac 47, 70
I'sma'ilites 53
Ishmael 51
Islam 51-57, 59, 284
Islamic world 50, 58, 68
Israel 46-49, 56, 69, 99, 250, 260-61, 263, 267-69, 279
Ithna' Ashari 53
Jacob 47, 70, 266
James I 67, 78, 81, 83, 89
Jamnia 49
Jastrow, Robert 177
Jehovah's Witnesses 140
Jeroboam 268
Jerusalem 48-49, 69-70, 261, 279
Jesus Christ 46, 70-71, 73, 87, 93-94, 98-99, 111, 114-15, 117, 132, 140, 143, 253, 265, 268-70, 275, 279
    of Nazareth 205
Jews 32-33, 46, 48-51
Jewish 34, 46, 57, 69, 259
jnana marga 36-37
John 280
John Templeton Foundation 101

Joseph 267
Joshua 267
Joyce, James 97
Judah 46, 48, 260-61, 267-68
Judaism 34, 46-51, 56, 59, 284
Judea 46
Jurassic Park 196
justice 24, 37, 51, 262, 269
karma 36
karma marga 36-37
Kauffman, Stuart 168
Kepler, Johannes 16, 77-78, 82, 125, 181, 282
Kepler satellite 173
Khariji 52
kinetics 15
King (God as) 79, 86-87, 89, 92, 97-99, 146
Kirkwood gaps 195
knowledge 247
Kobayahsi, Makoto 163
Koch snowflake 194-95
laboratory 206
Lake Malawi 218
Lake Tanganyika 218
Lake Victoria 218
Lamarck, Jean-Baptiste 102
lamas 45
Laplace, Pierre-Simon 16, 22, 126, 182, 206-7, 285
Lardner, Nathaniel 87
Large Hadron Collider 161
Large Magellanic Cloud 149
laser 183, 189
law (as moral development) 267-69
Law of Universal Gravitation 82, 289
Laws of Motion 82
laws of nature 16, 19, 21, 28-29, 31-32, 67, 81-82, 88, 92, 124, 134-36, 142, 146, 204, 207, 247, 254, 279, 281, 285, 288-89
Leclerc, Georges-Louis, Comte de Buffon 16
legalism 268
legalists 270
Lemaître, Georges, 282

lepton 163, 169, 176
level of organization 25, 26, 29, 120, 263, 284, 288, 290
levels of physical complexity 28
Lewis, C. S. 24, 118, 122, 203, 250, 263, 276-77
life 28-29, 167-68, 173, 180-81, 208, 244
Life magazine 236
life's characteristics 208
light 148, 163, 183
light year 149
limiting reagent 15
linear view 48, 56, 253-56, 263, 266
Linnaeus, Carl 127, 232
lithium 164
lithosphere 171, 208
living organisms 209
lobe-finned fish 222
Local Group Cluster 149
Locke 255
Logos 114
Loomer, Bernard 112
Lorentz, Edward 191-92, 207
love 24, 40, 110, 113-14, 118, 138, 141, 265
Luther, Martin 60-61, 64, 77, 82, 90
Lyell, Charles 16
M theory 24, 162, 286
Machen, J. Gresham 92
machine analogy 23
machine model 21, 179, 182
MACHOs (Massive Compact Halo Objects) 167
MacKay, Donald M. 16, 22
Madhva 37-38
Madhyamika 43
Maharishi, Sri Ramana Bhagavan 37
Mahayana 42-45
Mahdi 53
Maimonides 34, 49-50
Malikite 53-54
mammals 213
Mani 72
Manichaean(s) 72-73

Manichaeism 72
manipulate 28
manipulation 136, 288-89
Manu 36
Marx, Karl 103, 119, 131, 255-56
Maskawa, Toshihide 163
materialism 105, 107, 129-30, 249, 285, 291
materialistic 103, 107, 132, 249, 254, 286
mathematical model 21, 126
mathematician 13
matter 23-24, 26, 28, 112, 161, 163-64, 166, 169
matter-wave 184, 188
May, Robert 193
McGrath, Alister 120
meaning 28, 97, 252, 254-55, 257-58, 269
measles 195
measurement 183
mechanical model 86, 119, 127, 285, 291
mechanism 15, 22, 213, 245, 260-61
medicine 195
medieval 74-78, 81-83, 88, 95, 122-23, 129
medieval synthesis 122
megaparsec (Mpc) 149
Meland, Bernard 112
membrane 208
Mendel, Gregor 213, 235, 245
Mendelian genetics 224
mesosphere 172
metabolic pathways 210
metabolism 210, 215
metamorphic rock 172
metanarrative 25
metaphor 97-98, 256, 261, 289
metaphysic 124, 131-32
metaphysical 103, 118, 131, 249
metaphysical naturalism 16
metaphysics 78, 116, 125-26, 128-29, 133
method 25
methodological deist 17

methodological naturalism 16, 21, 117, 132-34, 179
methodological theism 59, 133
methyl rich diets 231
Michelangelo 82
microfossils 211
microwave radiation 149
Middle Ages 18, 76, 122, 126, 131
migration, genetic 222-23, 229
Milky Way Galaxy 149, 159
Miller, Kenneth 128
Milton 272
mimesis 256
minerals 25, 166-68
mints 219, 229
miracle 179, 203
Mishnah 49
mitigate 135
Mizrahi 49
modalism 119, 140
model(s) 21, 26, 28, 32, 57, 77, 81, 83, 85-87, 97-100, 102-3, 105, 110, 113, 116, 119-20, 122, 126-27, 142-43, 146, 259, 283-85, 289
model, scientific 21-22, 32, 150, 157
modern science 31, 33, 35, 46, 58, 59-60, 105, 122, 129, 130-31, 133-34
modern systhesis 224
Muhammad 51-53, 55
molecules 15-16, 25, 167-68
molecules of life 209
mollusks 212
momentum 186-87
monarchical model 28, 120, 137
monism 38, 41, 56
monotheistic 40, 45, 59
monotheism 41
Montesquieu 255
month 148
moon 174
moral judgment 263, 265
moral law 253

morality 262-63, 266-67, 269-70
Moreland, J. P. 132
Morgan, Lloyd 103-5
Morowitz, Harold, J. 168
Morris, Henry M. 94
Moses 47, 49-50, 250, 259, 267, 270, 278-79
moth 218
MRI machines 183
Muawiya 52
Muslim(s) 15, 33, 54-55, 57
mutable 214
mutation 222-23, 228, 244-46, 248
mysterium, tremendum, et fascinans 278
Nambu, Yoichiro 163
Napoleon 22, 182
natural causes 16, 285
natural explanation 16-17
natural knowledge 18
natural laws 59, 132
natural order 18
natural phenomena 15
natural philosophers 18, 181
natural selection 22, 91-92, 116, 128, 213, 222-24, 228, 239, 241-42, 257, 276
natural theology 204
naturalism 16-17, 129-30, 132, 285, 291
naturalism of the gaps 133
naturalists 16, 21, 286
nature 17, 23, 246
Nazi 51
Nebuchadnezzar 260-61
nebula 22
necessity 242
neo-orthodoxy 93-94, 107
Neo-Platonic 73-75, 81
neurology 170
neurosciences 25
neutron 163-64, 167, 175-76, 205
New Organum 65, 81
Newton, Isaac 16, 21-22, 82, 85, 89, 125-26, 129, 132, 159, 180-81, 274, 282, 291

Newtonian mechanics 22
nexus 106
Nicene Creed 71, 234
Niebuhr, Reinhold 93
Nigosian, S. A. 36
nirvana 42-44
Nizaris 53
Nominalism 61
nonbaryonic matter 167
nondynamic selection rule
    170
nonequilibrium state 165
nonlinear 191
nonreductionist 26
noosphere 110
nothing-buttery 16-17
Novum Organum. See New
    Organum
nuclei 197
Nuclei Era 162, 164
nucleic acids 210, 236
nucleosynthesis 170, 176
Nucleosynthesis Era
    162-63
nucleus 161, 163-64, 170,
    185
numinous 263, 278
Nyaya 37, 39
objectivity 133, 257
observation 19
Occam's Razor 19
Odyssey 250
Ogden, Schubert 112
Olber's paradox 290
Omar 52
Omega point 110-11
omnipotence 139, 141, 200
omnipresence 139
omniscience 139, 200
On Prescription Against
    Heretics 71
On the Origin of the Species
    88, 128, 213-16, 220,
    222, 224
ontological argument 23
ontological gaps 198
ontological naturalism 21
ontology 188-89
open universe 23, 29, 113,
    120, 136-38, 143, 146,
    196, 206-7, 235, 257, 292
openness 22-23, 29, 134,

180-81, 204, 236, 244,
    248, 281, 286, 289, 292
oral history 260
oral tradition 259
order 181, 204, 248
order of salvation 81
organic model 105, 114,
    116, 118, 127
organism 236
organization 25-26, 208
organs 209
Origen 71
origin of life 29
Orthodox Christianity 35
Orthodox Judaism 50
Otto, Rudolf 278
Owen, Richard 215
ozone layer 212
pagan 122
pain and suffering 24, 41,
    246, 258, 259, 265
Paley, William 233-34
Panchen Lama 45
panentheism 117
panentheist 137
panentheistic 113, 117-18
pantheism 41, 111
pantheistic 107, 113
paradigm shift 24
parallax, stellar 158
particle 163, 183, 205, 206
Particle Era 162
particular(s) 76-77, 82, 105
Pascal, Blaise 129, 131, 282
pattern formation 198
patterns 29
Paul 70, 264-65, 279-80
Pauli Exclusion Principle
    169-70, 178
Peacocke, Arthur 25, 116,
    146, 168, 188, 198-201,
    204
Peacocke's Levels of
    Complexity 27, 167-68
peas 245
Peirce, James 87
Pekah 260
peloria 232
Pentateuch 250
periodic table 170
periods 211
Perkins, William 79-85,

87-89, 92-93, 97-98,
    233-34
Persia 48-49, 260
Persian 259-60
personal agent 29, 201
personality 236
Pharisees 48-49
phenomenon 21, 26
Phenomenon of Man, The
    111
philosophy 20, 25, 189, 246
photoelectric effect 183
photon 162-64, 169
photosynthesis 242
phylogeny 220
physical laws 180
physical world 23-25
physics 206, 235
physics, high-energy 161
physiology 25
Pietism 90
Pietist(s) 137
Planck, Max 183, 205
Planck's constant 186
planets 25, 149, 167, 172
planets, gaseous 166
planets, rocky 166
plants 212-13, 219
plasma 164, 171, 196, 247
plastic model 127
plate tectonics 171, 174
Plato 24, 59, 61, 75-76, 79,
    81, 84, 89
Platonic 60, 122
Platonism 141
Podolsky, Boris 187
Poe, Edgar Allan 29,
    257-58, 273-74, 282-83,
    290
poetry 96-97, 99-100,
    250-51, 261, 273-274,
    283
poets 272, 277
point mutation 228
political science 25
Polkinghorne, John
    116-19, 136-38, 141,
    143, 186-89, 192, 196,
    198-200, 203-4
Polynesians 218
polynucleotides 209-10,
    215

polypeptides 209-10, 215
polysaccharides 209-10, 215
polytheism 41
polytheistic 40, 56
Pompey 48
position 186-87, 189
Prabhupada, A. C. Bhaktivedanta Swami 40
prayer 280
precipitation 172
predictability 248
"Preface to Lyrical Ballads" 272
Price, George McGready 94
Price, Huw 165
primary cause 18-19, 91
primary qualities 124
Prime Mover 21-22, 78, 81, 111, 151
probability 22, 185-86, 206
problem of evil 105, 108, 118
Problem of Pain, The 263
process 103-9, 113-14, 116-18, 135-36, 255
process theology 92, 119-20, 137, 140, 142, 262
progress 29, 48, 56, 243, 255, 258-59, 274, 280, 289-90
prokaryote 210-11, 215
protein 210, 215, 236
Protestant(s) 35, 36, 59-60, 68, 78, 96, 124, 285
Protestantism 79
proton 163-64, 167, 170, 175-76, 205
Providence 198, 203, 239
Proxima Centura 149
pruning agent 168-69, 171, 178
psychology 25
Ptolemy 21, 24, 73, 77, 152-53, 155, 157-58, 274, 277
punishment 265, 267, 270
Puritan(s) 64, 67, 83, 86, 90, 92, 98, 119
Puritanism 81

purpose(s) 28, 47, 51, 56, 81, 108, 120, 125, 131, 238-39, 242, 244, 254, 257, 263, 265, 269, 289
Purva-Mimansa 37, 39
quanta 183, 188, 201-2, 205-6
quantum fluctuations 165
quantum jumps 184, 188, 205
quantum mechanics 22-23, 26, 108, 115, 120, 143, 162, 169, 180, 182-83, 185-89, 197, 204-5, 255, 289-91
quantum theory 117, 131, 133
quantum wavefunction 188
quantum world 108
quarks 163, 167, 169
quintessence 152
Qur'an 51-55, 57
radio waves 148
radioactivity 160
radiometric dating 211
raisin-bread model 150, 161
Ramanuja 37-38
Ramus, Peter 79, 83
random 230
Ray, John 127
realism 189
reason 274-75, 278
Reconstructionist Judaism 51
red dwarfs 174
red in tooth and claw 233
redshift 150, 160
reductionism 19, 25-26, 29, 235
reductionist 119-20
Reform Judaism 50
Reformation 20, 50, 59-60, 63, 68, 77-79, 89, 99, 284-85
regularity 18
reincarnation 36, 45, 55
relativism 269
relativity 179, 273, 283
religion 17
Renaissance 60, 63-64, 75, 78, 88, 181
reproduction 208

resistance 225
resurrection 70-71, 93, 112, 138, 143, 278-79
retrograde motion 152
revelation 45, 48, 51, 55, 68, 75, 77, 86, 90, 94, 108, 118, 120, 130, 265, 279, 281, 283
reverse causality 143
reward 266-67
rewinding the tape of life 240-41
Reynolds, John Mark 132
Rezin 260
righteousness 264, 269
ring species 218
RNA 236
rock cycle 172
rock-paper-scissors 135
rocks 25, 166-68
rocky planets 170
Roman Empire 46, 49, 70, 72-74, 250-51, 254
Rosen, Nathan 187
Ross, Hugh 177
rubidium 190
Russell, Robert 143
Rust, Eric 108, 111, 114, 125
Sadducees 48-49
salvation 117
samara 36
Sankara 37-38
Sankhya 37, 39
Sarah 250
satellite 174
Saul 268
Savonarola 66
Sayers, Dorothy L. 63-64, 140
Schleiermacher, Friedrich 278
Schrödinger, Erwin 184-86, 188, 205
science 15-16, 19, 24, 26, 28-29, 247
scientific age 23
scientific method 19, 34-35, 63-66, 68, 81-82, 90, 123-24, 130, 133, 253, 257
scientific naturalism 16-17

scientist 16-17, 24
Scofield, C. I. 90
Scofield Reference Bible
    90-91
Scotus, John Duns 76
Scripture(s) 18, 61-64, 67,
    71, 74, 77, 98, 130, 139,
    141, 214, 282
Search for Extraterrestrial
    Intelligence (SETI) 173
second law of
    thermodynamics 164-65
second-generation stars
    166-67, 170, 175, 181,
    197
secondary causes 18-20, 89
secondary qualities 124
sedimentary rock 172, 210
selection 246
self-contained machine 21
self-limitation 204
self-organization 168
semiconductor 183
sensitivity 208
sentience 243
Sephardi 49
Seventh-Day Adventists
    94-95
sexual beings 28
sexual selection 222-23,
    227-28
Shafiite 53-54
Shakespeare, William 67
shepherd 98-99
Shi'ah 52
Shiites 52-54
sickle cell hemoglobin 228
simile 97
simplicity 26, 28-29
Simpson, George Gayland
    238
sin 108, 114
singularity 26, 161-62
Slipher, Vesto 160
Small Magellanic Cloud
    149
Smuts, Jan 105
social sciences 25, 195
sociology 25
sodium 190
sodium hydrogen carbonate
    14-15

software 245
soil 212
Solar system 22, 166, 182
solution 14
Son 28, 59, 68, 78, 103,
    137-43, 284
soteriology 85
soul 130, 262, 278
Soviet state 274
space 26, 28
space-time 104, 141, 143,
    263
special revelation 204
species 209, 214
Spener, Philip Jacob 90
Spengler, Oswald 255-56
Spenser, Edmund 67
spheres 21
Spinoza 117
spirit 261, 265, 271, 275,
    280
St. Batholomew massacre
    79
Staph infection 225-26
star 25, 149, 165-66,
    169-70, 174, 196, 247
star dust 166
states of matter 15
static universe 28
sterility 219
Stoical 122
Stonehenge 148
strange attractor 192, 202
stratigraphy 220
stratosphere 172
string theory 24, 162, 286,
    288
strong nuclear force 24,
    143, 161, 163, 169, 176
Study of History, A 256
subatomic particles 196,
    197
sublunary region 151
Suetonius 217
suffering 24, 42, 51, 114,
    118, 141, 246-47, 252,
    269-70
Sufis 53-55
Sukhavati 43-44
Summa Theologiae 19
sun 149
sun-like star 172

Sunni(s) 52-54
superatom 190
superclusters 169
superlunary region 151
supernatural 16-17
supernova 166
superposition principle 186
superstring theory 162
survival 244, 246
symbol 97
symbolic 97
synagogue 48, 49
Synod of Dort 81, 83
Talmud 49-50
tantricism 44
Teilhard de Chardin, Pierre
    92, 109-12
Temple, William 92, 107-8,
    112
temporal bias 165
Ten Commandments 268
Tennyson, Alfred Lord 233
terapods 221
Tertiary Period 220
Tertullian 71
theist(s) 13, 134, 138
theistic 103, 113
theodicy 141
theologian 13, 17
theology 26, 29
theory 18
Theosophical Society 40
"theotoxin" 23
Theravada 41-43
thermosphere 172
Thirty Years' War 82, 124
Thomist 36, 61
Thompson, George Paget
    205
Thomson, J. J. 205
three laws of motion 181
Tibetan Buddhism 44-45
Tibetan greenish warbler
    218-19, 227-28
Tien-t'ai 43-44
Tiktaalik 222
Tillich, Paul 93
time and space 24, 26, 28,
    46, 70, 84, 94, 105,
    138-43, 269, 271
tissue 209
Toland, John 86

top-down causality 197-98, 202, 204
Torah 50, 250-51
Toynbee, Arnold 256-57
tradition(s) 59, 61-66, 68, 77-78, 89, 91, 93, 95, 116-18, 124-25, 130, 250-51, 262, 281, 285, 290-91
transcendence 108-9, 111, 138, 142, 255
transcendent 68, 139-40, 142, 277, 281
Transcendental Meditation 40
transcends 107, 271, 281
transistor 189
transit method 172
trilobites 212, 221
trinitarian 28, 103, 137-38, 141, 284
Trinity 26, 28, 109, 119, 137, 141
troposphere 172
truth 20, 107-8
turbulent flow 22
two books of God 20
Tyndall, John 16
ultraviolet radiation 149
uncertainity 186-87
unified field 24, 143
Unitarianism 87
universal acid 239
universals 76
universe 21, 24, 26, 28, 30, 168, 179-81, 196, 247
universe
   expanding 150
   expansion rate 166
Umayyad Dynasty 52
Upanishads 36-38
U-shape wire 193, 202
Ussher, James 89-91, 96
Uthman 52
vacuum 83-84, 282
Vaisheshika 37-38

value(s) 107-8, 119, 250, 258, 263, 265, 269, 280
Vajrayana 43-44
Vayu 38
Vedanta 37-38
Vedas 37, 39
Venter, J. Craig 237
Venus, phases 159
vestigial structures 216
vinegar 13-16
violation 135-36, 269, 281, 288-89
Virgil 250, 252, 272
Virgo Super Cluster 149
Vishnu 38, 40
visible light 149
vitality 262
vocabulary 25
Voltaire 182, 255
Walcott, Charles 240
Walker, Williston 61
Wallace, Alfred Russel 213, 224
Ward, Peter D. 173
Warfield, B. B. 20-21, 91-92
watchmaker 233
water 14, 172, 241
Watson, James 17
wave 183, 205-6
wavefunction 183-85
wave-particle duality 183-84
weak nuclear force 24, 161, 163
weather 172
week 148
Wesley, Charles 86
Wesley, John 86, 92
West 31, 33-34, 40, 42, 44, 46, 55-56, 58-59, 68, 73-75, 122, 137, 252-54, 262, 278, 284
Western 31, 34, 41, 57, 59-60, 68-69, 74, 96-98, 103, 124, 263

Western culture 33
Western logic 205
Westerners 31
Westminster Assembly 81
whales 213, 217
Whewell, William 16
Whitcomb, John C. 94
Whitehead, Alfred North 60, 92, 105-6, 112, 114-15, 123
Whitfield, George 86
Whittington, Harry B. 240
Wilkinson Microwave Anisotropy Probe (WMAP) 161, 163
will 262, 275, 278
will of God 57, 59, 82, 90, 142
William of Occam 19, 60-61, 76-78
Williams, Daniel Day 112
WIMPs (Weakly Interacting Massive Particles) 167
Word 138
Wordsworth, William 272-73
World War I 93, 97
World War II 94
worldview 59, 87-88
Wycliffe, John 60, 61-63, 66-67, 77
x-rays 149
Yahweh 47-48, 139
year 148
Yemenite Jews 49
Yezid 52
yoga 37, 39
Zaidites 53
Zedekiah 260
Zen 43, 45, 57
zero-sum game 17
zoology 25
Zoroastrianism 72
Zygon Center 101

Scripture Index

Genesis
1:3, *95*
1:11, *88, 95, 253*
1:20, *88, 253*
1:24, *88, 253*
28:20-22, *266*

Numbers
13:26–14:9, *267*

Deuteronomy
18:15-22, *279*

2 Kings
15:37, *260*

2 Chronicles
36:22, *262*

Psalms
1:1, *267-68*
19:1, *148*
51:10, *261*

Isaiah
10:5, *261*
10:7, *261*
10:12, *261*
10:15, *261*
30:16, *261*
41:2-4, *261*
45:1, *260*
45:4-5, *260*

Jeremiah
18:1-11, *99*
25:12, *261*
25:15-38, *260*
27:8, *260*
44:30, *260*
51:11, *261*

Amos
5:21-24, *268-69*

Jonah
1:9, *69*

Haggai
1:14, *261*

Zechariah
7:8-14, *262*

Matthew
5:17-18, *279*
13:44, *98*
13:45-46, *98*
13:47-50, *98*
22:1-14, *99*
24:36, *140*

Mark
2:8, *140*

Luke
5:22, *140*
15:3-7, *98*
15:8-10, *98*
15:11-24, *98*

John
1:1-3, *70*
1:14, *70*
10:1-2, *99*
10:3-5, *99*
10:11, *99*

Acts
14:11-18, *70*
17:16-34, *70*
17:30, *264*

Romans
1, *280*
1:20-23, *70*
1:21, *279*
8:26, *280*

1 Corinthians
13:12, *265*
15:3-4, *279*
15:28, *143*

Ephesians
1:16-19, *265*
3:18-19, *265*

Philippians
2:6-8, *141*

Colossians
1:15-20, *70*

1 Thessalonians
5:17, *280*

Hebrews
1:1-4, *70*
1:9-18, *270*
4:14-16, *270*
11:3, *204*

1 Peter
4:19, *70*

1 John
4:1, *280*

Revelation
22:1, *143*